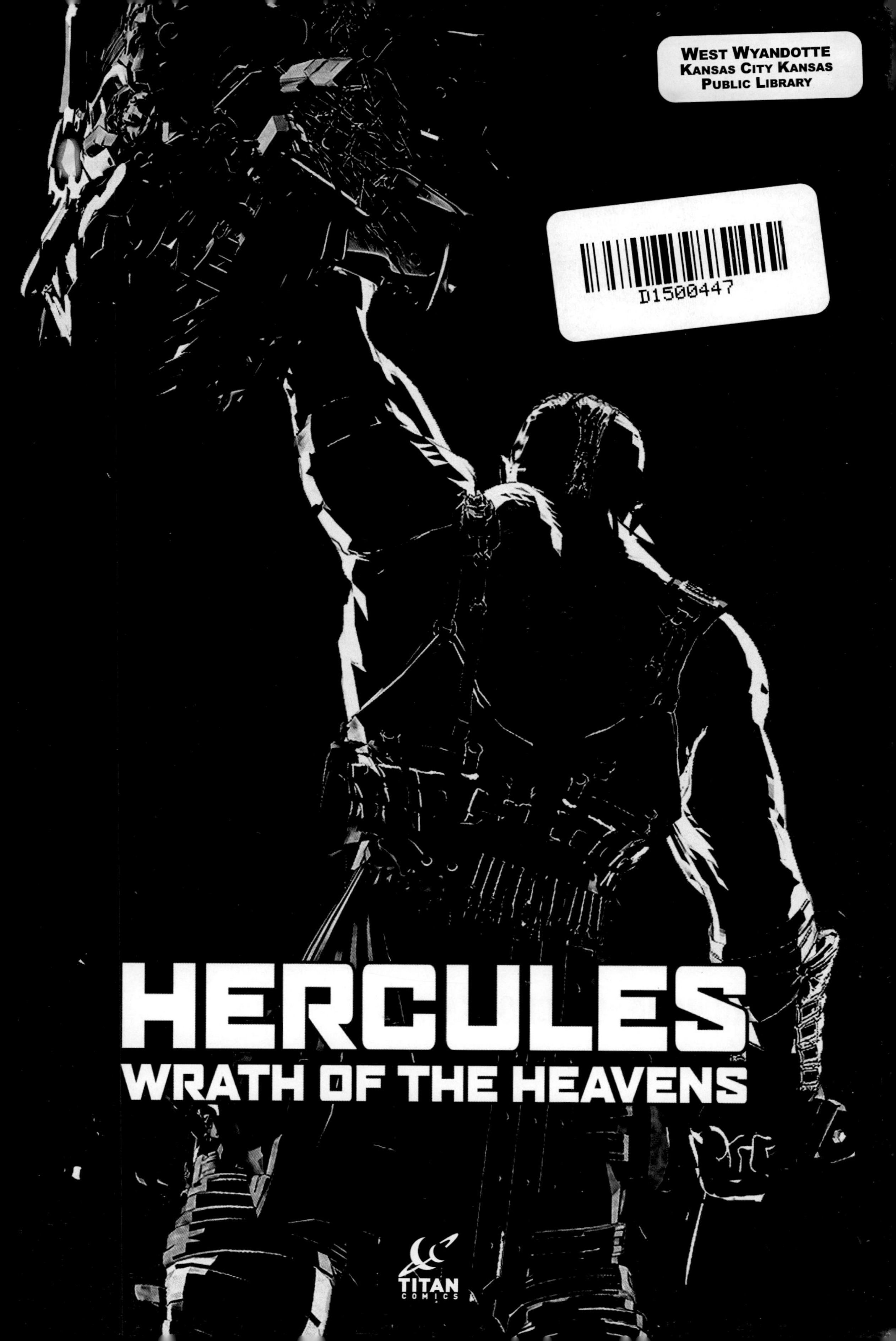
HERCULES
WRATH OF THE HEAVENS
TITAN
COMICS

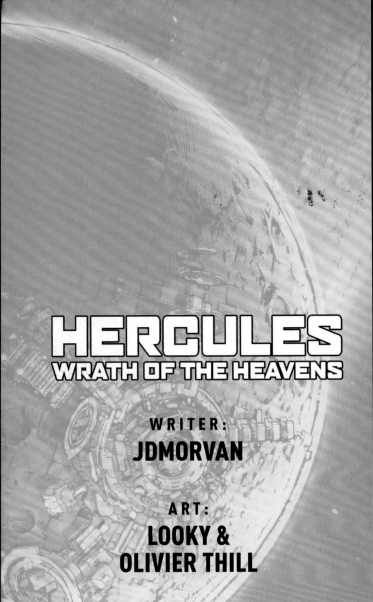

HERCULES
WRATH OF THE HEAVENS

WRITER:

JDMORVAN

ART:

**LOOKY &
OLIVIER THILL**

TRANSLATION:

**VIRGINIE SÉLAVY
&
MARC BOURBON-CROOK**

TITAN EDITORIAL

COLLECTION EDITOR
Jonathan Stevenson

MANAGING AND LAUNCH EDITOR
Andrew James

DESIGNER
Donna Askem

PRODUCTION ASSISTANT
Natalie Bolger

PRODUCTION SUPERVISOR
Maria Pearson

PRODUCTION CONTROLLER
Peter James

SENIOR PRODUCTION CONTROLLER
Jackie Flook

ART DIRECTOR
Oz Browne

SENIOR SALES MANAGER
Steve Tothill

CIRCULATION ASSISTANT
Frances Hallam

PRESS OFFICER
Will O'Mullane

BRAND MANAGER
Chris Thompson

ADS & MARKETING ASSISTANT
Tom Miller

DIRECT SALES & MARKETING MANAGER
Ricky Claydon

COMMERCIAL MANAGER
Michelle Fairlamb

HEAD OF RIGHTS
Jenny Boyce

PUBLISHING MANAGER
Darryl Tothill

PUBLISHING DIRECTOR
Chris Teather

OPERATIONS DIRECTOR
Leigh Baulch

EXECUTIVE DIRECTOR
Vivian Cheung

PUBLISHER
Nick Landau

HERCULES: WRATH OF THE HEAVENS
ISBN: 9781785855863

Published by Titan Comics
A division of Titan Publishing Group Ltd.
144 Southwark St.
London
SE1 0UP

Originally published in French as: Hercule 1 - 3 by Morvan,
Looky and Thill. © Editions Soleil – 2012, 2013, 2017. All rights
reserved.

A CIP catalogue record for this title is available from the
British Library.

First edition: April 2018

10 9 8 7 6 5 4 3 2 1

Printed in China.

www.titan-comics.com
Follow us on Twitter @ComicsTitan
Visit us at facebook.com/comicstitan

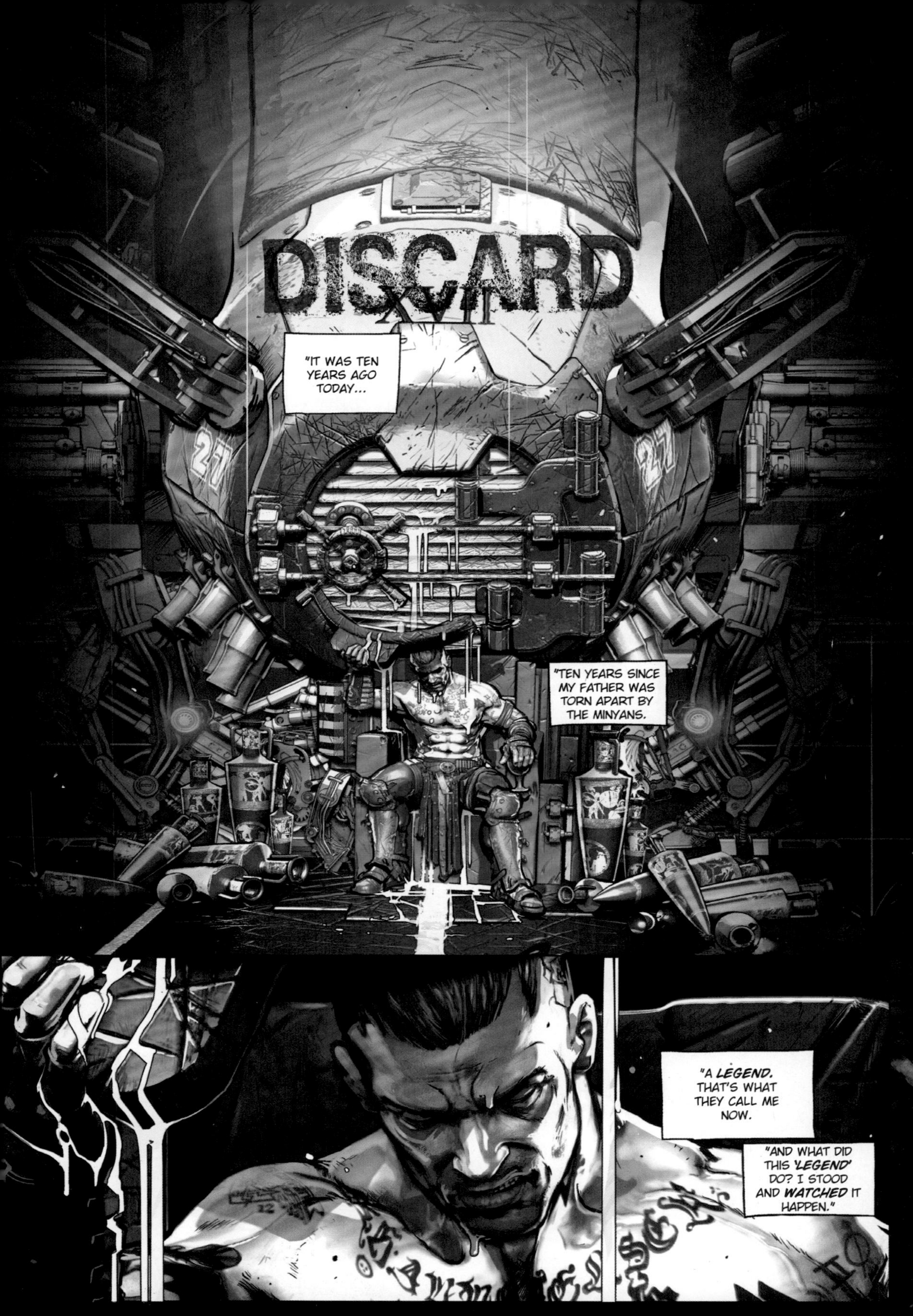
DISCARD
"IT WAS TEN YEARS AGO TODAY...
"TEN YEARS SINCE MY FATHER WAS TORN APART BY THE MINYANS.
"A LEGEND. THAT'S WHAT THEY CALL ME NOW.
"AND WHAT DID THIS 'LEGEND' DO? I STOOD AND WATCHED IT HAPPEN."

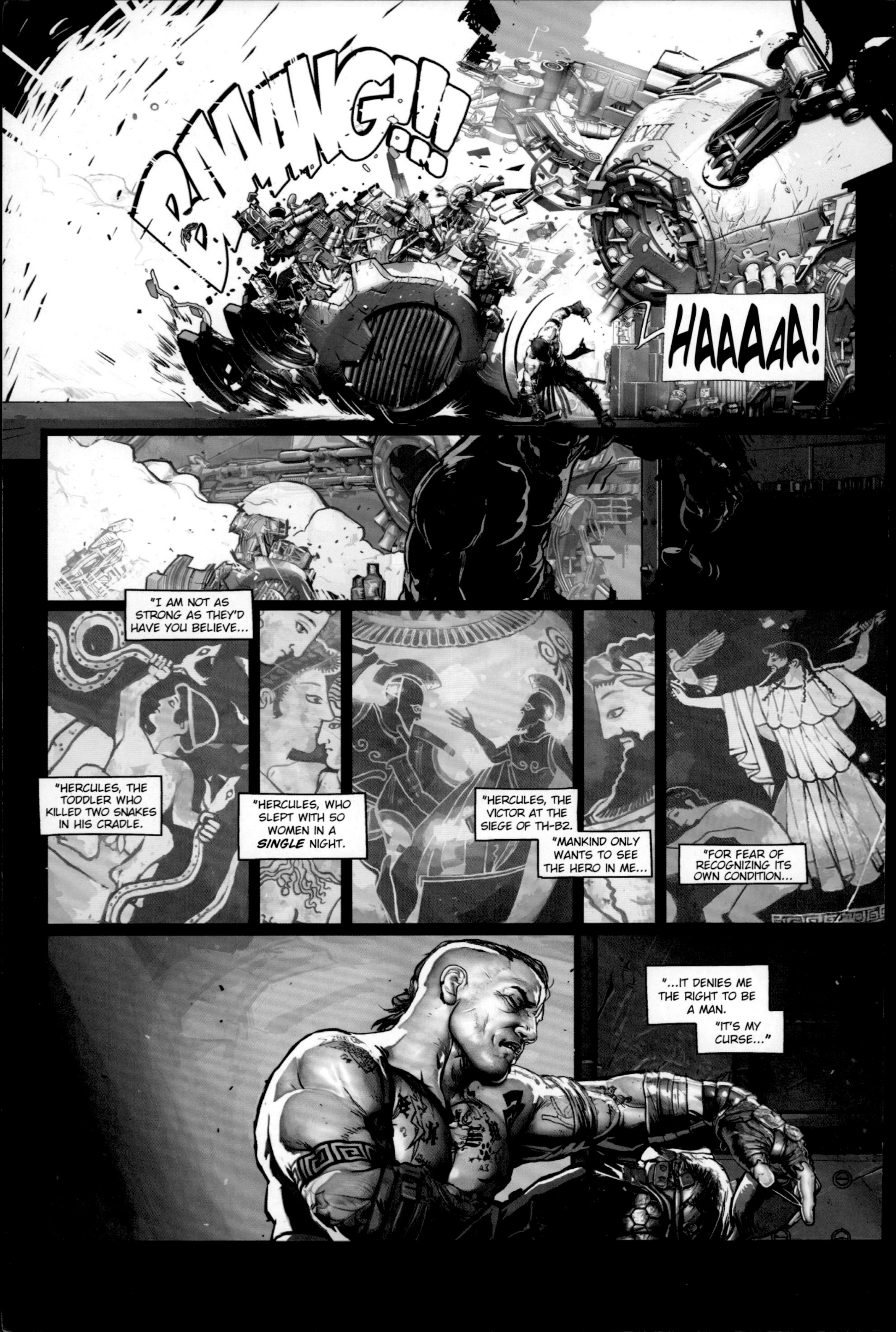
BANNNG!!!
HAAAAA!
"I AM NOT AS STRONG AS THEY'D HAVE YOU BELIEVE...
"HERCULES, THE TODDLER WHO KILLED TWO SNAKES IN HIS CRADLE.
"HERCULES, WHO SLEPT WITH 50 WOMEN IN A SINGLE NIGHT.
"HERCULES, THE VICTOR AT THE SIEGE OF TH-B2.
"MANKIND ONLY WANTS TO SEE THE HERO IN ME...
"FOR FEAR OF RECOGNIZING ITS OWN CONDITION...
"...IT DENIES ME THE RIGHT TO BE A MAN.
"IT'S MY CURSE..."

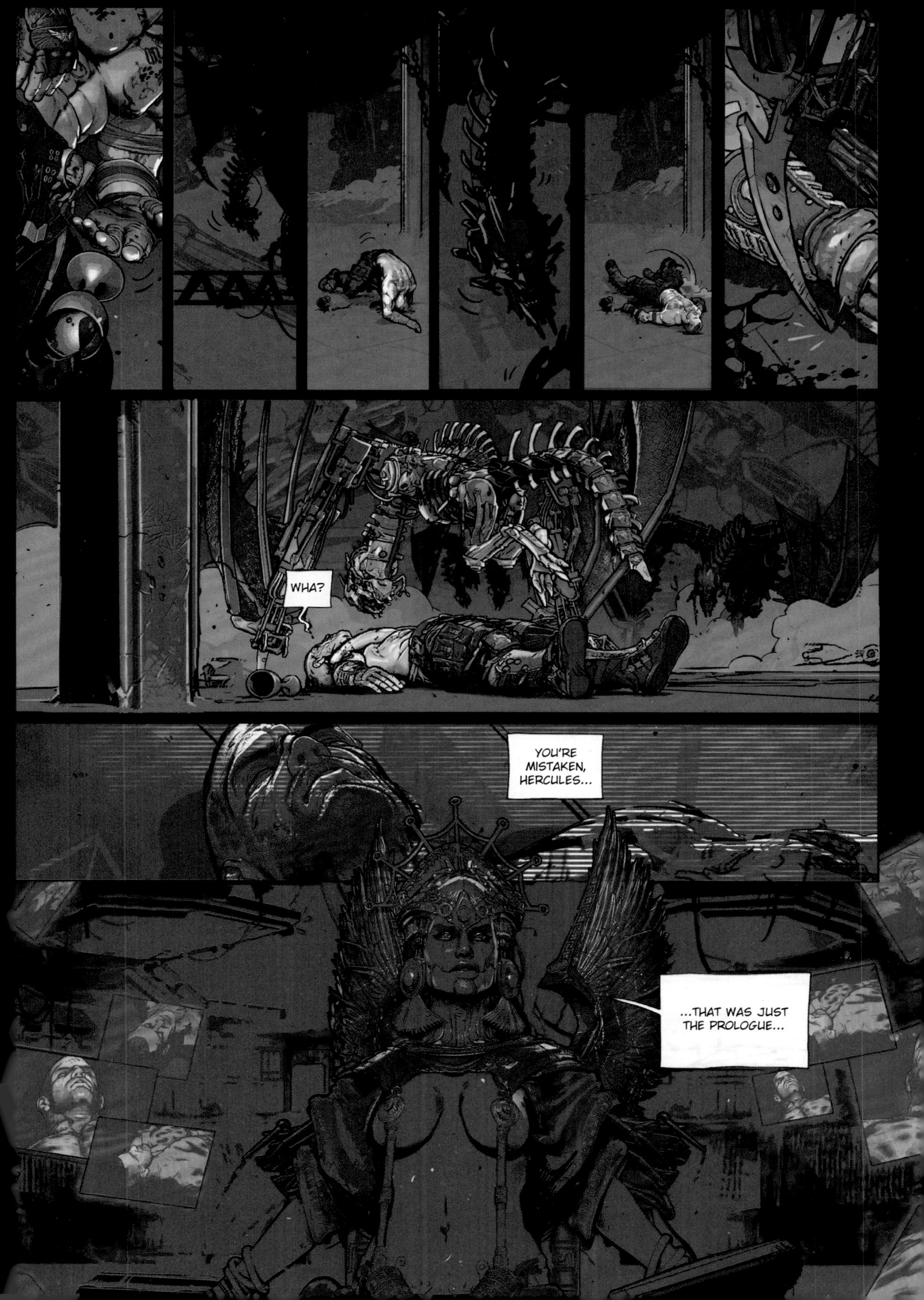
WHA?
YOU'RE MISTAKEN, HERCULES...
...THAT WAS JUST THE PROLOGUE...

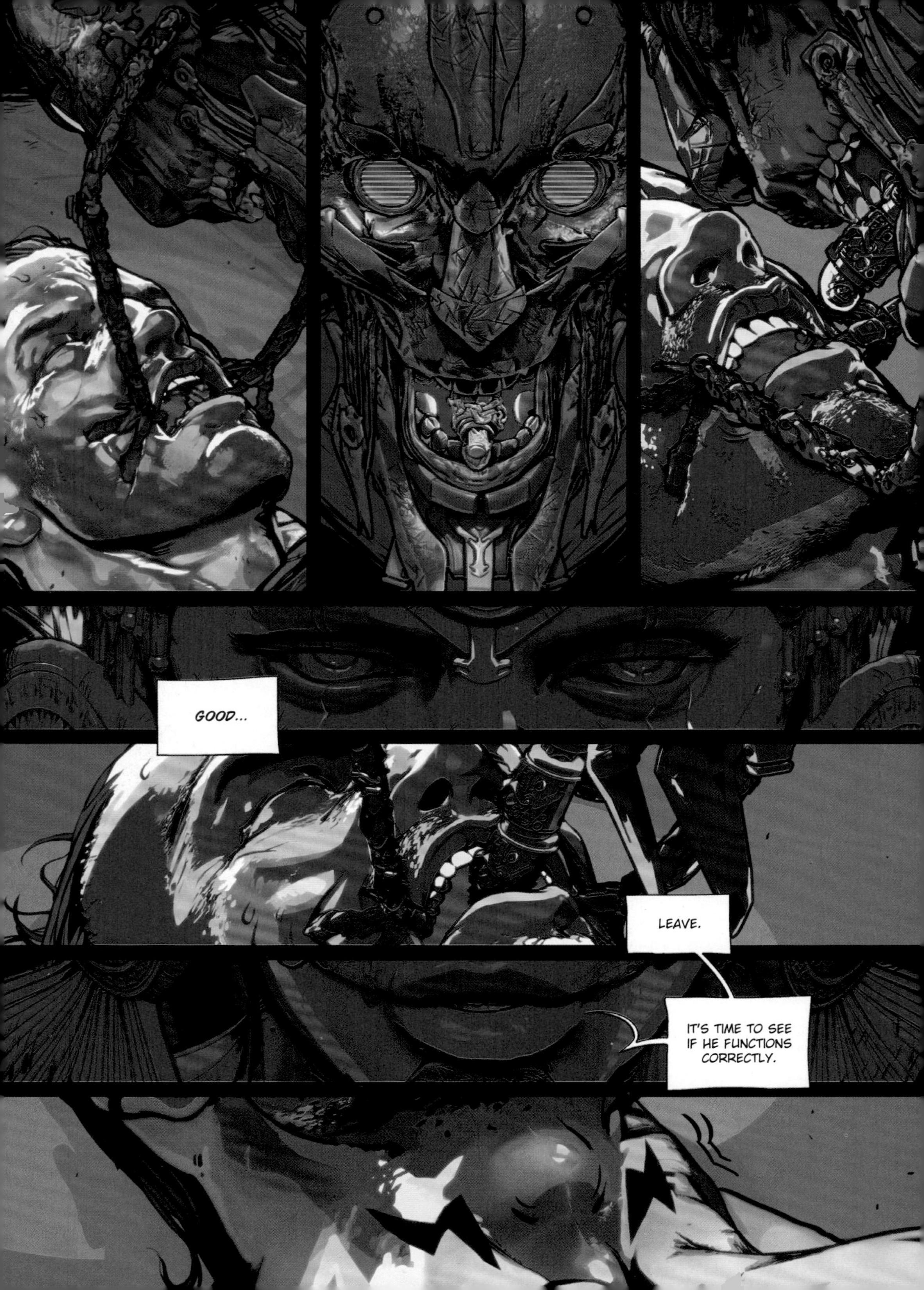
GOOD...
LEAVE.
IT'S TIME TO SEE IF HE FUNCTIONS CORRECTLY.

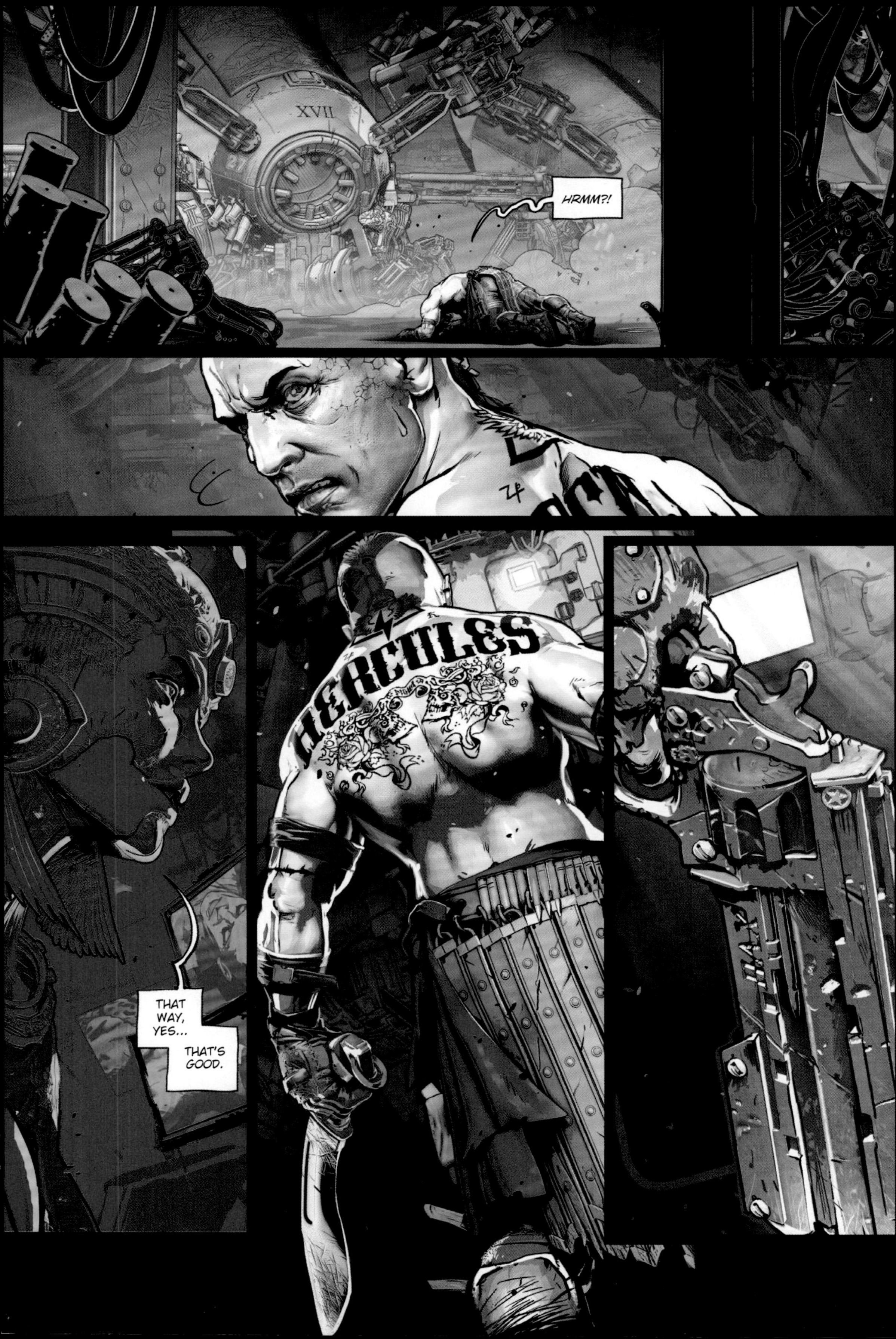
HRMM?!
THAT WAY, YES...
THAT'S GOOD.

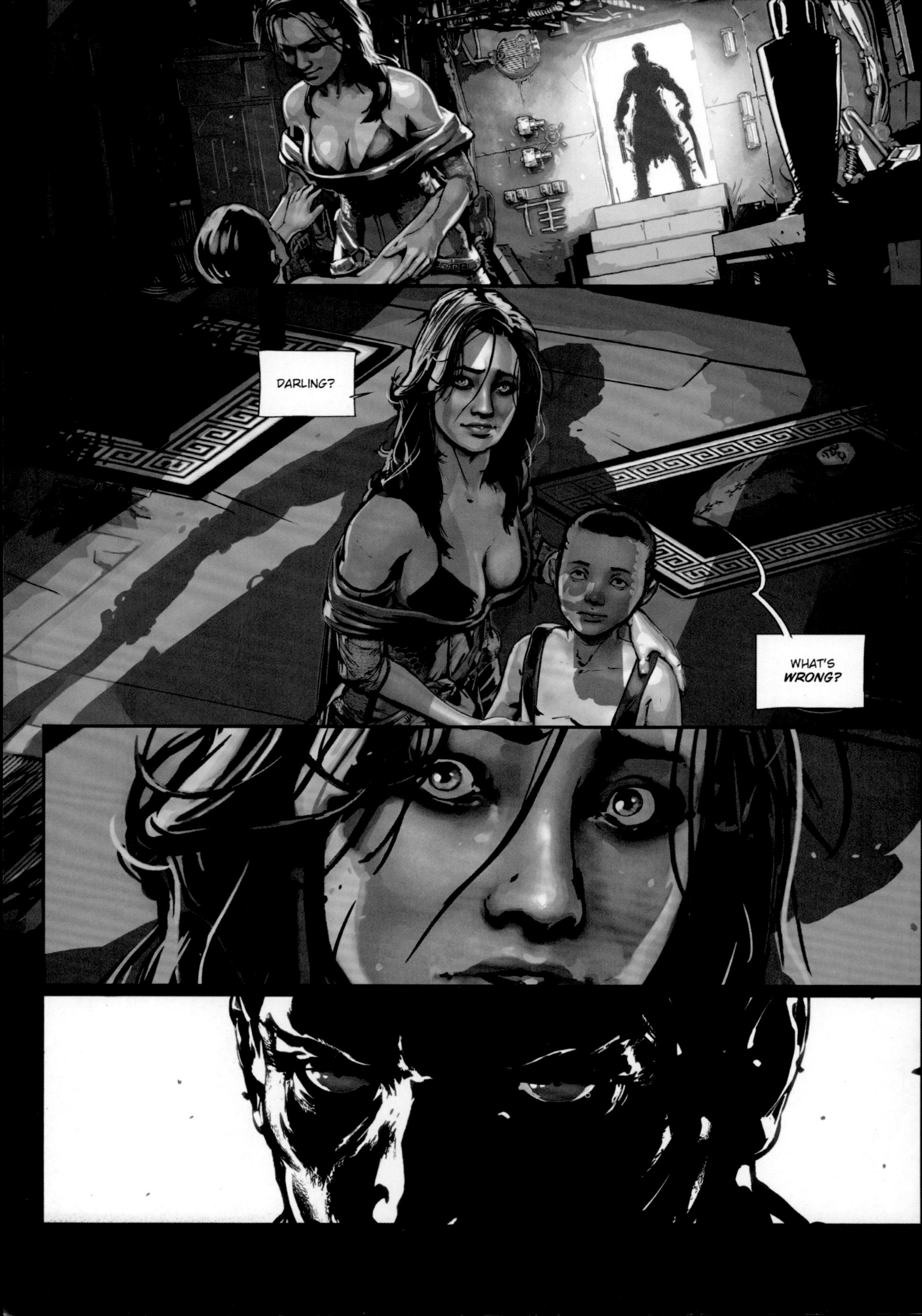
DARLING?
WHAT'S *WRONG?*

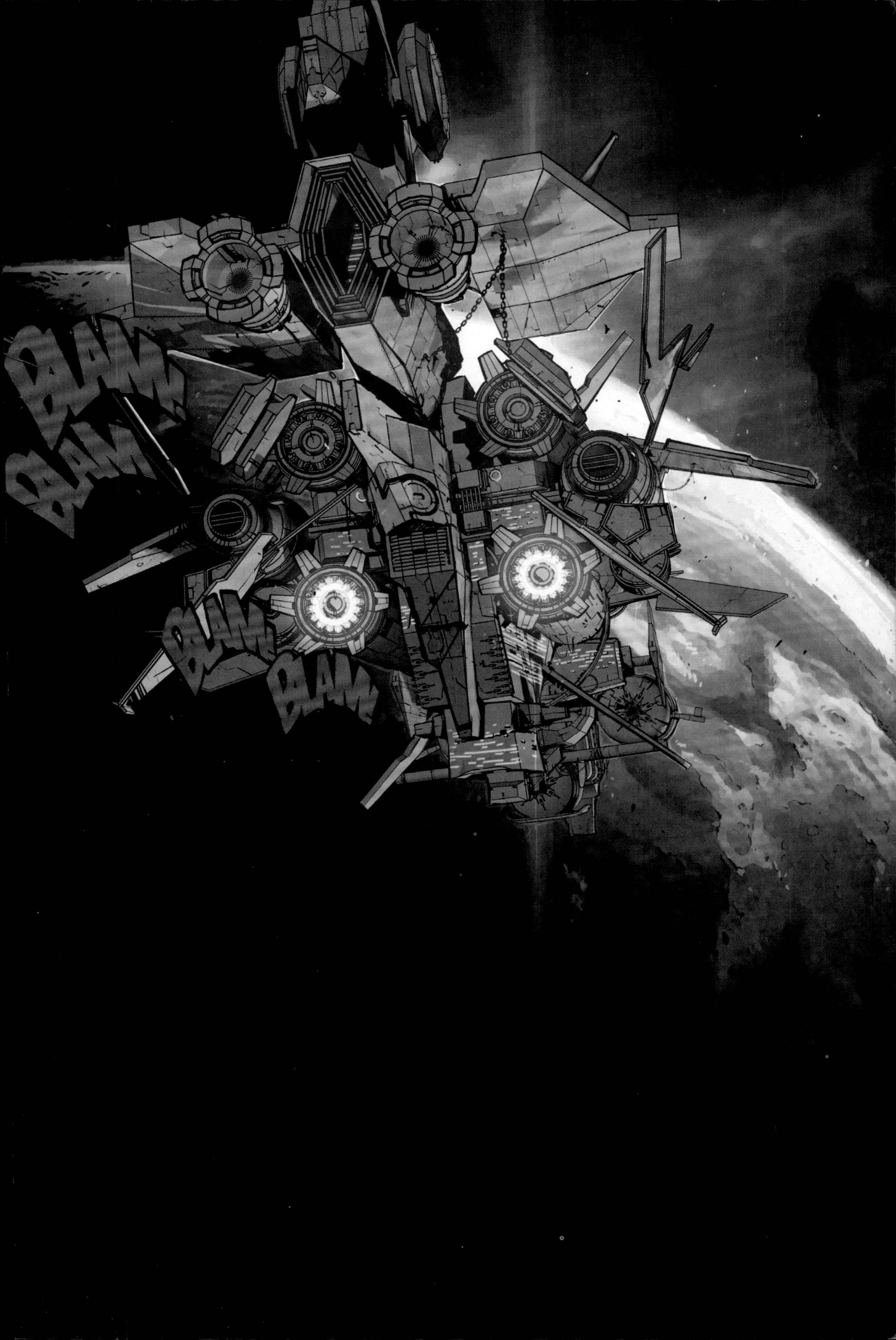
BLAM!
BLAM!
BLAM!
BLAM!

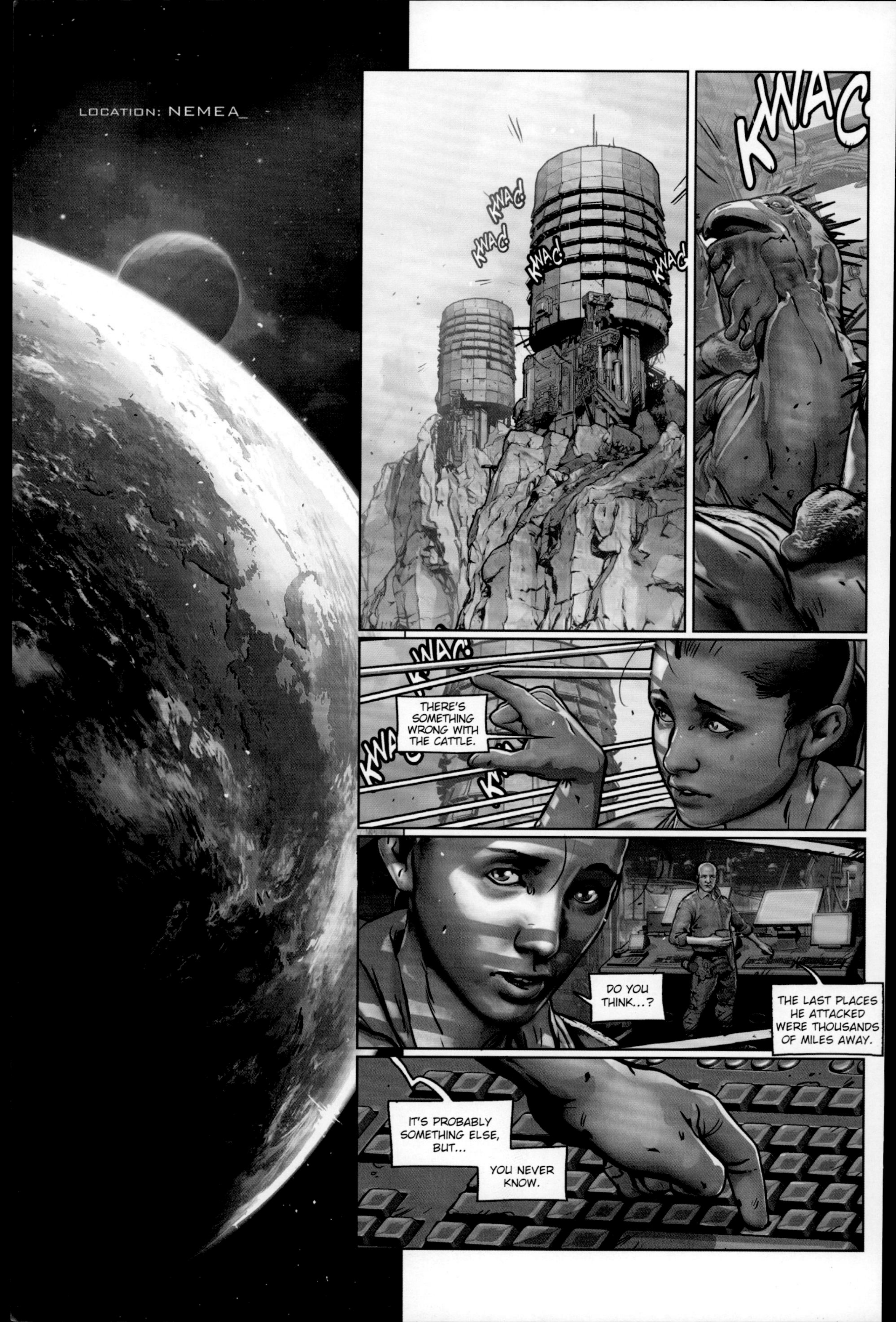
LOCATION: NEMEA_
KWAC!
KWAC!
KWAC!
KWAC!
KWAC
KWAC!
THERE'S SOMETHING WRONG WITH THE CATTLE.
KWAC
DO YOU THINK...?
THE LAST PLACES HE ATTACKED WERE THOUSANDS OF MILES AWAY.
IT'S PROBABLY SOMETHING ELSE, BUT...
YOU NEVER KNOW.

CLONG!

CLONG!

CLONG!

CLONG

THOSE FORTIFICATIONS ARE BUILT TO RESIST TYPHOONS OF OVER 2000 MILES PER HOUR.

NOTHING'S GETTIN' THROUGH THESE WALLS.

?!

ROA AR

IMPOSSIBLE!

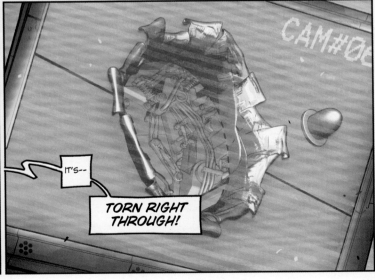

CAM#06

IT'S--

TORN RIGHT THROUGH!

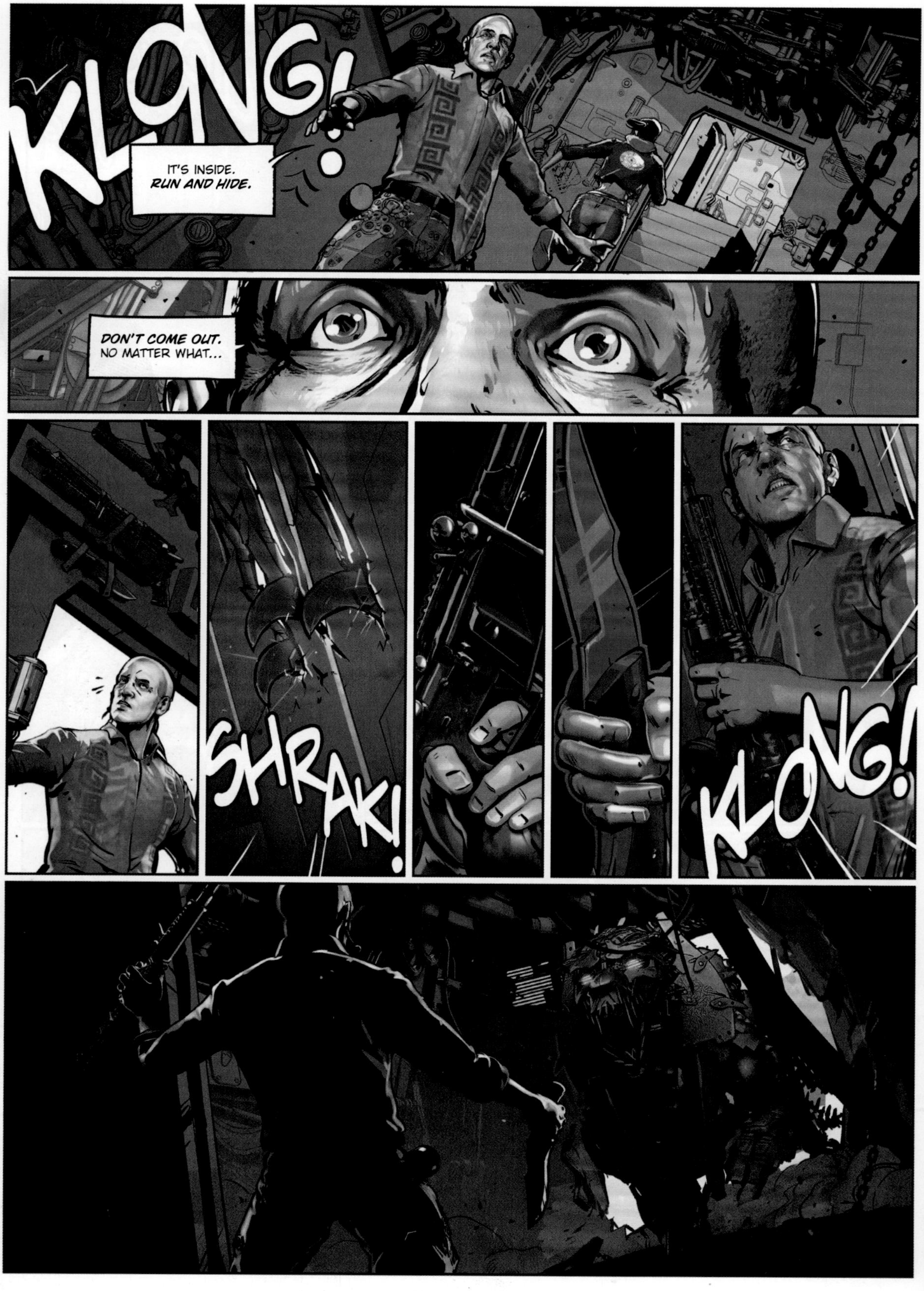
KLONG!
IT'S INSIDE.
RUN AND HIDE.
DON'T COME OUT.
NO MATTER WHAT...
SHRAK!
KLONG!

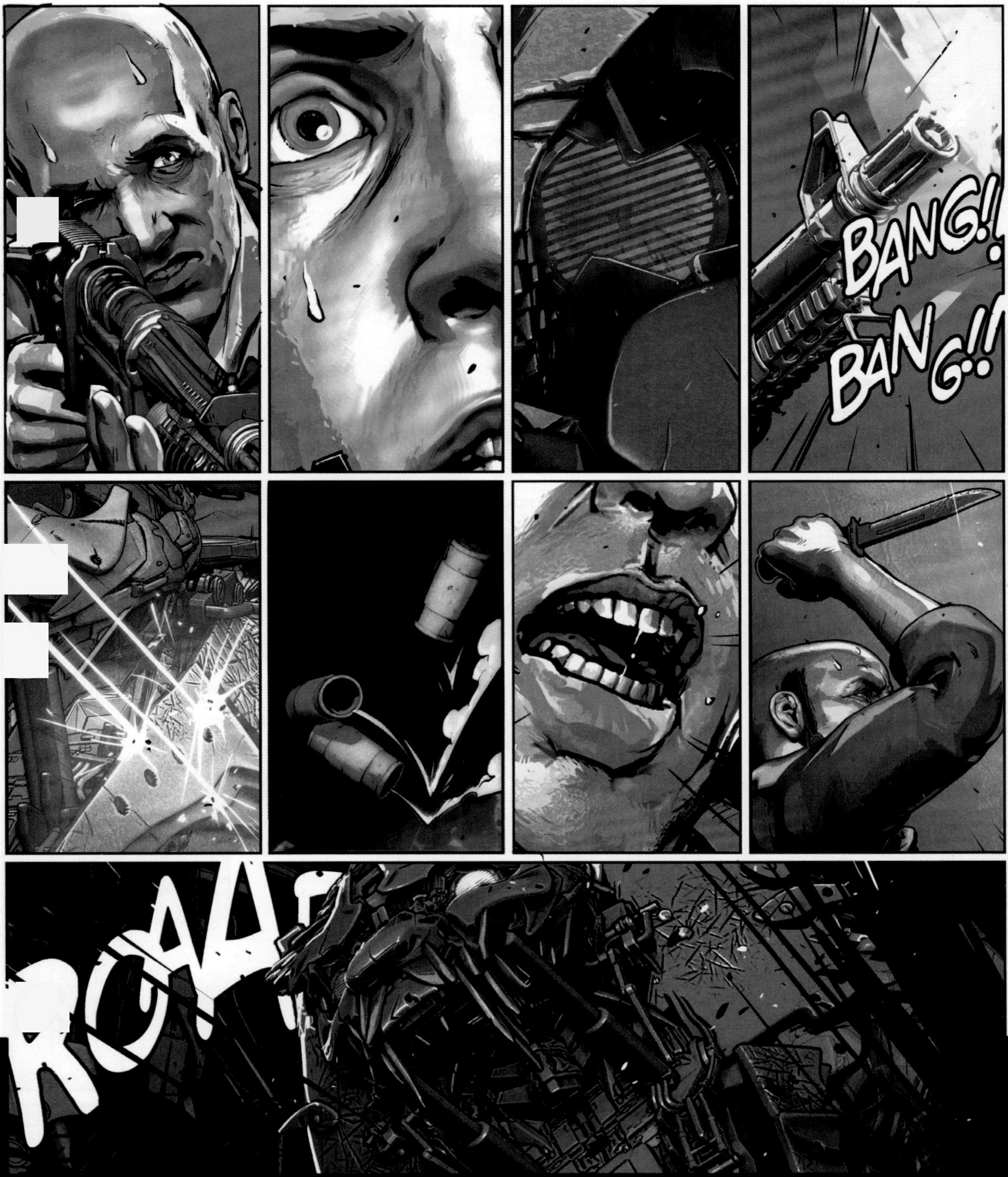
BANG!!
BANG!!

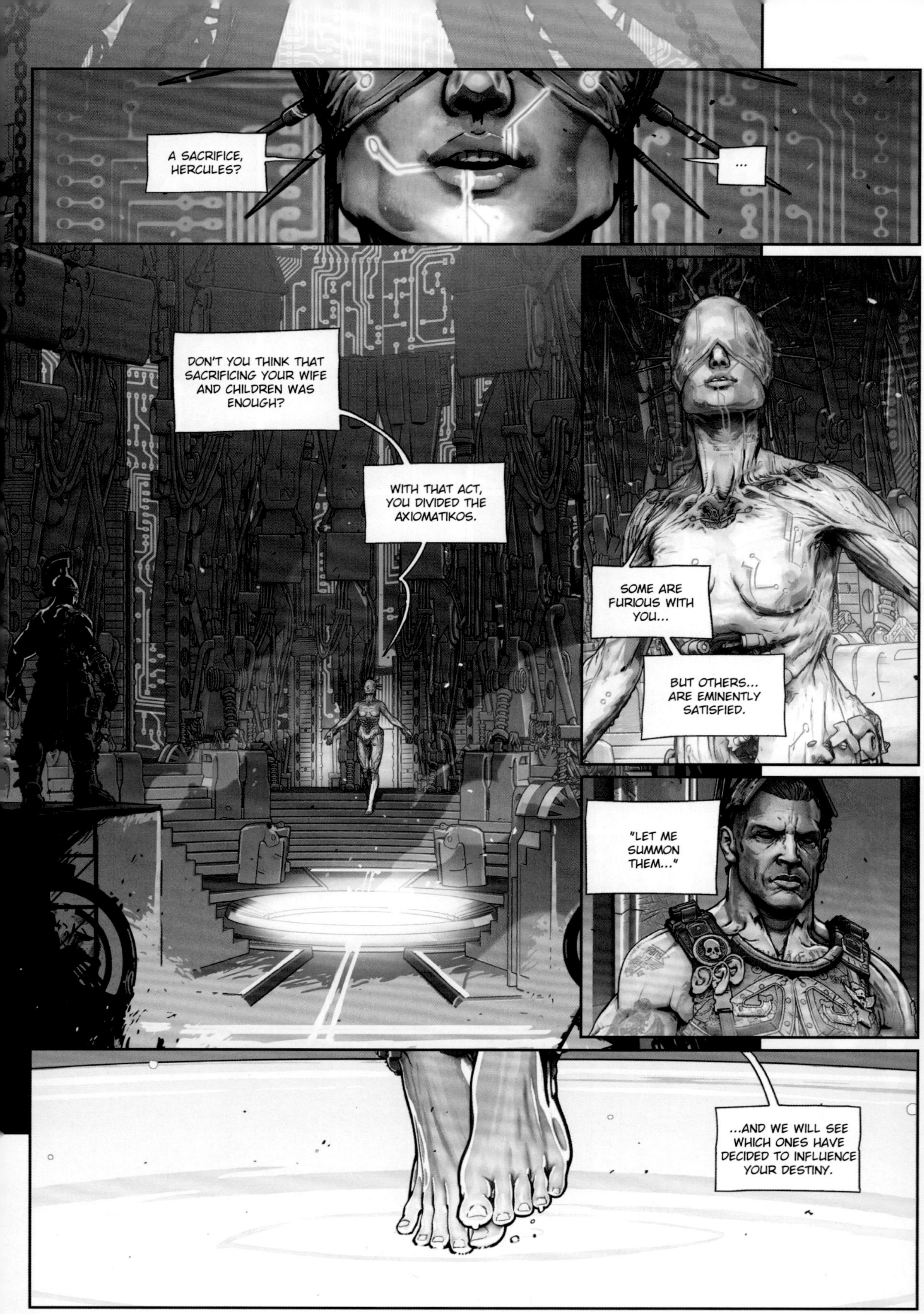
A SACRIFICE, HERCULES?
...
DON'T YOU THINK THAT SACRIFICING YOUR WIFE AND CHILDREN WAS ENOUGH?
WITH THAT ACT, YOU DIVIDED THE AXIOMATIKOS.
SOME ARE FURIOUS WITH YOU...
BUT OTHERS... ARE EMINENTLY SATISFIED.
"LET ME SUMMON THEM..."
...AND WE WILL SEE WHICH ONES HAVE DECIDED TO INFLUENCE YOUR DESTINY.

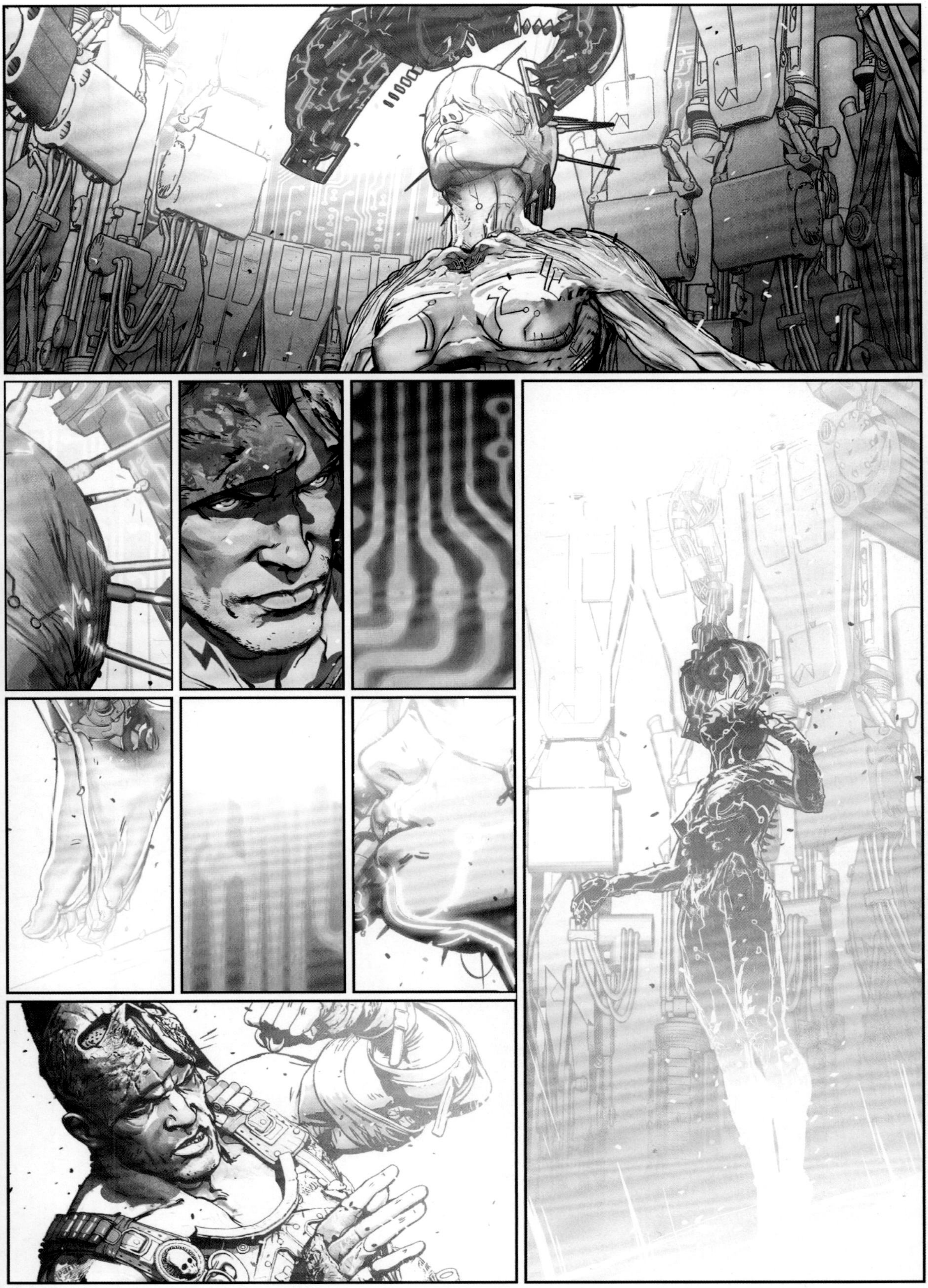

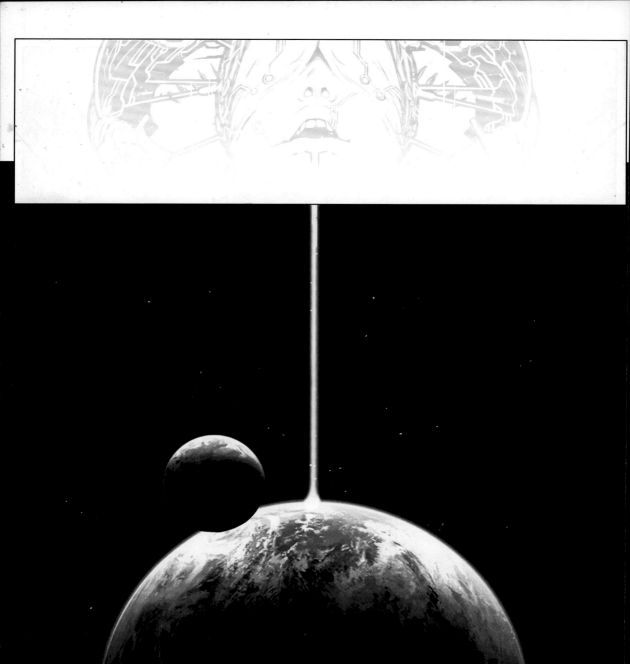

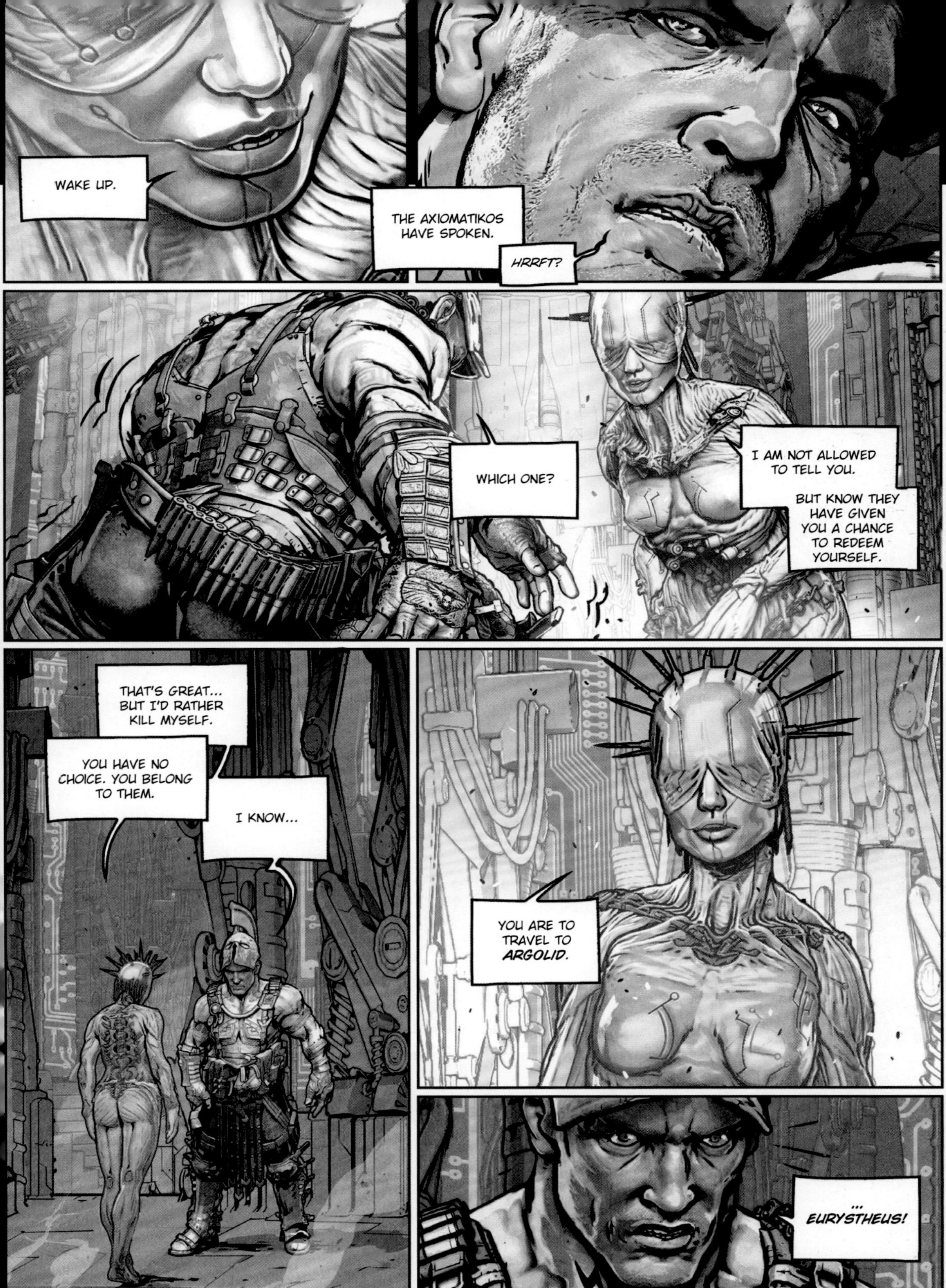

WAKE UP.
THE AXIOMATIKOS HAVE SPOKEN.
HRRFT?
WHICH ONE?
I AM NOT ALLOWED TO TELL YOU.
BUT KNOW THEY HAVE GIVEN YOU A CHANCE TO REDEEM YOURSELF.
THAT'S GREAT... BUT I'D RATHER KILL MYSELF.
YOU HAVE NO CHOICE. YOU BELONG TO THEM.
I KNOW...
YOU ARE TO TRAVEL TO ARGOLID.
... EURYSTHEUS!

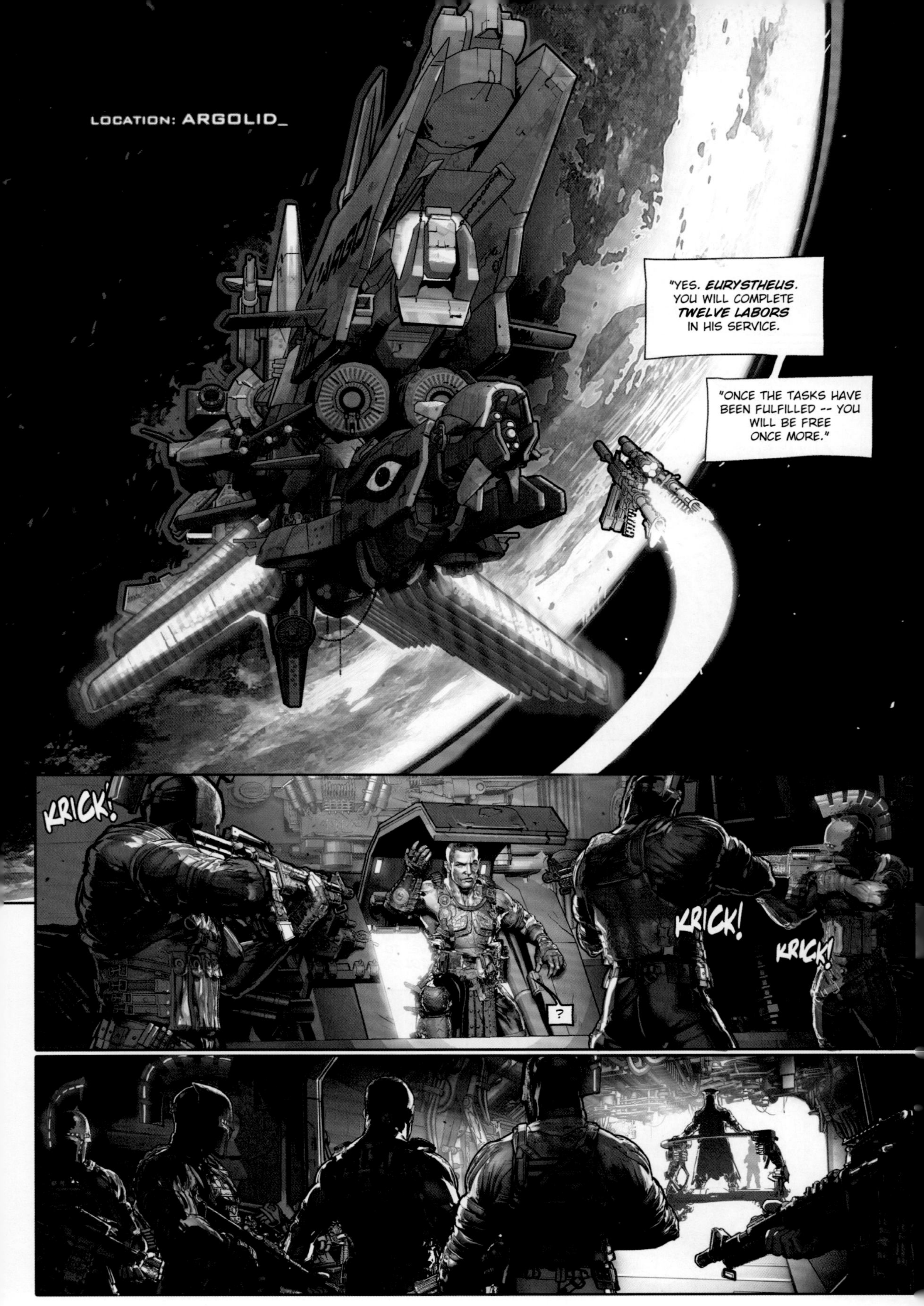
LOCATION: ARGOLID_
"YES. EURYSTHEUS. YOU WILL COMPLETE TWELVE LABORS IN HIS SERVICE.
"ONCE THE TASKS HAVE BEEN FULFILLED -- YOU WILL BE FREE ONCE MORE."
KRICK!
KRICK!
KRICK!
?

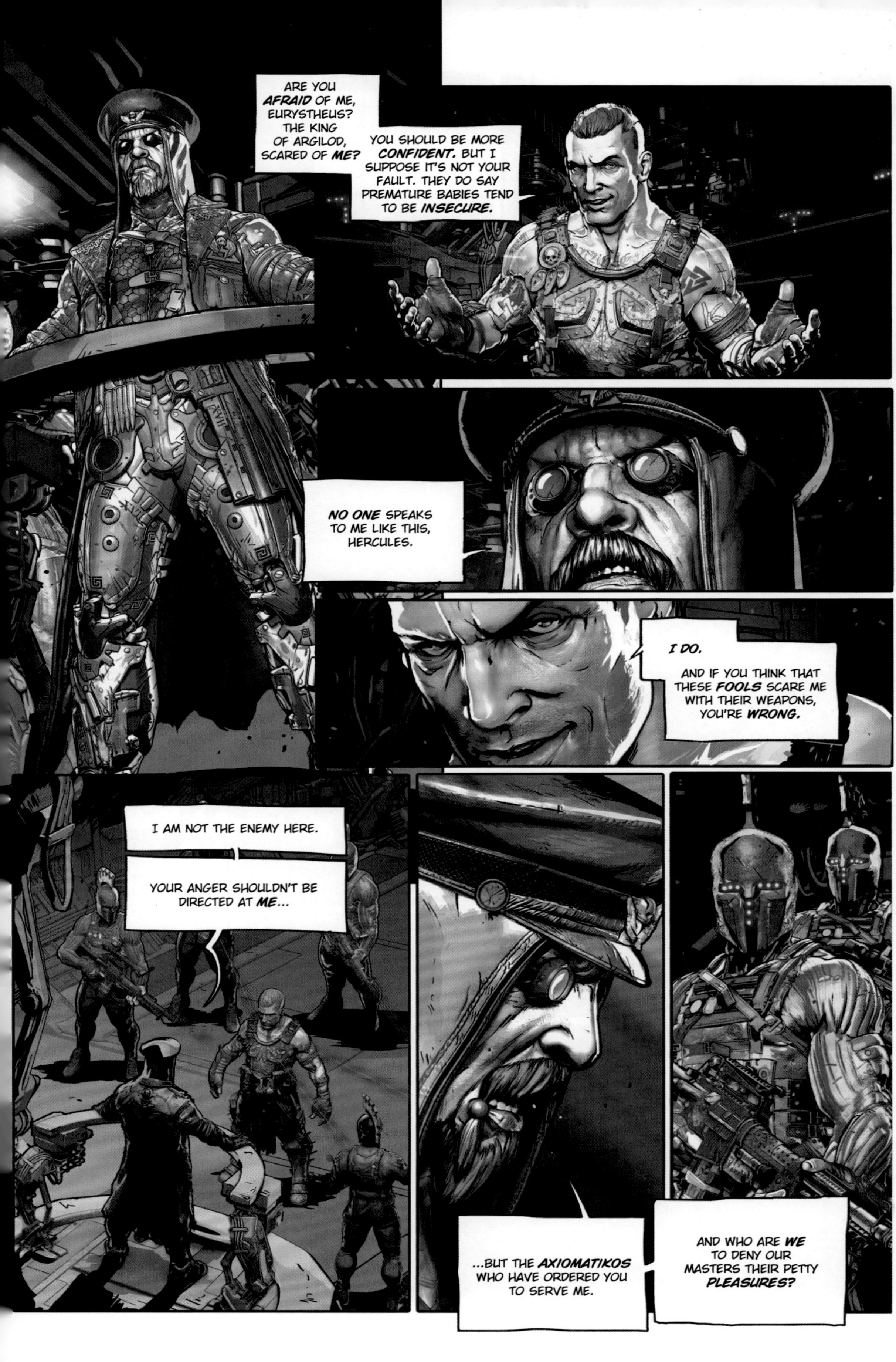
ARE YOU *AFRAID* OF ME, EURYSTHEUS? THE KING OF ARGILOD, SCARED OF *ME?*
YOU SHOULD BE MORE *CONFIDENT.* BUT I SUPPOSE IT'S NOT YOUR FAULT. THEY DO SAY PREMATURE BABIES TEND TO BE *INSECURE.*
NO ONE SPEAKS TO ME LIKE THIS, HERCULES.
I DO.
AND IF YOU THINK THAT THESE *FOOLS* SCARE ME WITH THEIR WEAPONS, YOU'RE *WRONG.*
I AM NOT THE ENEMY HERE.
YOUR ANGER SHOULDN'T BE DIRECTED AT *ME*...
...BUT THE *AXIOMATIKOS* WHO HAVE ORDERED YOU TO SERVE ME.
AND WHO ARE *WE* TO DENY OUR MASTERS THEIR PETTY *PLEASURES?*

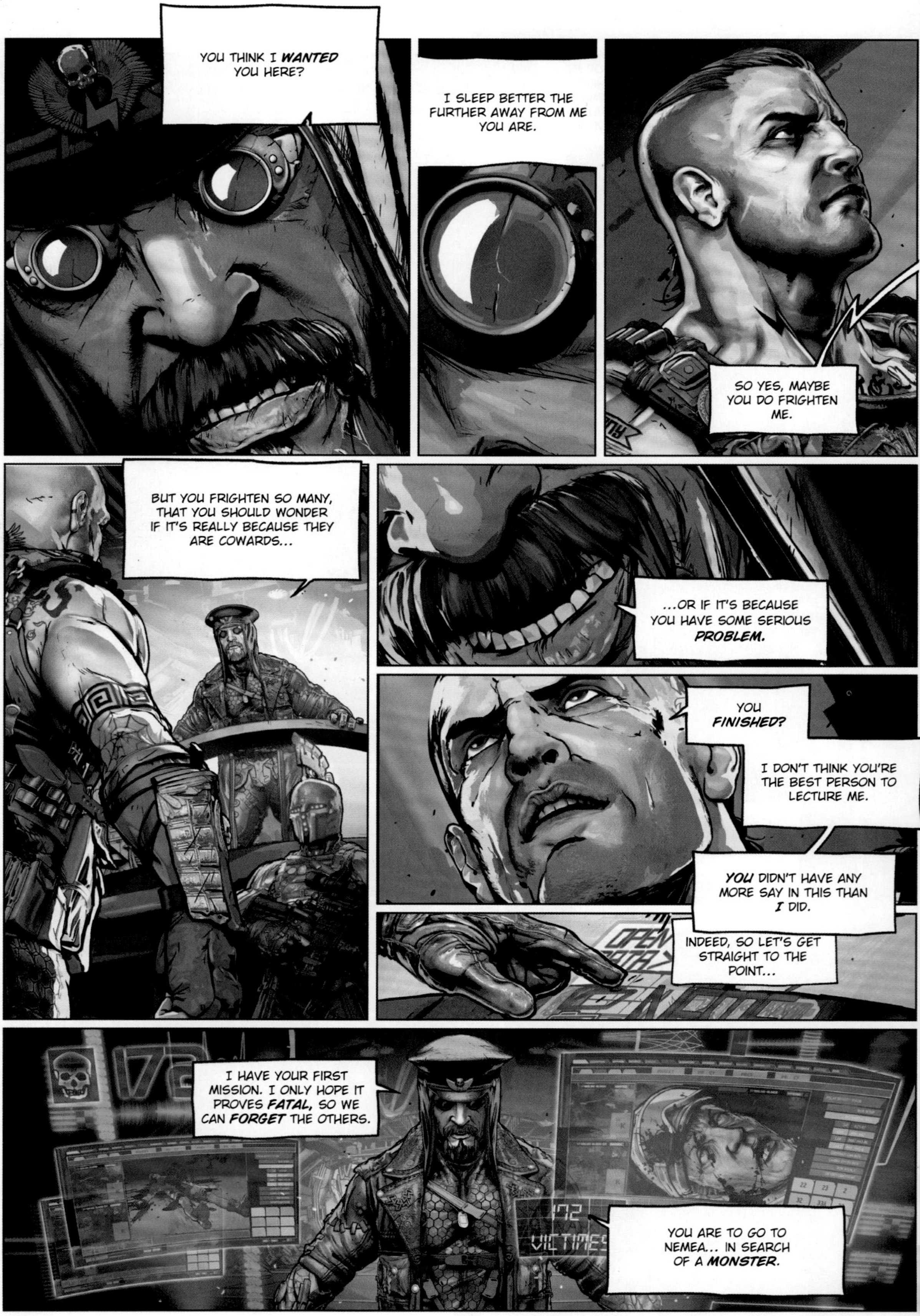
YOU THINK I WANTED YOU HERE?
I SLEEP BETTER THE FURTHER AWAY FROM ME YOU ARE.
SO YES, MAYBE YOU DO FRIGHTEN ME.
BUT YOU FRIGHTEN SO MANY, THAT YOU SHOULD WONDER IF IT'S REALLY BECAUSE THEY ARE COWARDS...
...OR IF IT'S BECAUSE YOU HAVE SOME SERIOUS PROBLEM.
YOU FINISHED?
I DON'T THINK YOU'RE THE BEST PERSON TO LECTURE ME.
YOU DIDN'T HAVE ANY MORE SAY IN THIS THAN I DID.
INDEED, SO LET'S GET STRAIGHT TO THE POINT...
I HAVE YOUR FIRST MISSION. I ONLY HOPE IT PROVES FATAL, SO WE CAN FORGET THE OTHERS.
VICTIMES
YOU ARE TO GO TO NEMEA... IN SEARCH OF A MONSTER.

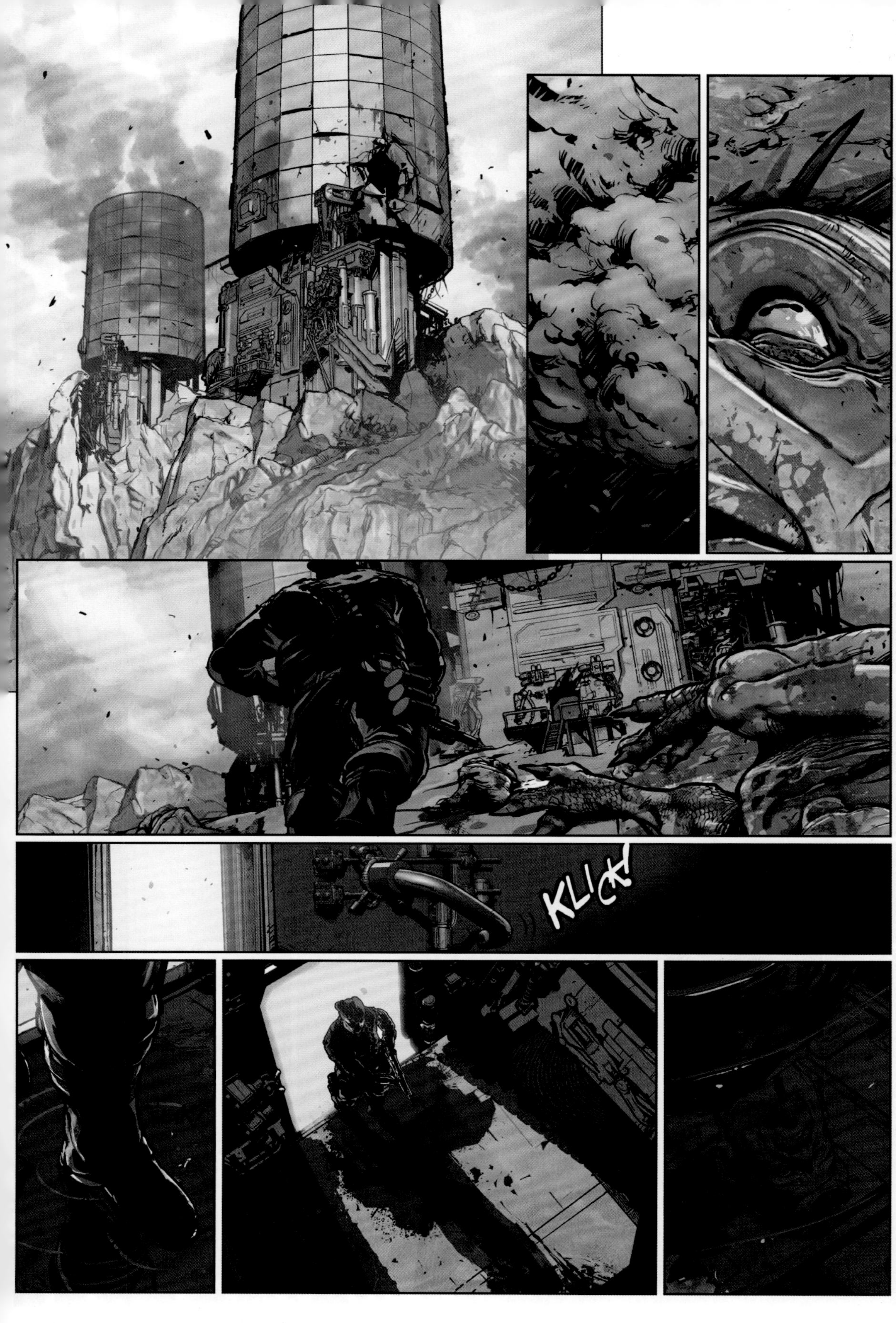
KLICK!

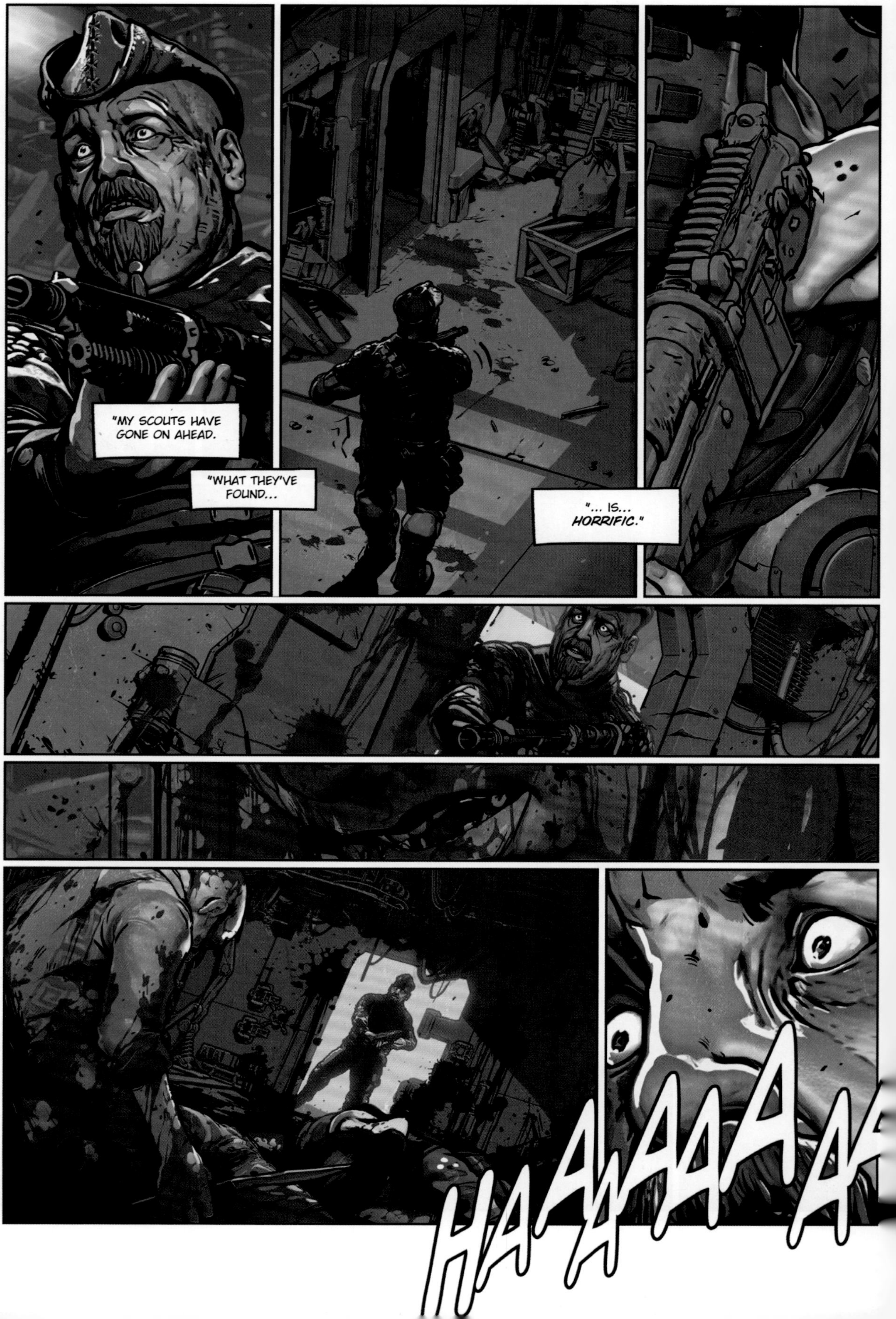
"MY SCOUTS HAVE GONE ON AHEAD.
"WHAT THEY'VE FOUND...
"... IS... HORRIFIC."
HAAAAAA

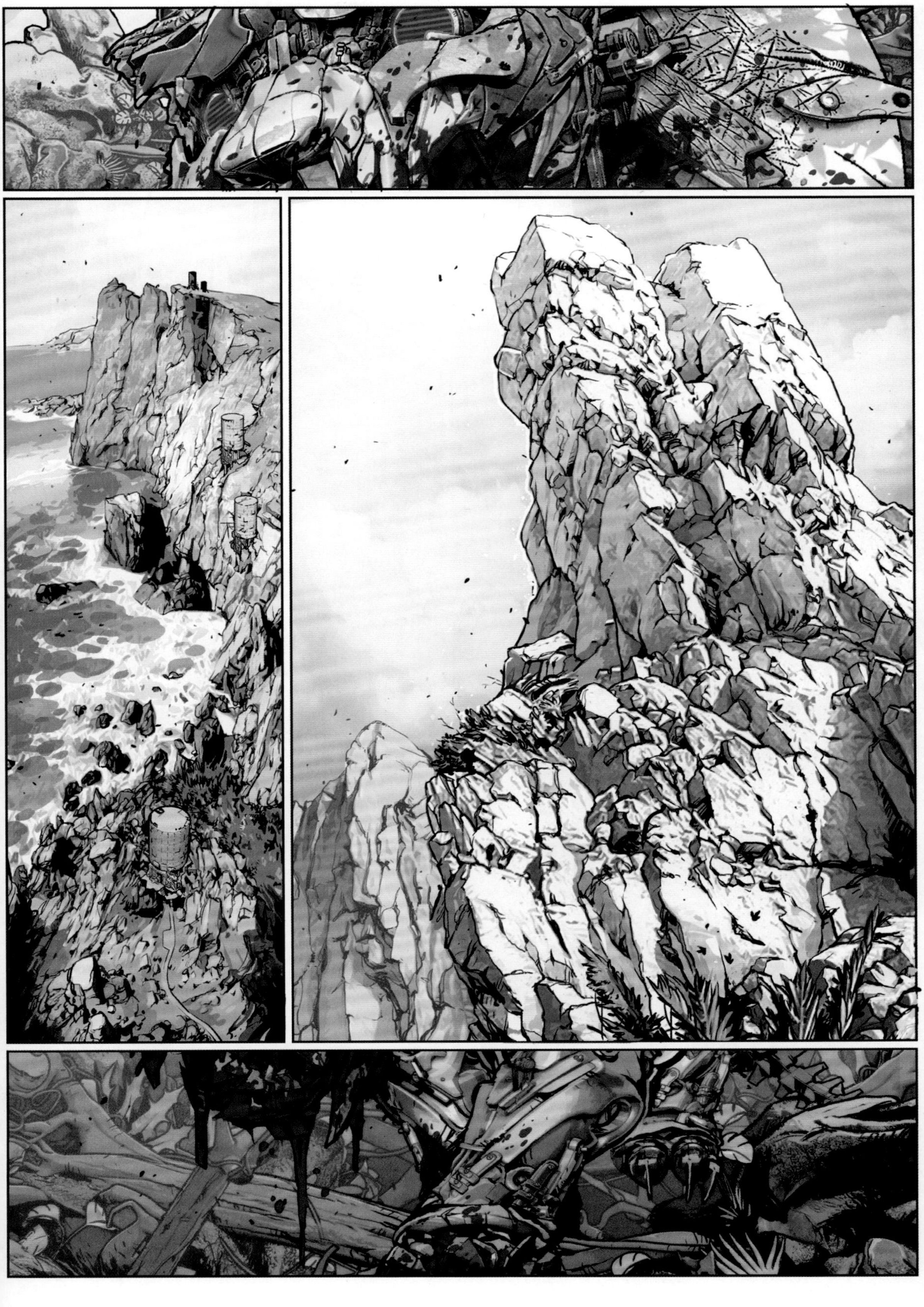

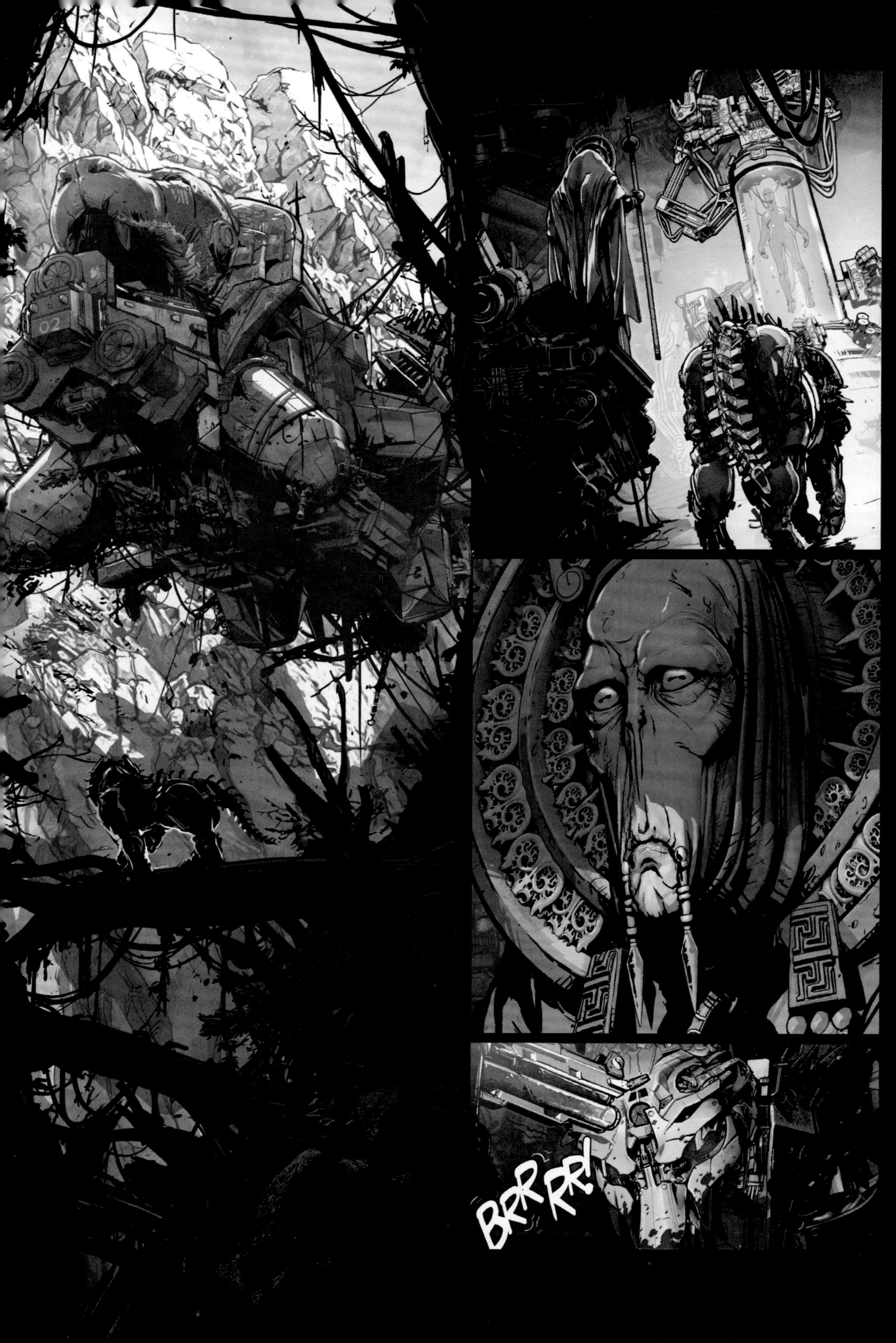
BRRRR!

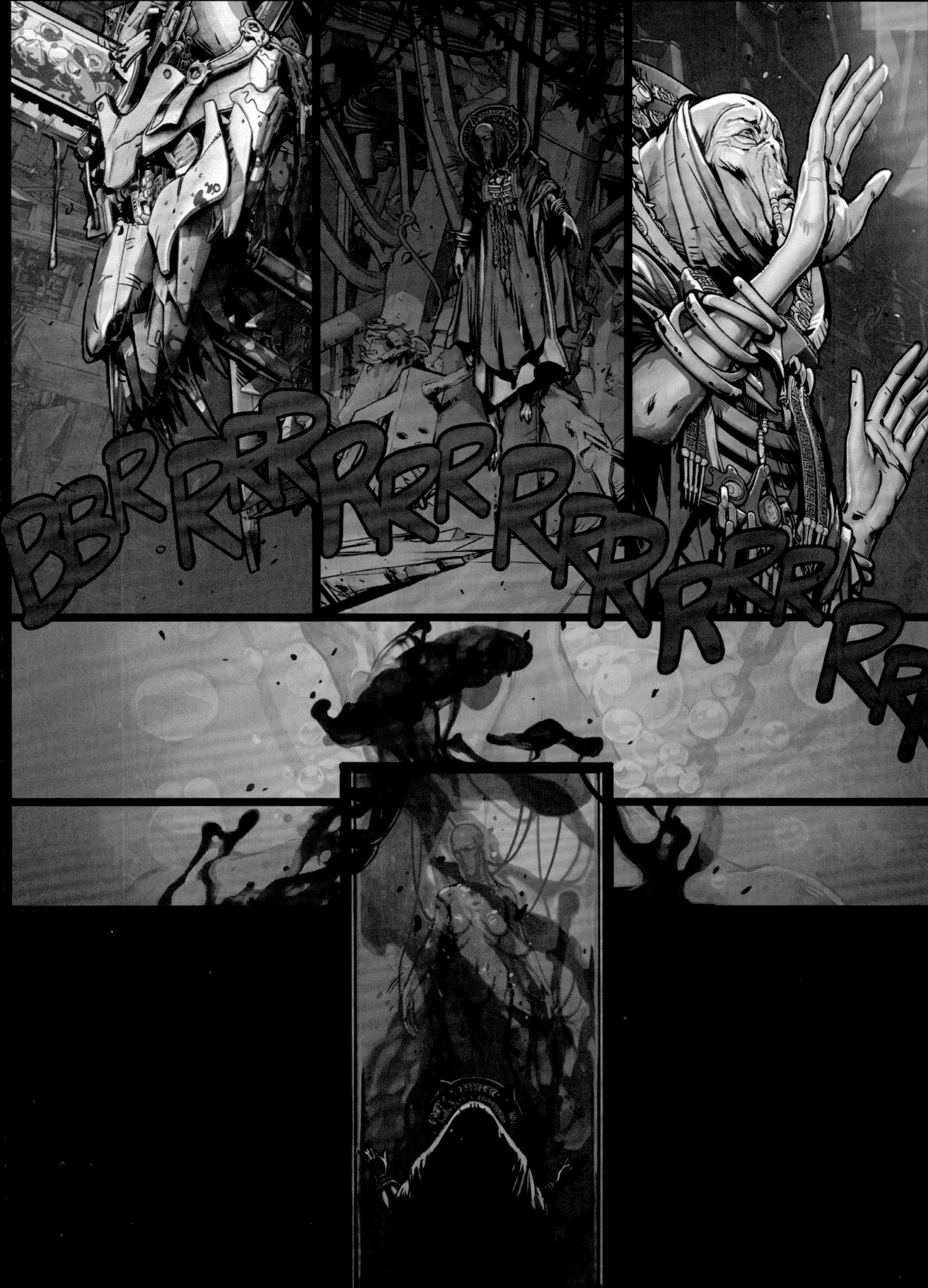
BBRRRRRRRRRRRRRRRRRR

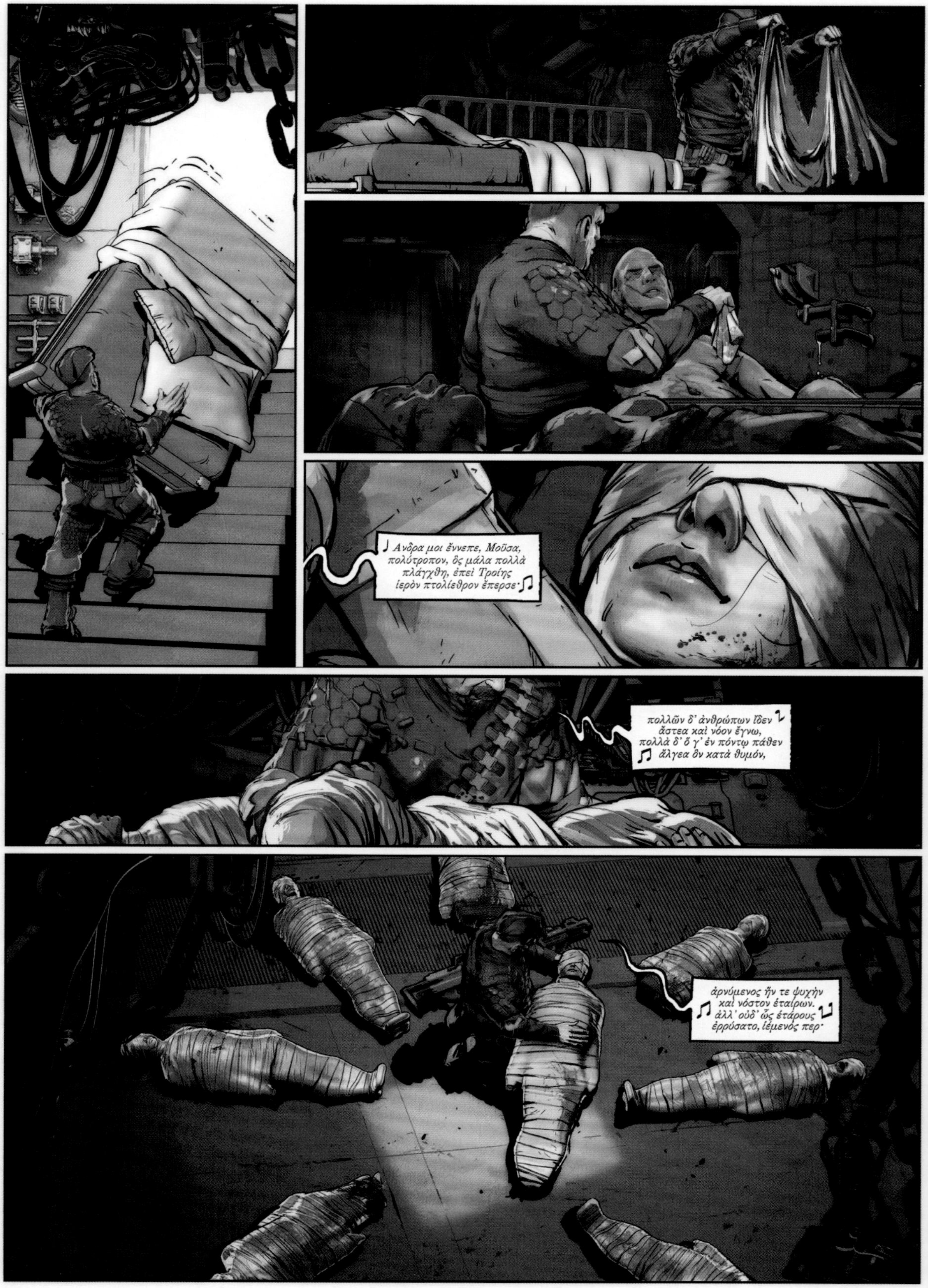
Ανδρα μοι ἔννεπε, Μοῦσα, πολύτροπον, ὃς μάλα πολλὰ πλάγχθη, ἐπεὶ Τροίης ἱερὸν πτολίεθρον ἔπερσε·
πολλῶν δ' ἀνθρώπων ἴδεν ἄστεα καὶ νόον ἔγνω, πολλὰ δ' ὅ γ' ἐν πόντῳ πάθεν ἄλγεα ὃν κατὰ θυμόν,
ἀρνύμενος ἥν τε ψυχὴν καὶ νόστον ἑταίρων. ἀλλ' οὐδ' ὧς ἑτάρους ἐρρύσατο, ἱέμενός περ·

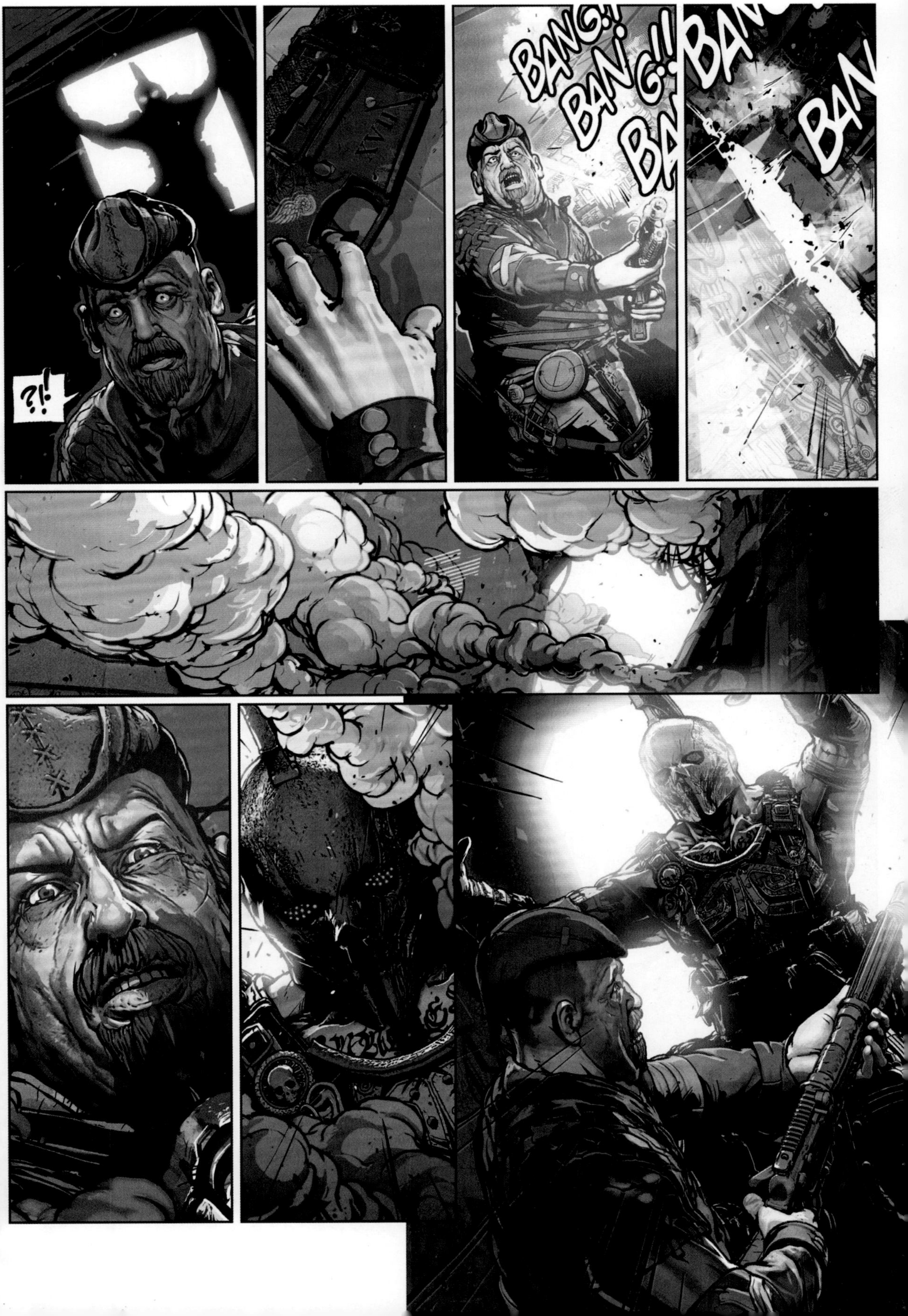
?!
BANG!!
BANG!!
BA
BAN
BAN

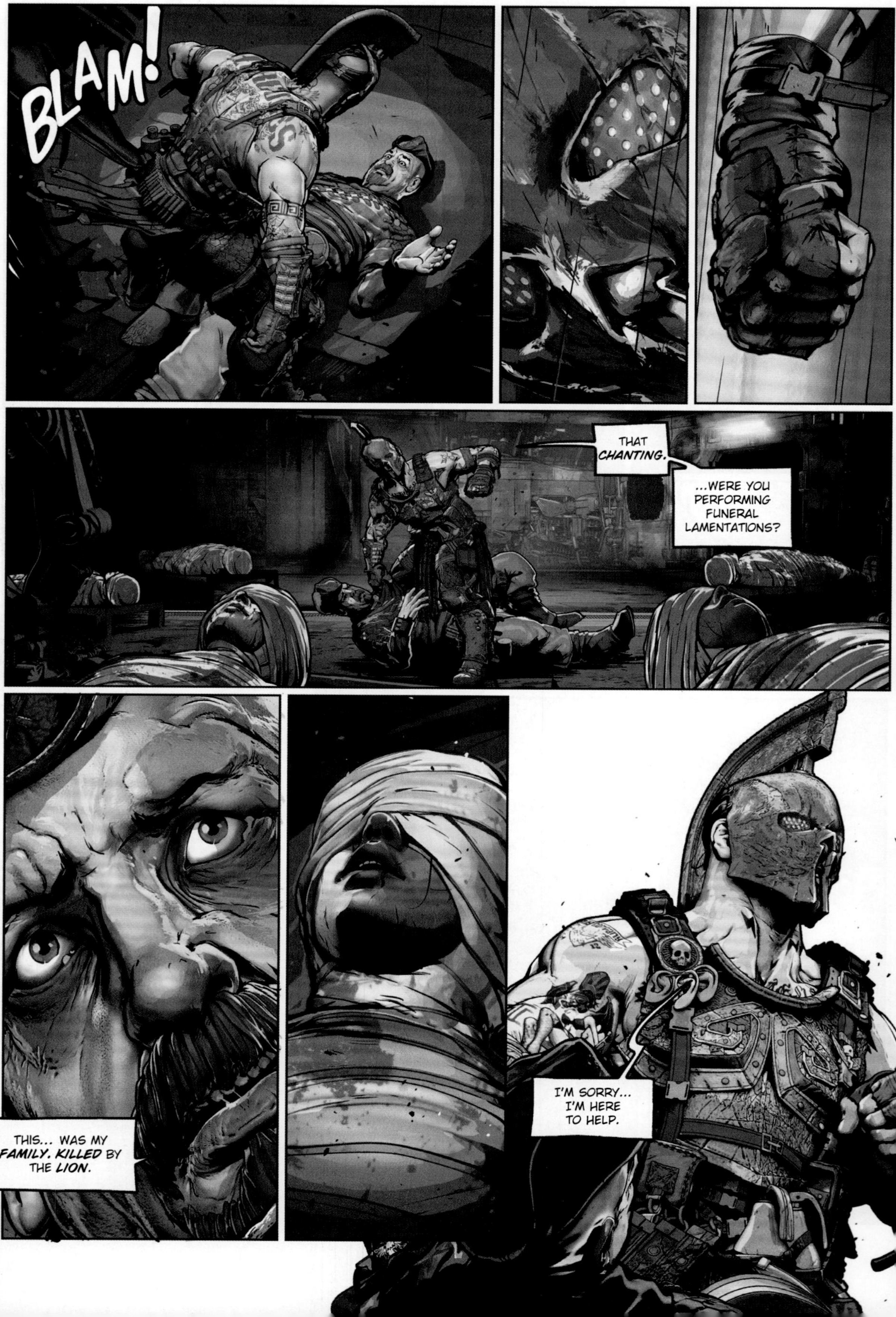
BLAM!
THAT CHANTING.
...WERE YOU PERFORMING FUNERAL LAMENTATIONS?
THIS... WAS MY FAMILY. KILLED BY THE LION.
I'M SORRY... I'M HERE TO HELP.

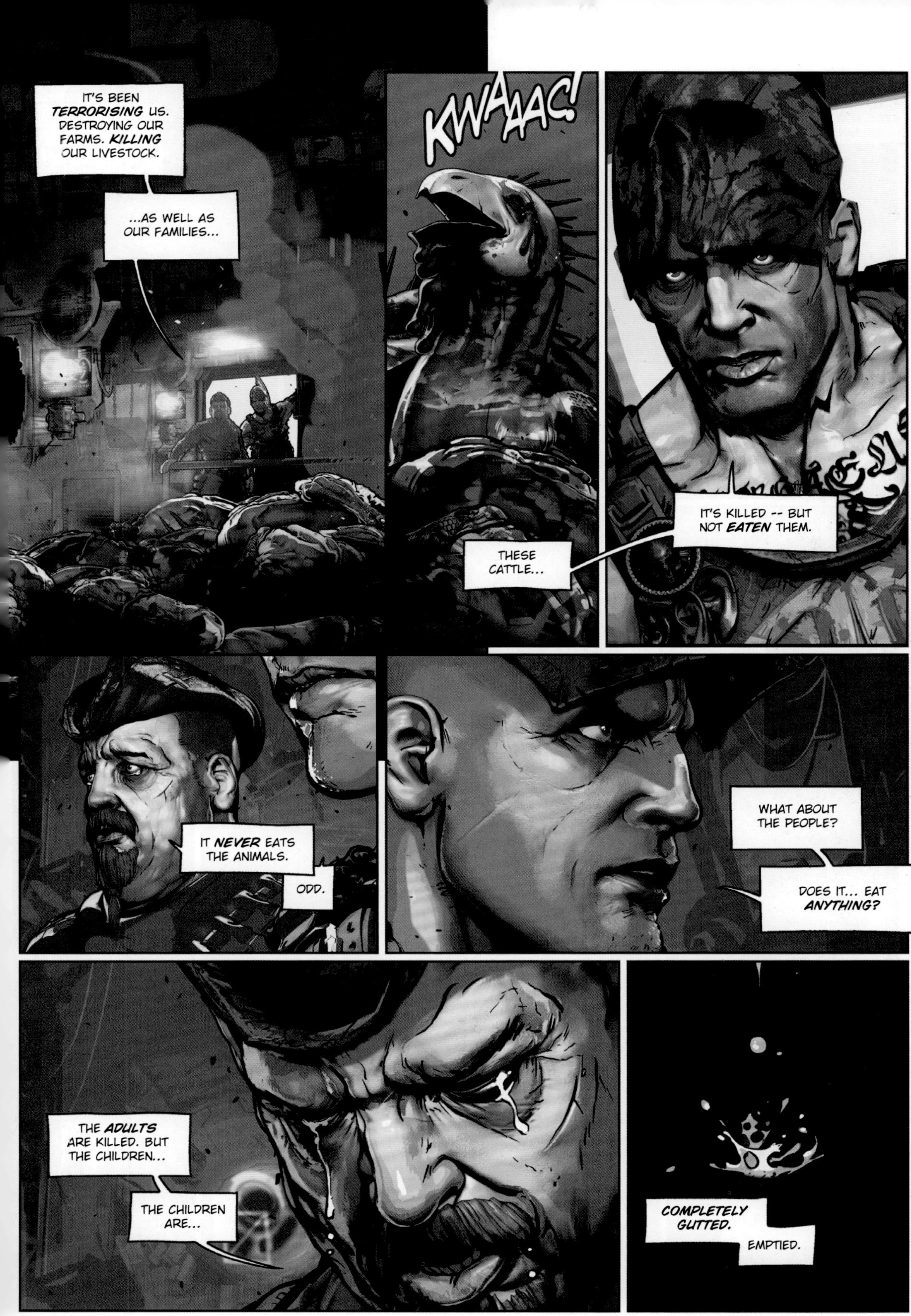
IT'S BEEN TERRORISING US. DESTROYING OUR FARMS. KILLING OUR LIVESTOCK.
...AS WELL AS OUR FAMILIES...
KWAAAAC!
THESE CATTLE...
IT'S KILLED -- BUT NOT EATEN THEM.
IT NEVER EATS THE ANIMALS.
ODD.
WHAT ABOUT THE PEOPLE?
DOES IT... EAT ANYTHING?
THE ADULTS ARE KILLED. BUT THE CHILDREN...
THE CHILDREN ARE...
COMPLETELY GUTTED.
EMPTIED.

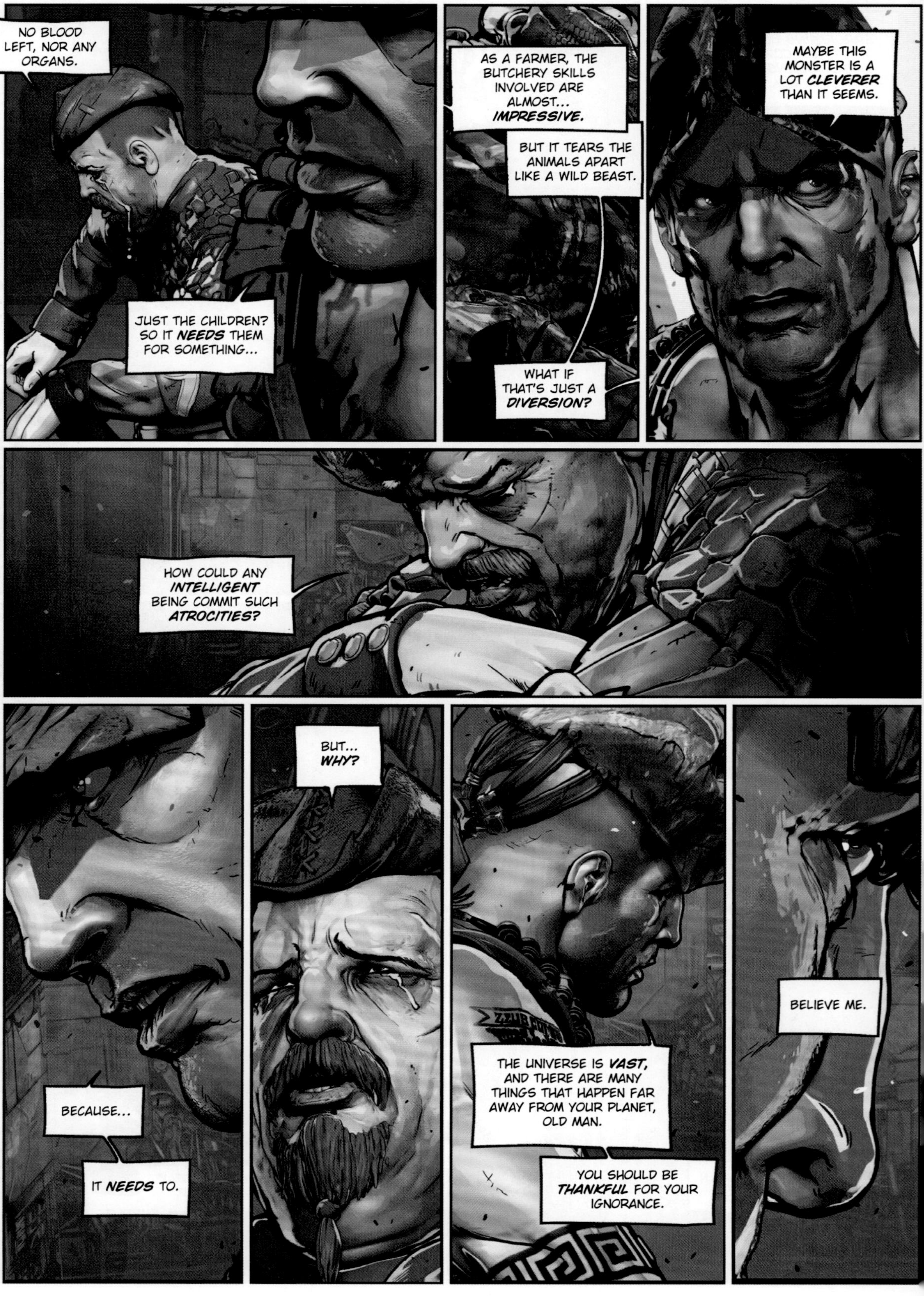
NO BLOOD LEFT, NOR ANY ORGANS.
JUST THE CHILDREN? SO IT NEEDS THEM FOR SOMETHING...
AS A FARMER, THE BUTCHERY SKILLS INVOLVED ARE ALMOST... IMPRESSIVE.
BUT IT TEARS THE ANIMALS APART LIKE A WILD BEAST.
WHAT IF THAT'S JUST A DIVERSION?
MAYBE THIS MONSTER IS A LOT CLEVERER THAN IT SEEMS.
HOW COULD ANY INTELLIGENT BEING COMMIT SUCH ATROCITIES?
BECAUSE...
IT NEEDS TO.
BUT... WHY?
THE UNIVERSE IS VAST, AND THERE ARE MANY THINGS THAT HAPPEN FAR AWAY FROM YOUR PLANET, OLD MAN.
YOU SHOULD BE THANKFUL FOR YOUR IGNORANCE.
BELIEVE ME.

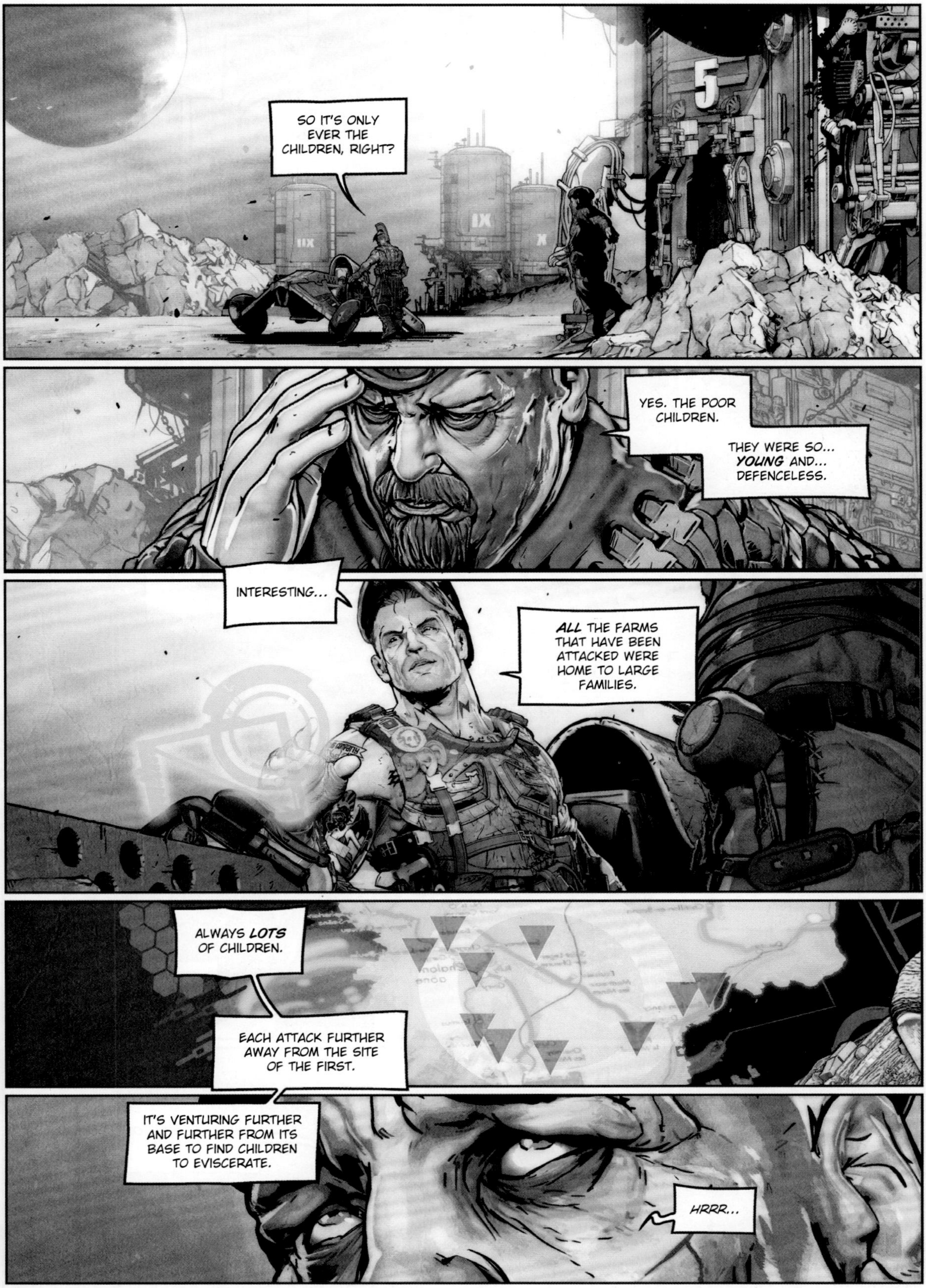

SO IT'S ONLY EVER THE CHILDREN, RIGHT?
5
YES. THE POOR CHILDREN.
THEY WERE SO... *YOUNG* AND... DEFENCELESS.
INTERESTING...
ALL THE FARMS THAT HAVE BEEN ATTACKED WERE HOME TO LARGE FAMILIES.
ALWAYS *LOTS* OF CHILDREN.
EACH ATTACK FURTHER AWAY FROM THE SITE OF THE FIRST.
IT'S VENTURING FURTHER AND FURTHER FROM ITS BASE TO FIND CHILDREN TO EVISCERATE.
HRRR...

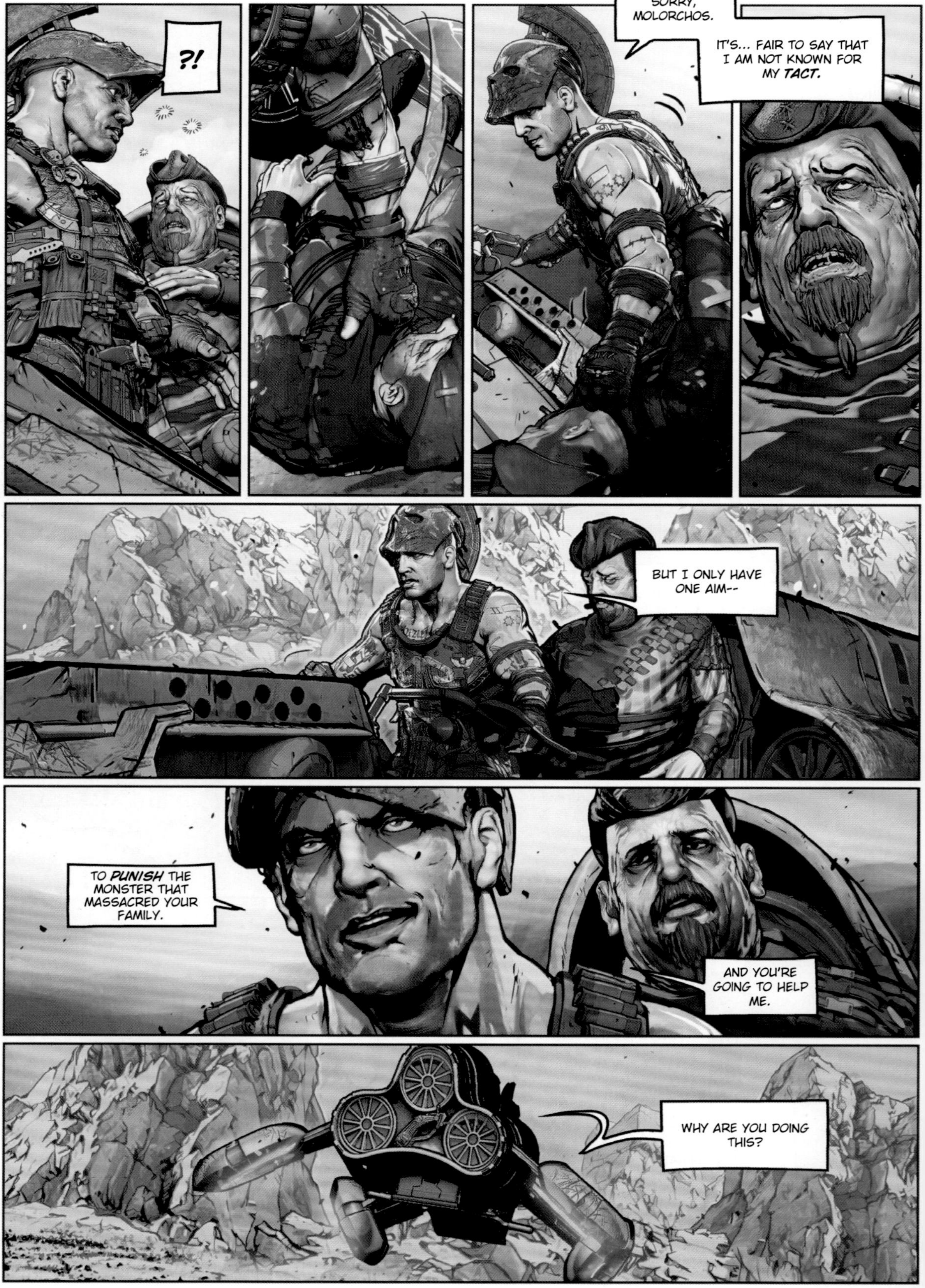
?!
SORRY, MOLORCHOS.
IT'S... FAIR TO SAY THAT I AM NOT KNOWN FOR MY *TACT.*
BUT I ONLY HAVE ONE AIM--
TO *PUNISH* THE MONSTER THAT MASSACRED YOUR FAMILY.
AND YOU'RE GOING TO HELP ME.
WHY ARE YOU DOING THIS?

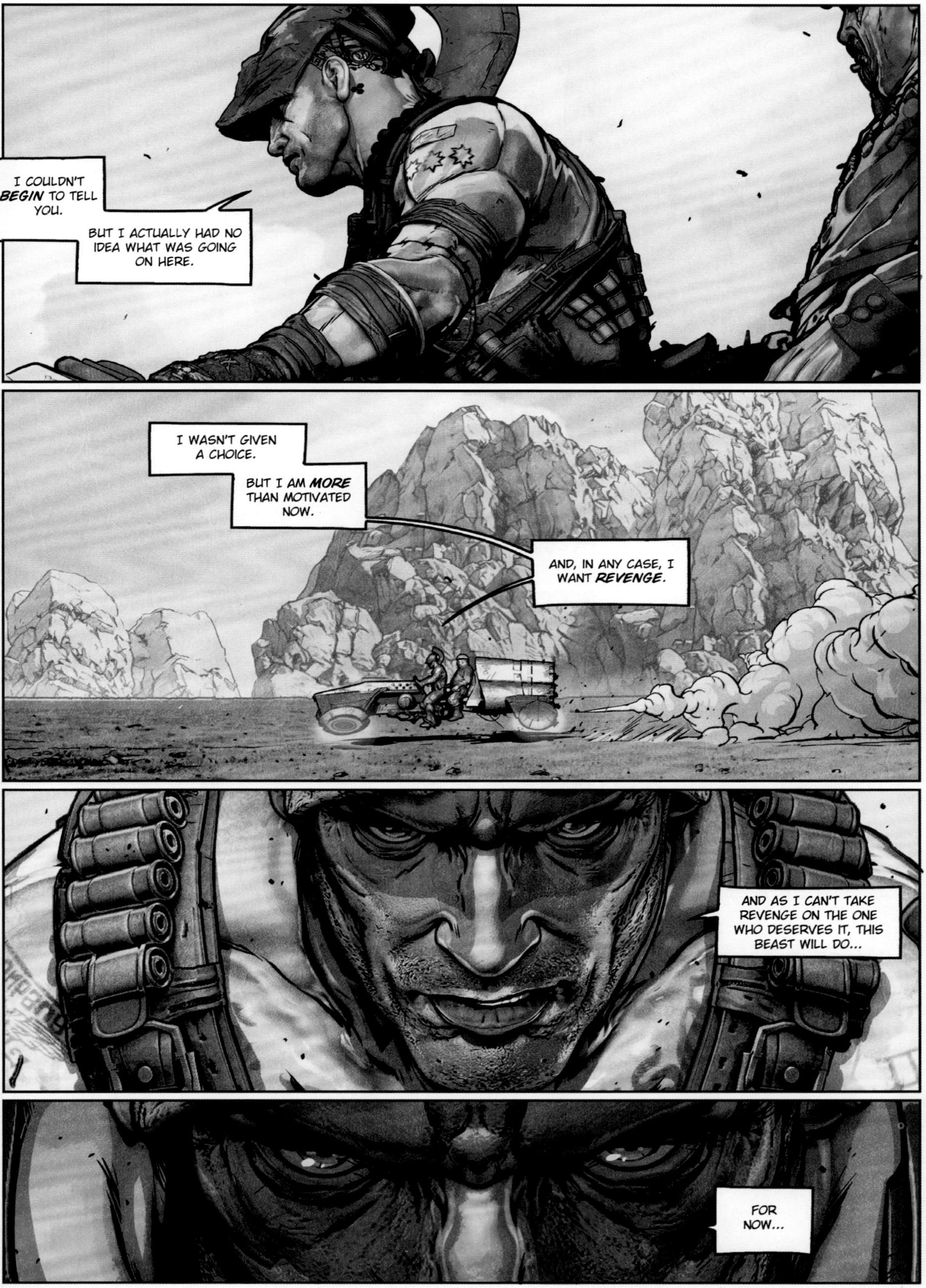
I COULDN'T BEGIN TO TELL YOU.
BUT I ACTUALLY HAD NO IDEA WHAT WAS GOING ON HERE.
I WASN'T GIVEN A CHOICE.
BUT I AM MORE THAN MOTIVATED NOW.
AND, IN ANY CASE, I WANT REVENGE.
AND AS I CAN'T TAKE REVENGE ON THE ONE WHO DESERVES IT, THIS BEAST WILL DO...
FOR NOW...

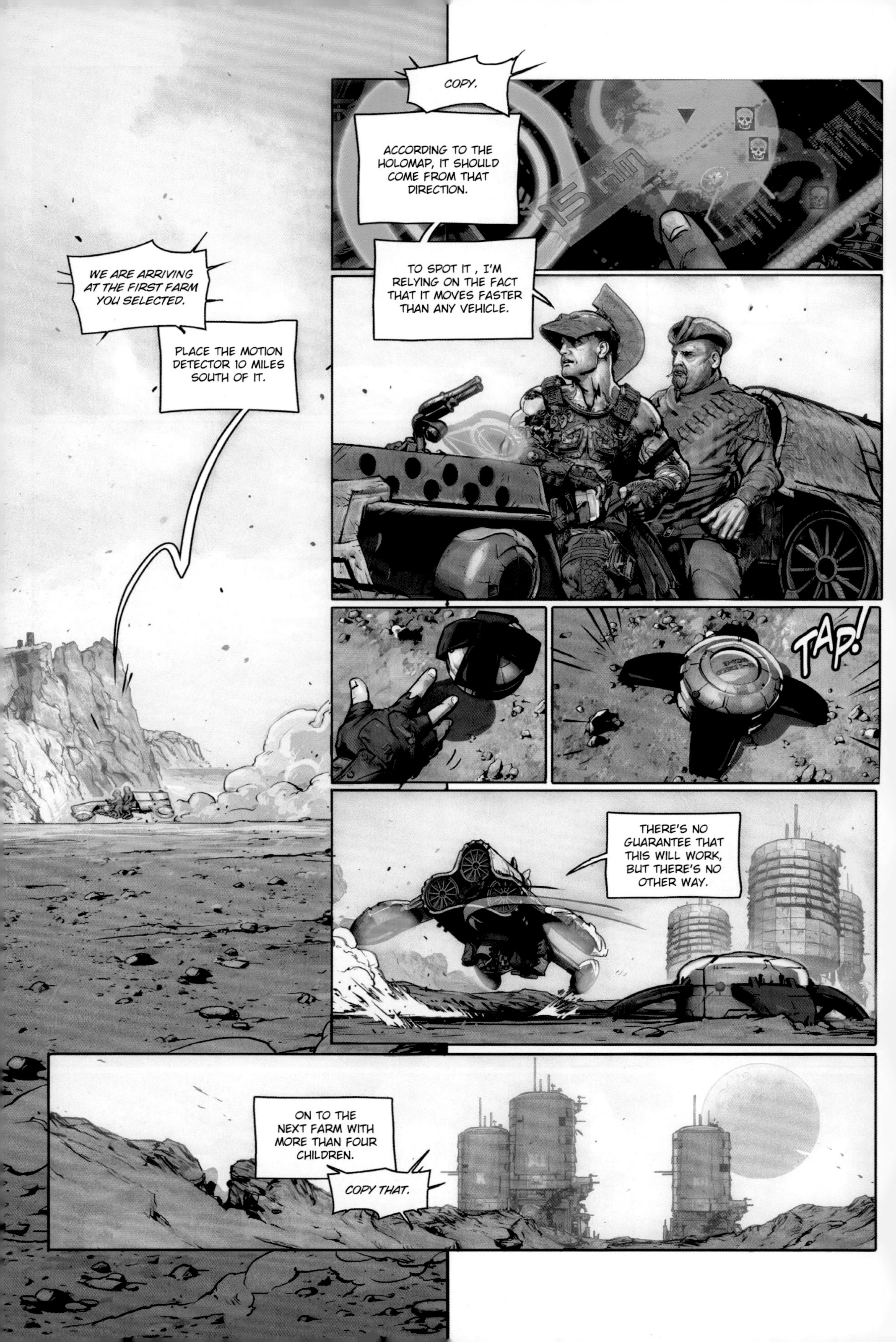
WE ARE ARRIVING AT THE FIRST FARM YOU SELECTED.
PLACE THE MOTION DETECTOR 10 MILES SOUTH OF IT.
COPY.
ACCORDING TO THE HOLOMAP, IT SHOULD COME FROM THAT DIRECTION.
15 km
TO SPOT IT , I'M RELYING ON THE FACT THAT IT MOVES FASTER THAN ANY VEHICLE.
TAP!
THERE'S NO GUARANTEE THAT THIS WILL WORK, BUT THERE'S NO OTHER WAY.
ON TO THE NEXT FARM WITH MORE THAN FOUR CHILDREN.
COPY THAT.

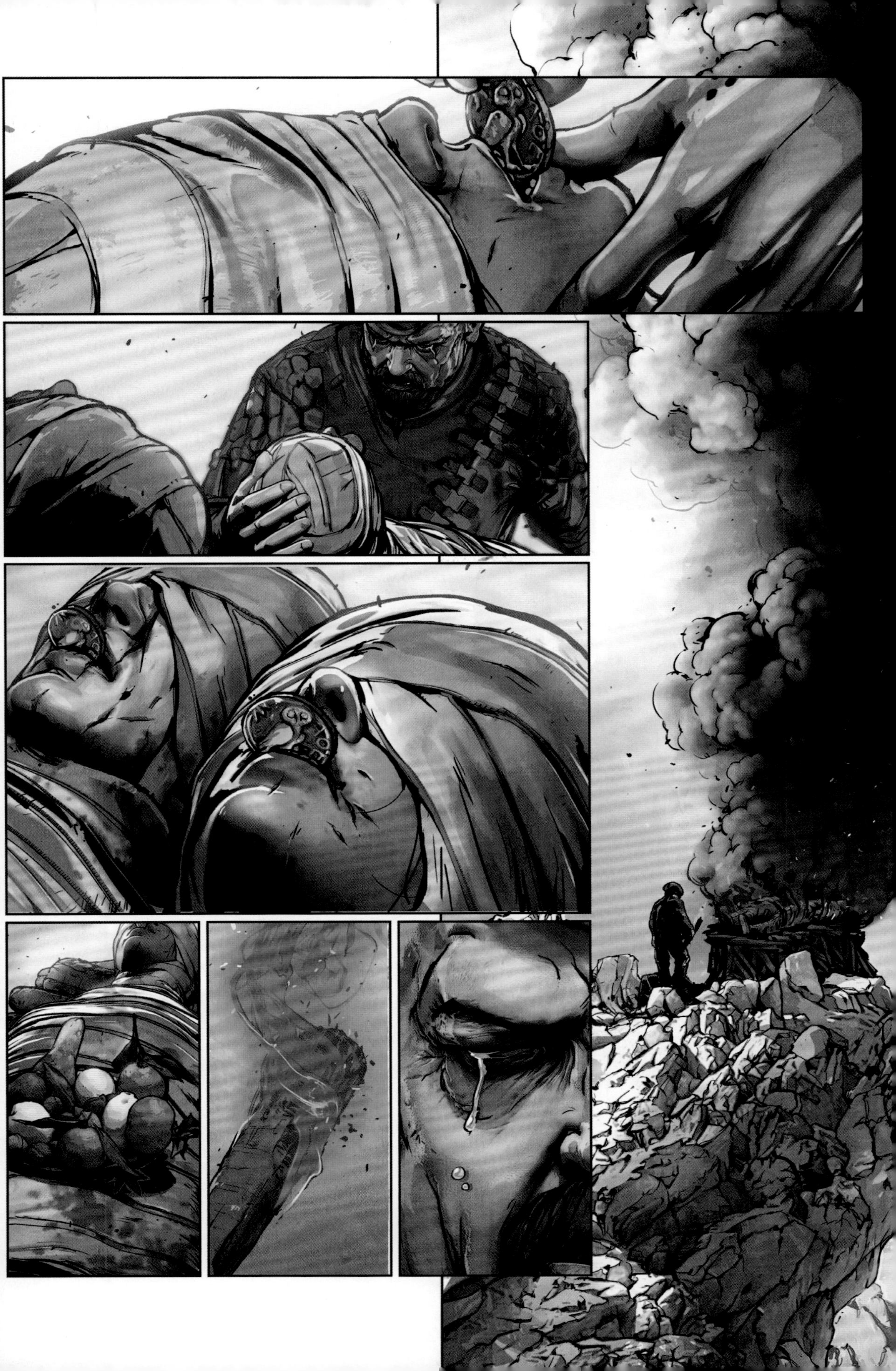

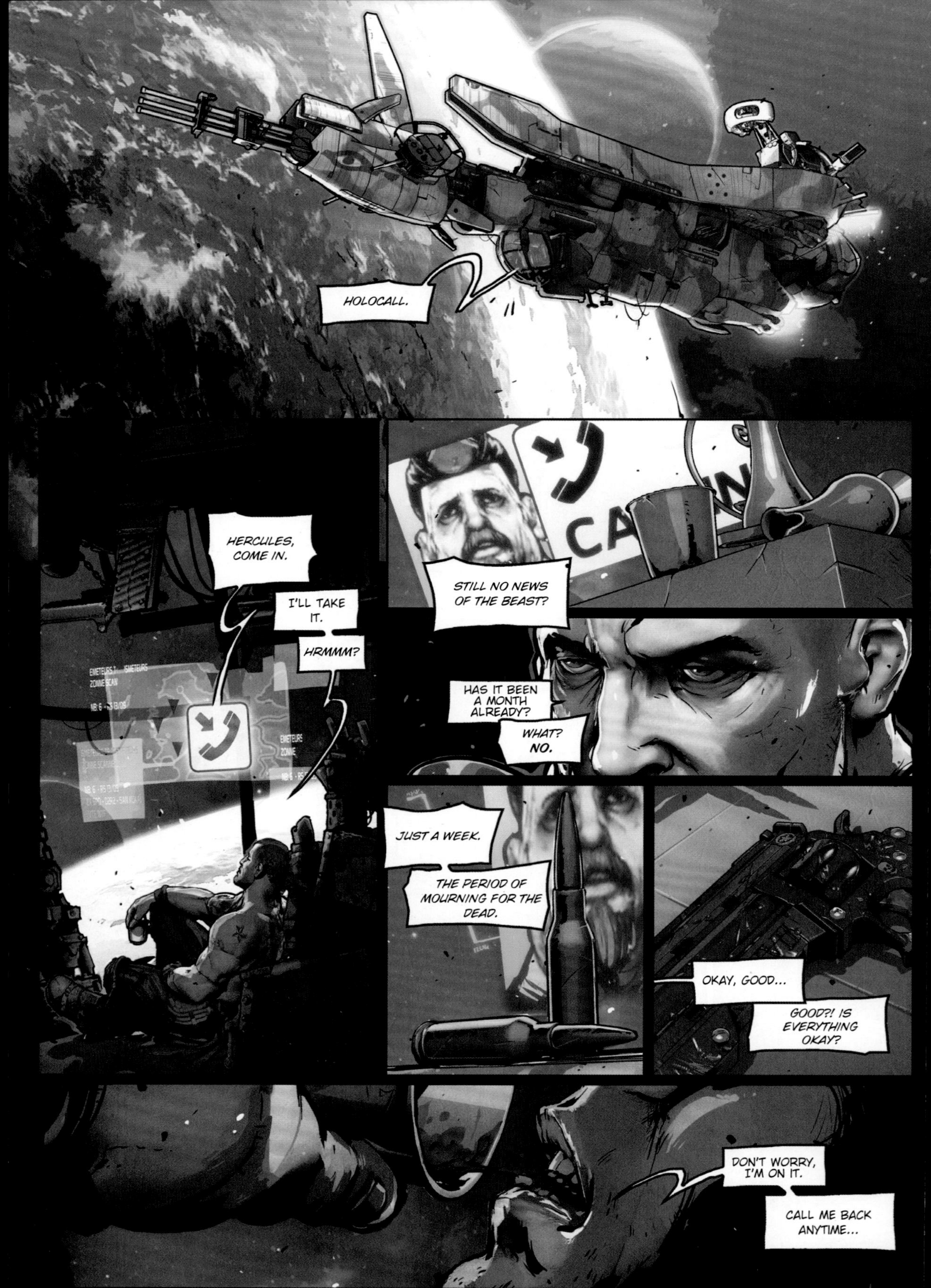
HOLOCALL.
HERCULES, COME IN.
I'LL TAKE IT.
HRMMM?
STILL NO NEWS OF THE BEAST?
HAS IT BEEN A MONTH ALREADY?
WHAT? NO.
JUST A WEEK.
THE PERIOD OF MOURNING FOR THE DEAD.
OKAY, GOOD...
GOOD?! IS EVERYTHING OKAY?
DON'T WORRY, I'M ON IT.
CALL ME BACK ANYTIME...

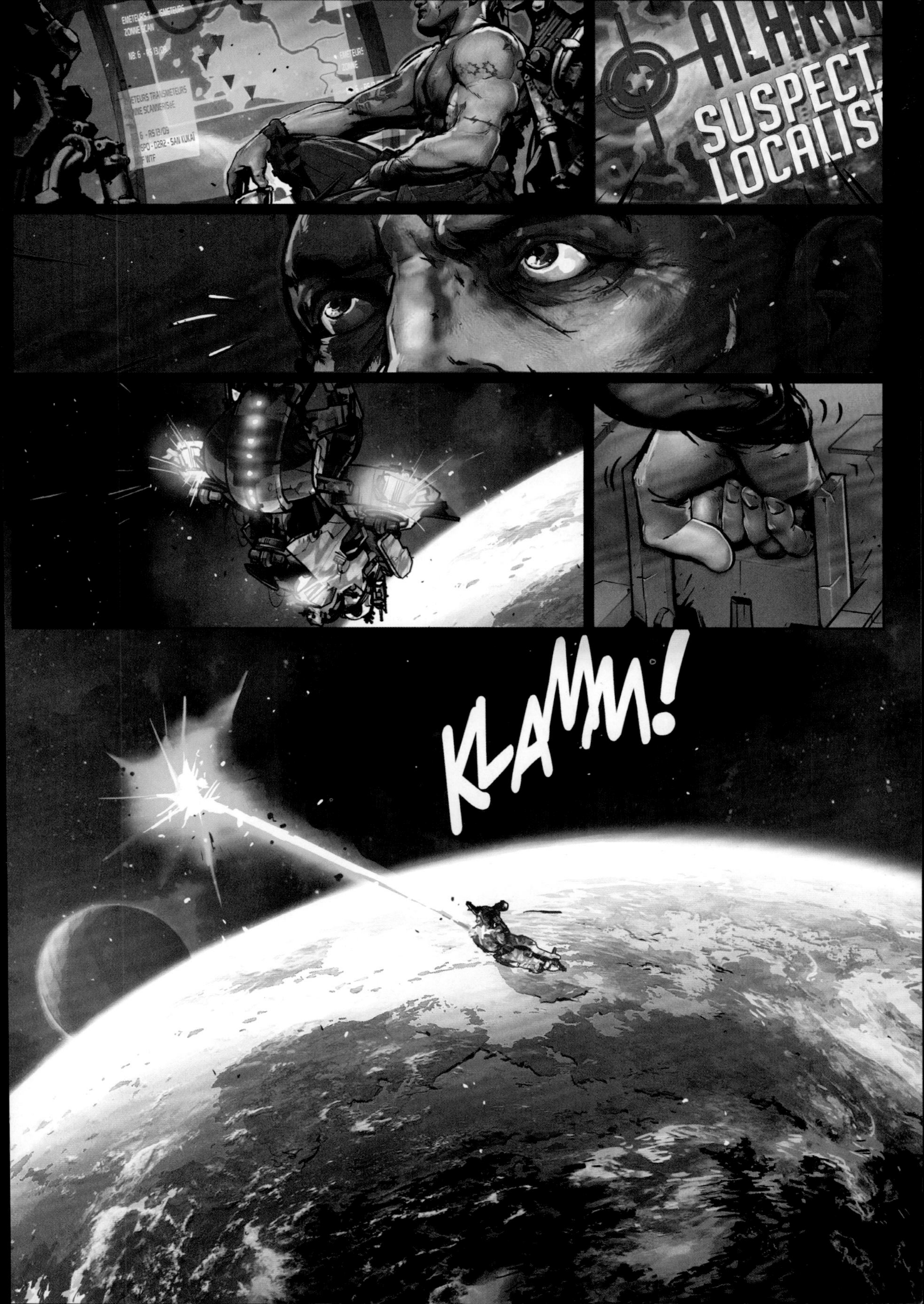

ALARM
SUSPECT,
LOCALIS
KLAMM!

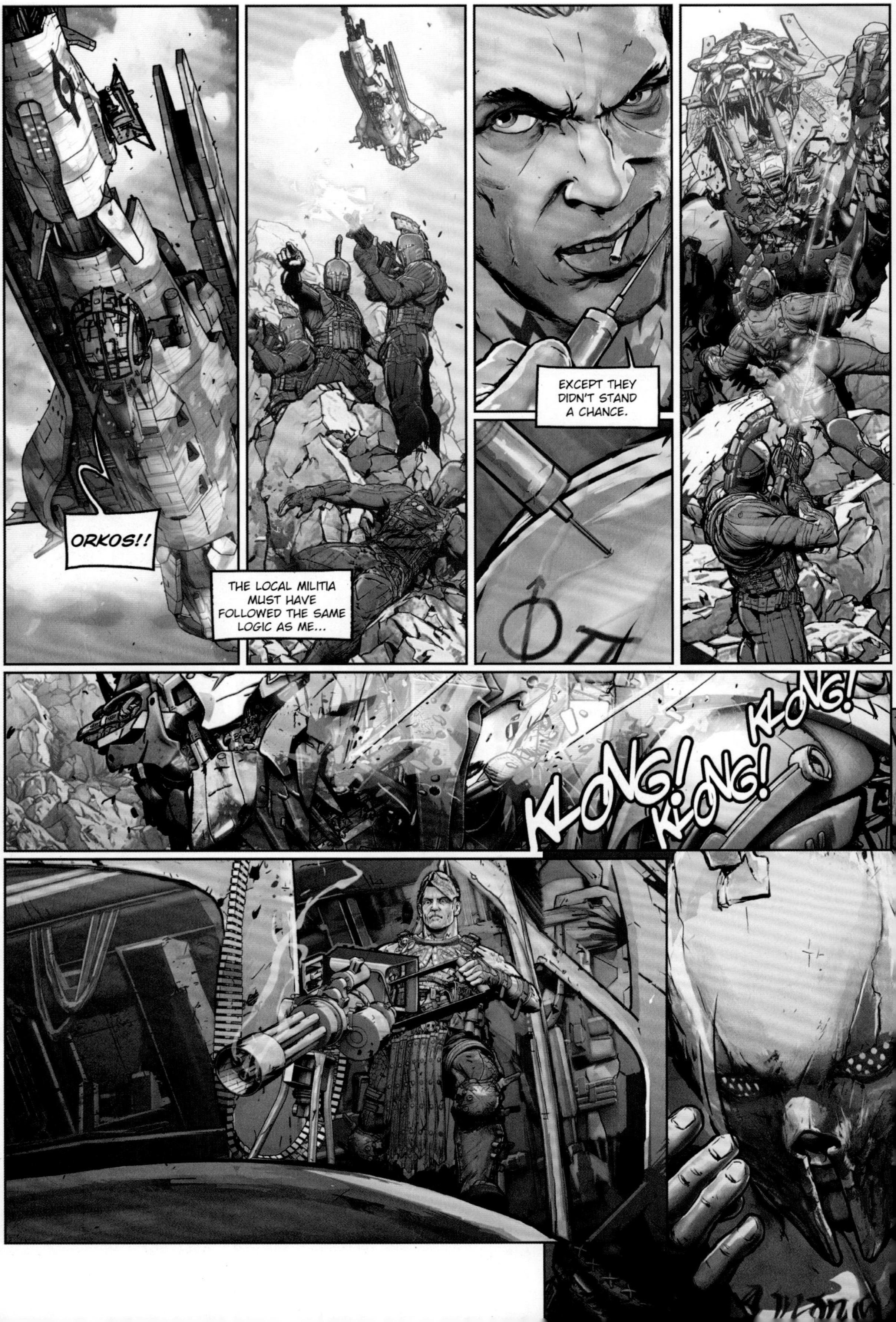
ORKOS!!
THE LOCAL MILITIA MUST HAVE FOLLOWED THE SAME LOGIC AS ME...
EXCEPT THEY DIDN'T STAND A CHANCE.
KLONG!
KLONG!
KLONG!

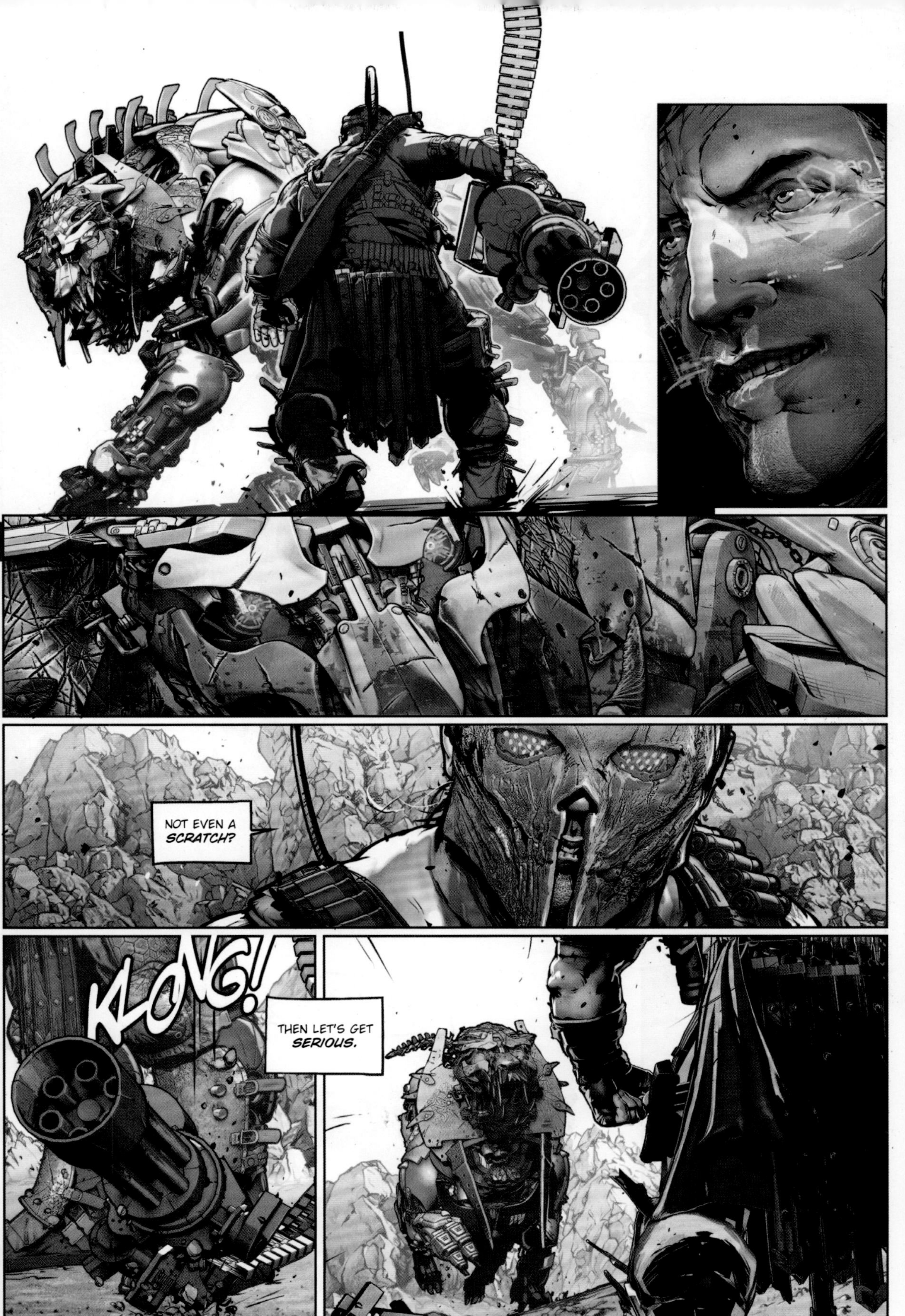
NOT EVEN A SCRATCH?
KLONG!
THEN LET'S GET SERIOUS.

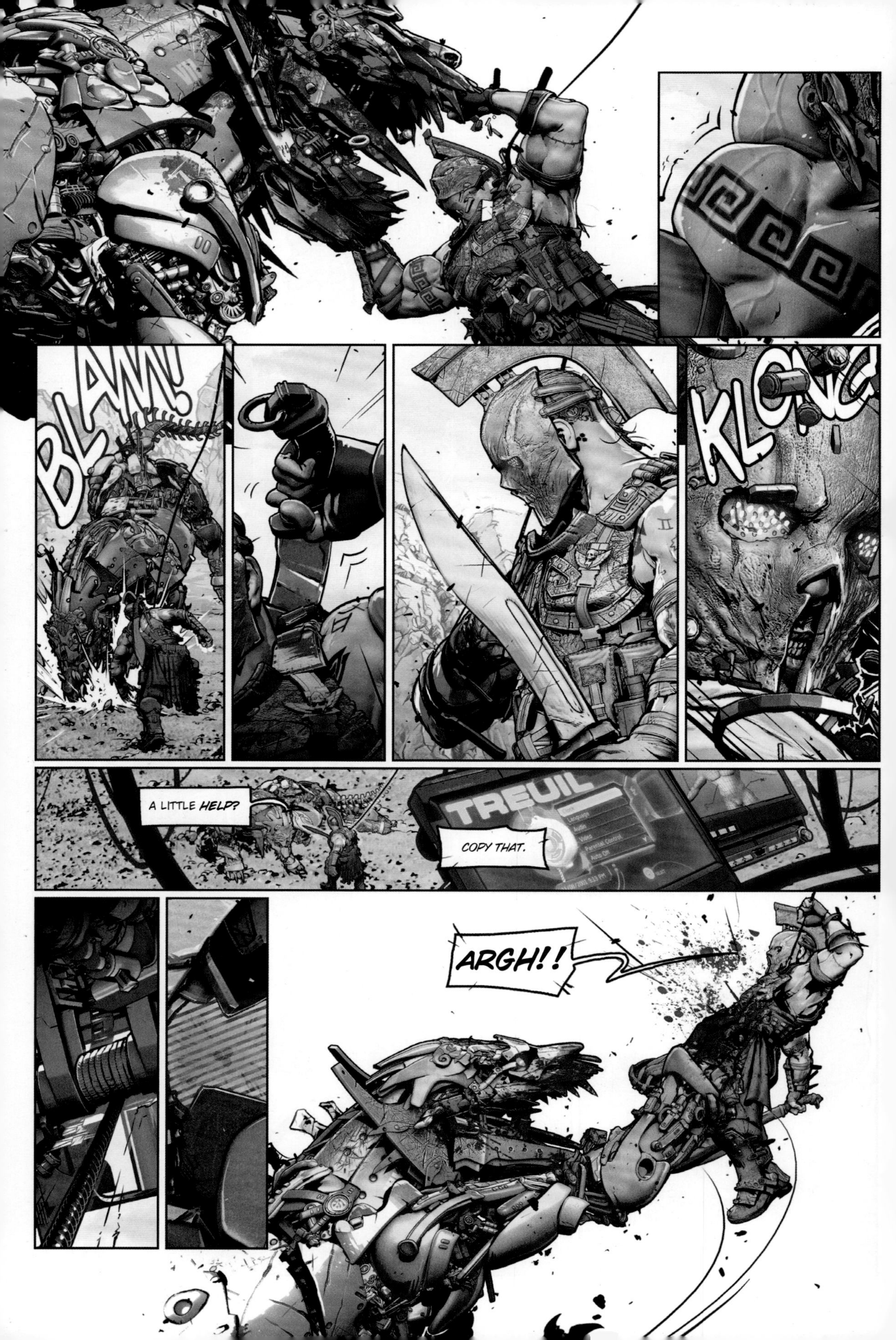
BLAM!
KLONG
A LITTLE HELP?
TREUIL
COPY THAT.
ARGH!!

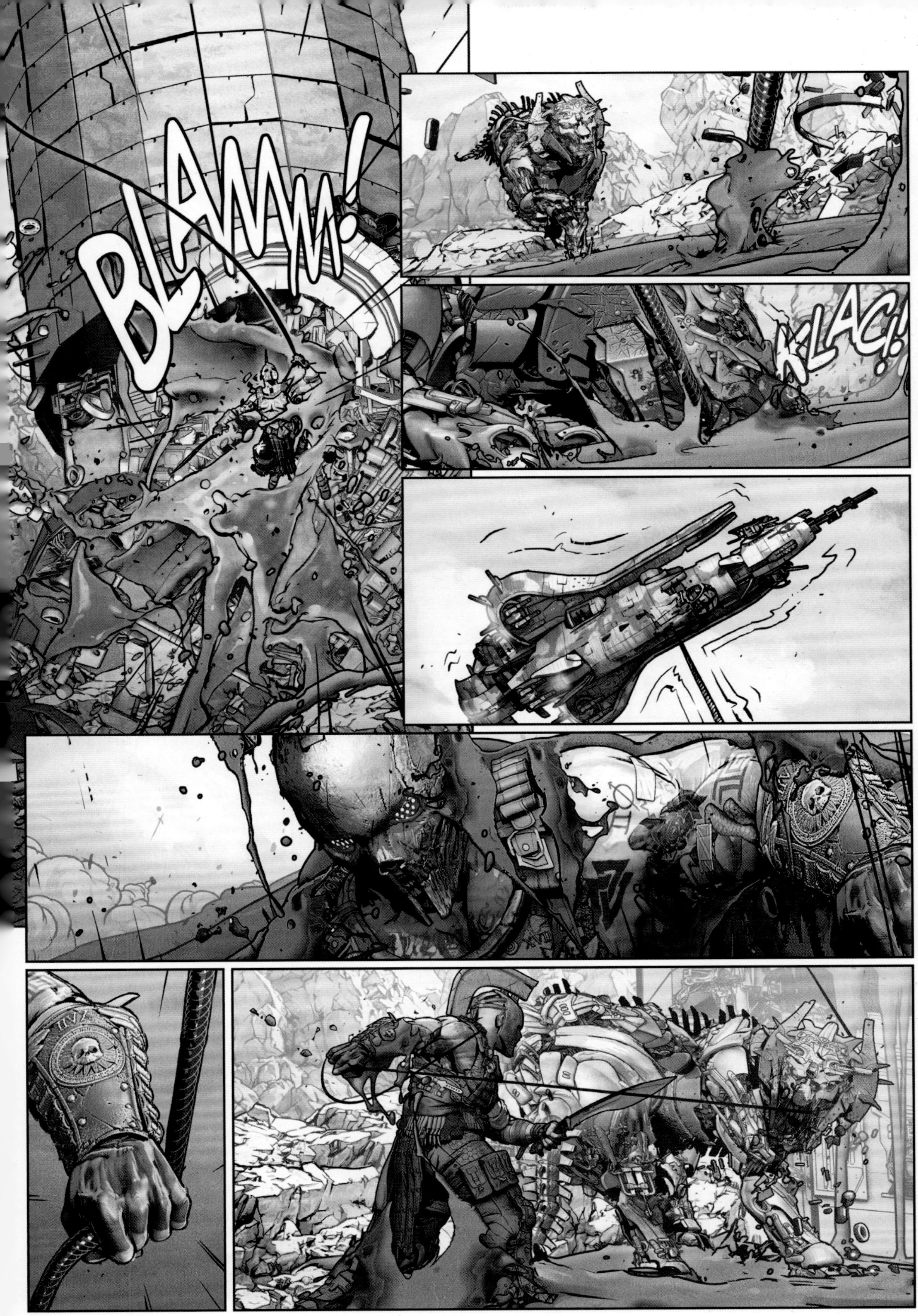
BLAMM!
KLAC!

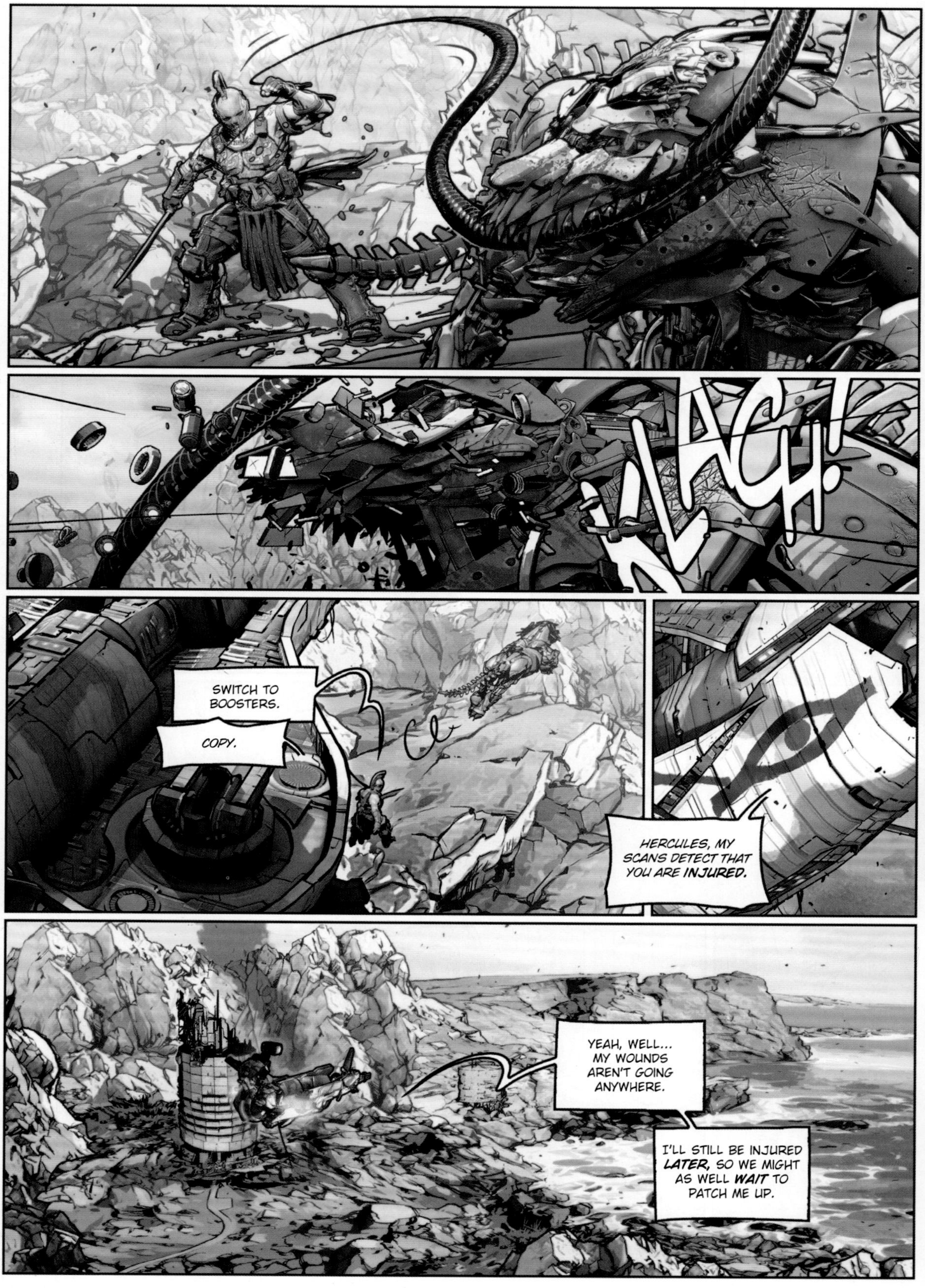
SWITCH TO BOOSTERS.
COPY.
HERCULES, MY SCANS DETECT THAT YOU ARE **INJURED.**
YEAH, WELL... MY WOUNDS AREN'T GOING ANYWHERE.
I'LL STILL BE INJURED **LATER,** SO WE MIGHT AS WELL **WAIT** TO PATCH ME UP.

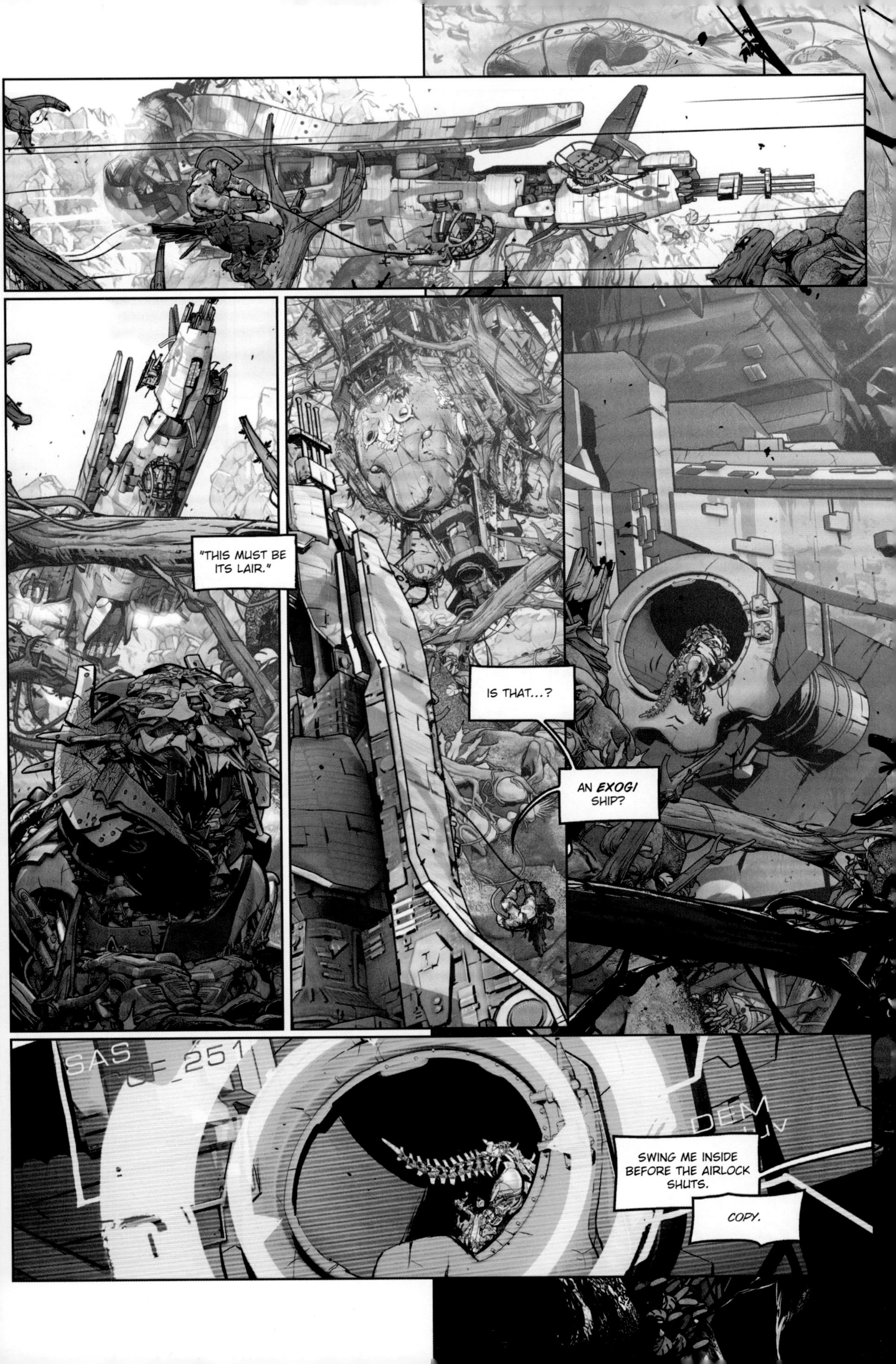
"THIS MUST BE ITS LAIR."
IS THAT...?
AN *EXOGI* SHIP?
SAS
251
DEM
SWING ME INSIDE BEFORE THE AIRLOCK SHUTS.
COPY.

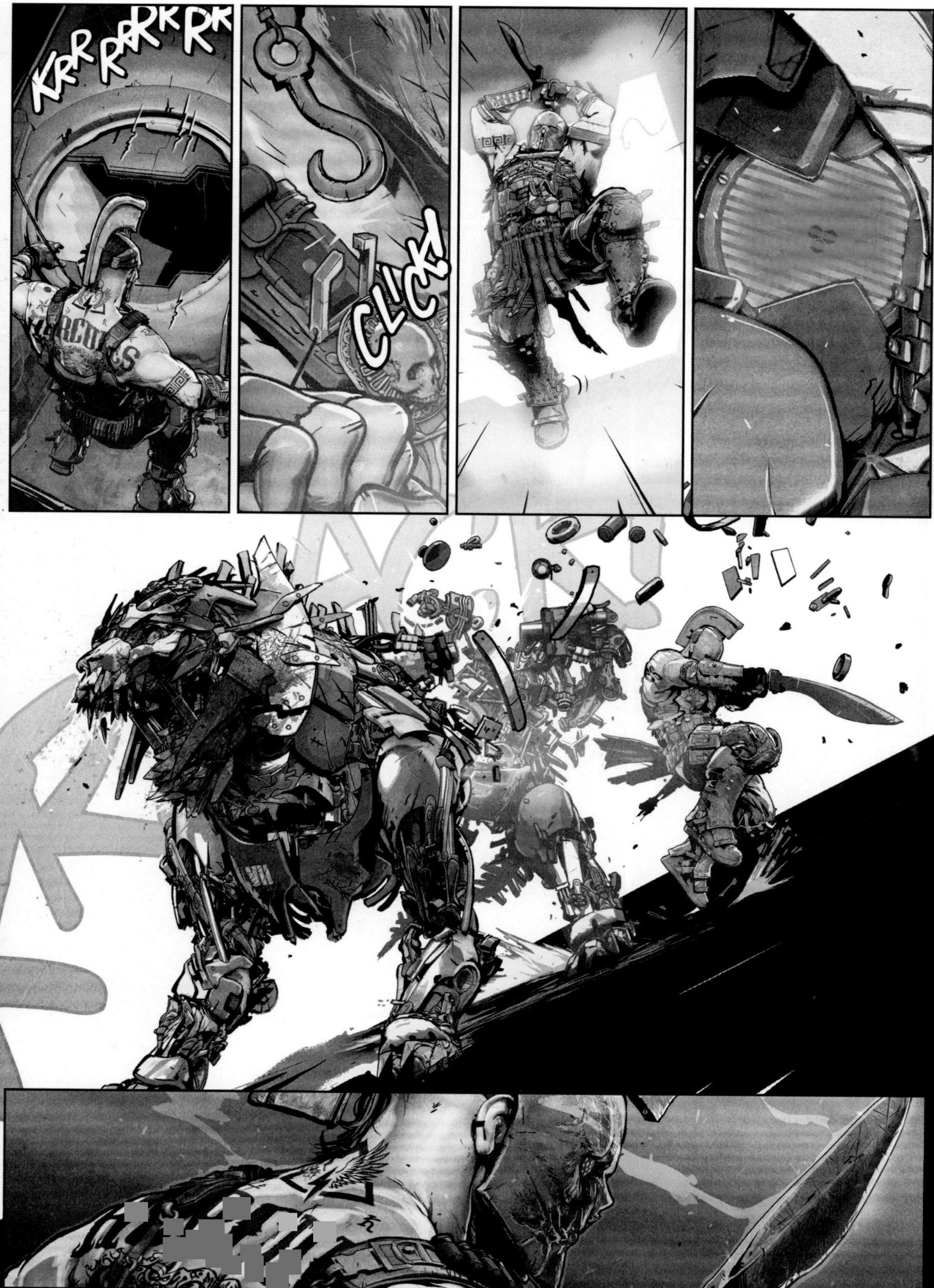
KRRRRRKRRK
CLICK!

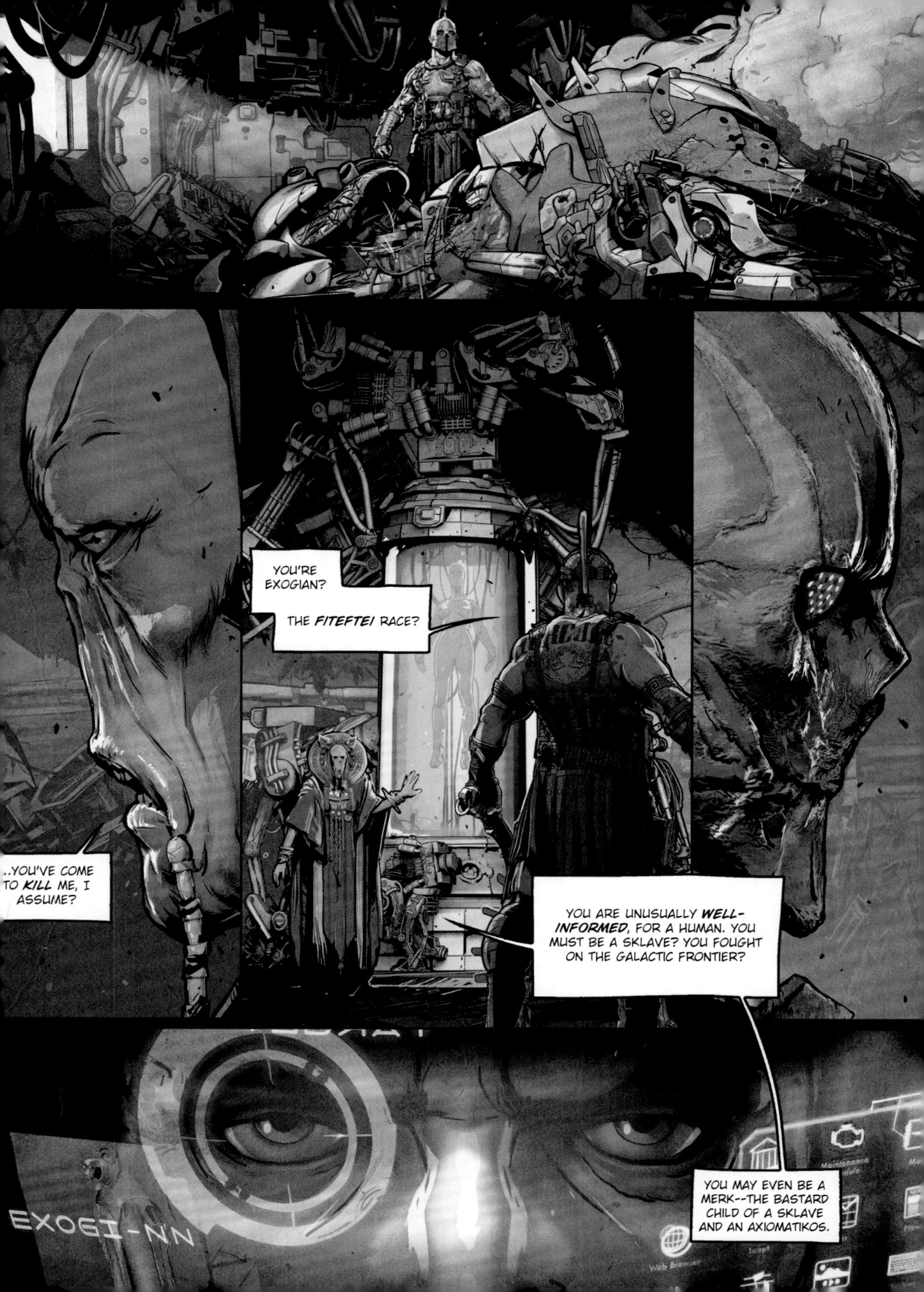
YOU'RE EXOGIAN?
THE FITEFTEI RACE?
..YOU'VE COME TO KILL ME, I ASSUME?
YOU ARE UNUSUALLY WELL-INFORMED, FOR A HUMAN. YOU MUST BE A SKLAVE? YOU FOUGHT ON THE GALACTIC FRONTIER?
EXOGI-NN
YOU MAY EVEN BE A MERK--THE BASTARD CHILD OF A SKLAVE AND AN AXIOMATIKOS.

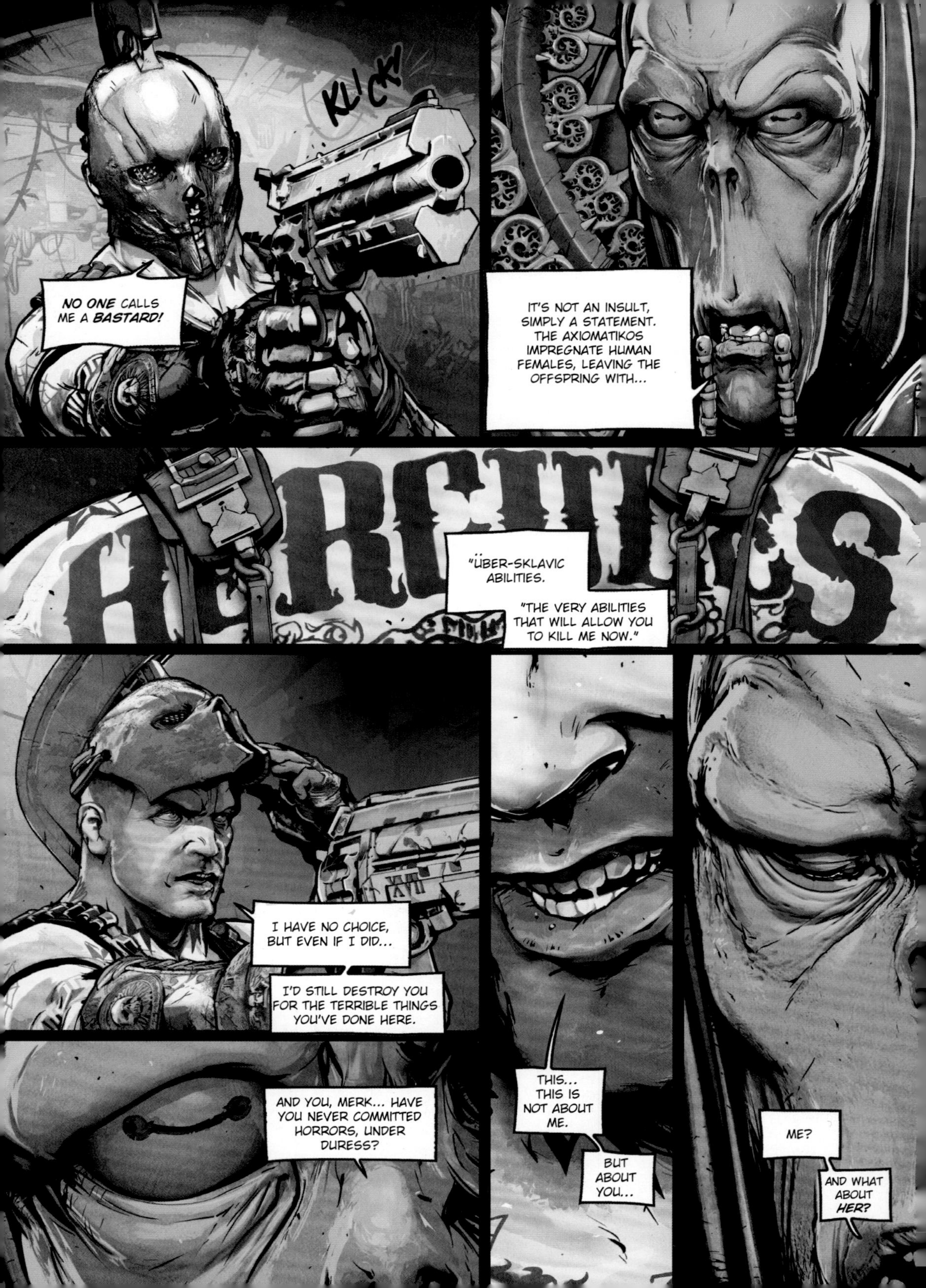
KL'CK!
NO ONE CALLS ME A BASTARD!
IT'S NOT AN INSULT, SIMPLY A STATEMENT. THE AXIOMATIKOS IMPREGNATE HUMAN FEMALES, LEAVING THE OFFSPRING WITH...
"ÜBER-SKLAVIC ABILITIES.
"THE VERY ABILITIES THAT WILL ALLOW YOU TO KILL ME NOW."
I HAVE NO CHOICE, BUT EVEN IF I DID...
I'D STILL DESTROY YOU FOR THE TERRIBLE THINGS YOU'VE DONE HERE.
AND YOU, MERK... HAVE YOU NEVER COMMITTED HORRORS, UNDER DURESS?
THIS... THIS IS NOT ABOUT ME.
BUT ABOUT YOU...
ME?
AND WHAT ABOUT HER?

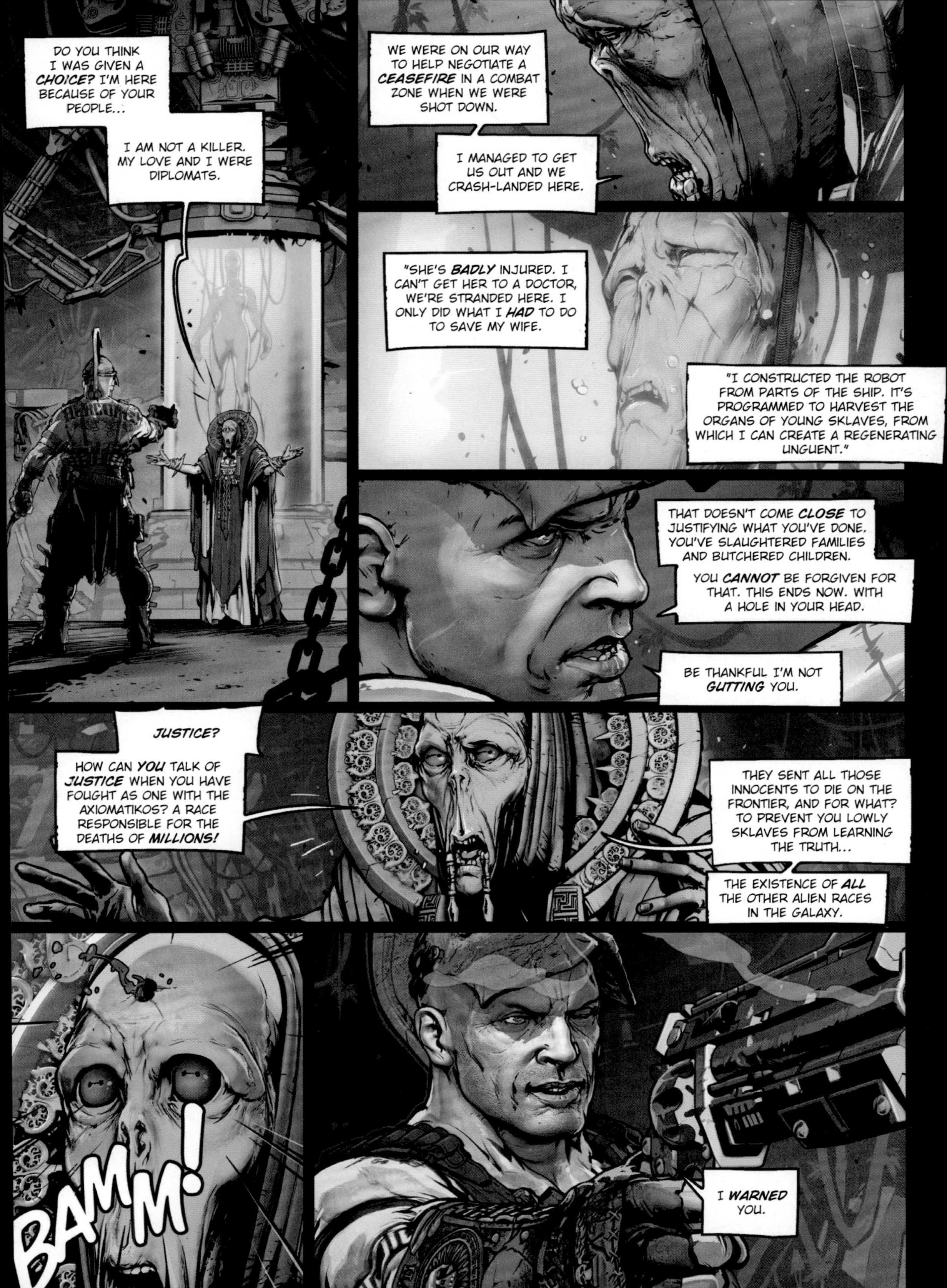
DO YOU THINK I WAS GIVEN A CHOICE? I'M HERE BECAUSE OF YOUR PEOPLE...
I AM NOT A KILLER. MY LOVE AND I WERE DIPLOMATS.
WE WERE ON OUR WAY TO HELP NEGOTIATE A CEASEFIRE IN A COMBAT ZONE WHEN WE WERE SHOT DOWN.
I MANAGED TO GET US OUT AND WE CRASH-LANDED HERE.
"SHE'S BADLY INJURED. I CAN'T GET HER TO A DOCTOR, WE'RE STRANDED HERE. I ONLY DID WHAT I HAD TO DO TO SAVE MY WIFE.
"I CONSTRUCTED THE ROBOT FROM PARTS OF THE SHIP. IT'S PROGRAMMED TO HARVEST THE ORGANS OF YOUNG SKLAVES, FROM WHICH I CAN CREATE A REGENERATING UNGUENT."
THAT DOESN'T COME CLOSE TO JUSTIFYING WHAT YOU'VE DONE. YOU'VE SLAUGHTERED FAMILIES AND BUTCHERED CHILDREN.
YOU CANNOT BE FORGIVEN FOR THAT. THIS ENDS NOW. WITH A HOLE IN YOUR HEAD.
BE THANKFUL I'M NOT GUTTING YOU.
JUSTICE?
HOW CAN YOU TALK OF JUSTICE WHEN YOU HAVE FOUGHT AS ONE WITH THE AXIOMATIKOS? A RACE RESPONSIBLE FOR THE DEATHS OF MILLIONS!
THEY SENT ALL THOSE INNOCENTS TO DIE ON THE FRONTIER, AND FOR WHAT? TO PREVENT YOU LOWLY SKLAVES FROM LEARNING THE TRUTH...
THE EXISTENCE OF ALL THE OTHER ALIEN RACES IN THE GALAXY.
BAMM!
I WARNED YOU.

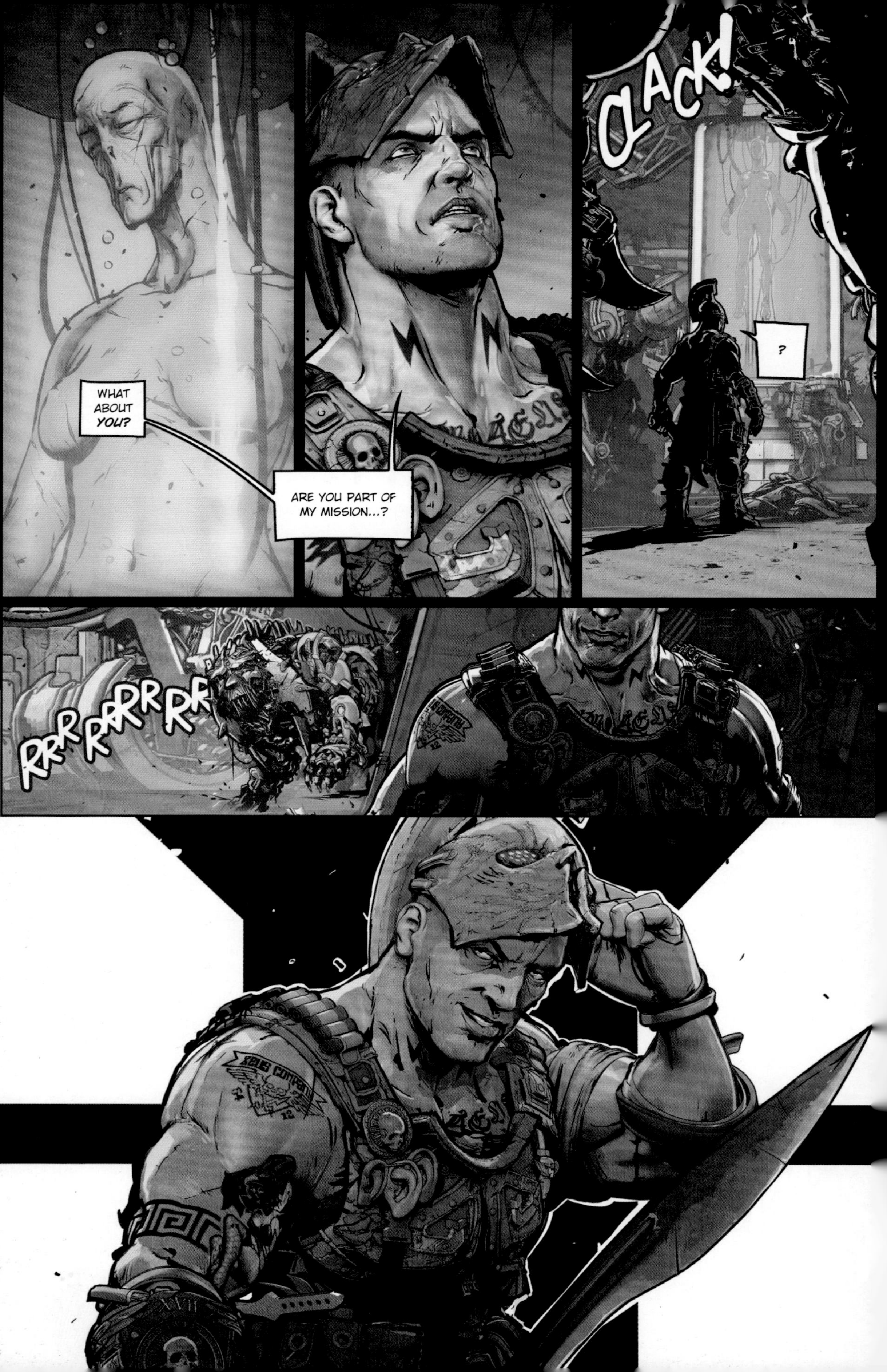
CLACK!
WHAT ABOUT YOU?
ARE YOU PART OF MY MISSION...?
?
RRRRRRRRR

LOCATION: HERNE_

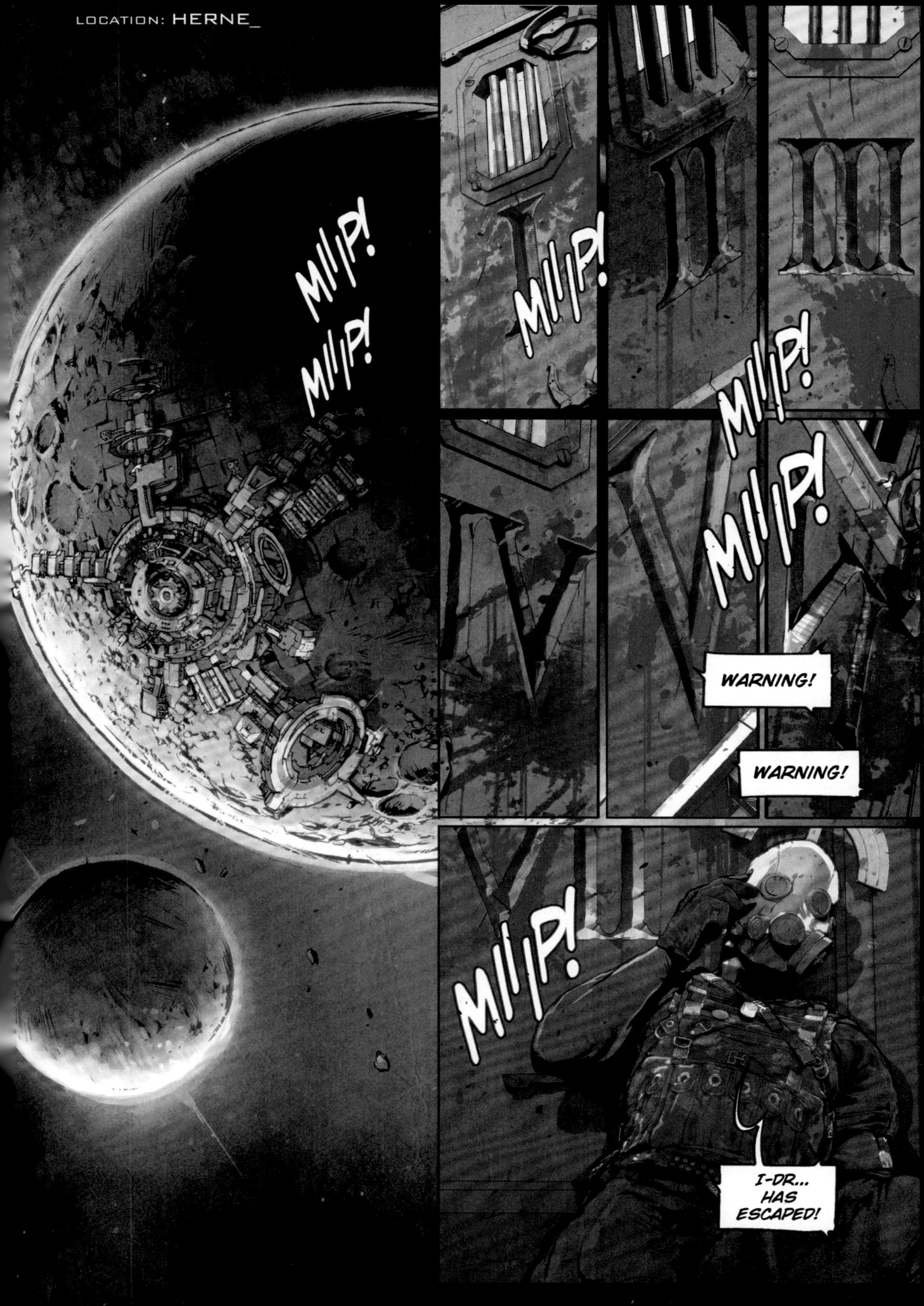
MIIIP!
MIIIP!
MIIIP!
MIIIP!
MIIIP!
WARNING!
WARNING!
MIIIP!
I-DR... HAS ESCAPED!

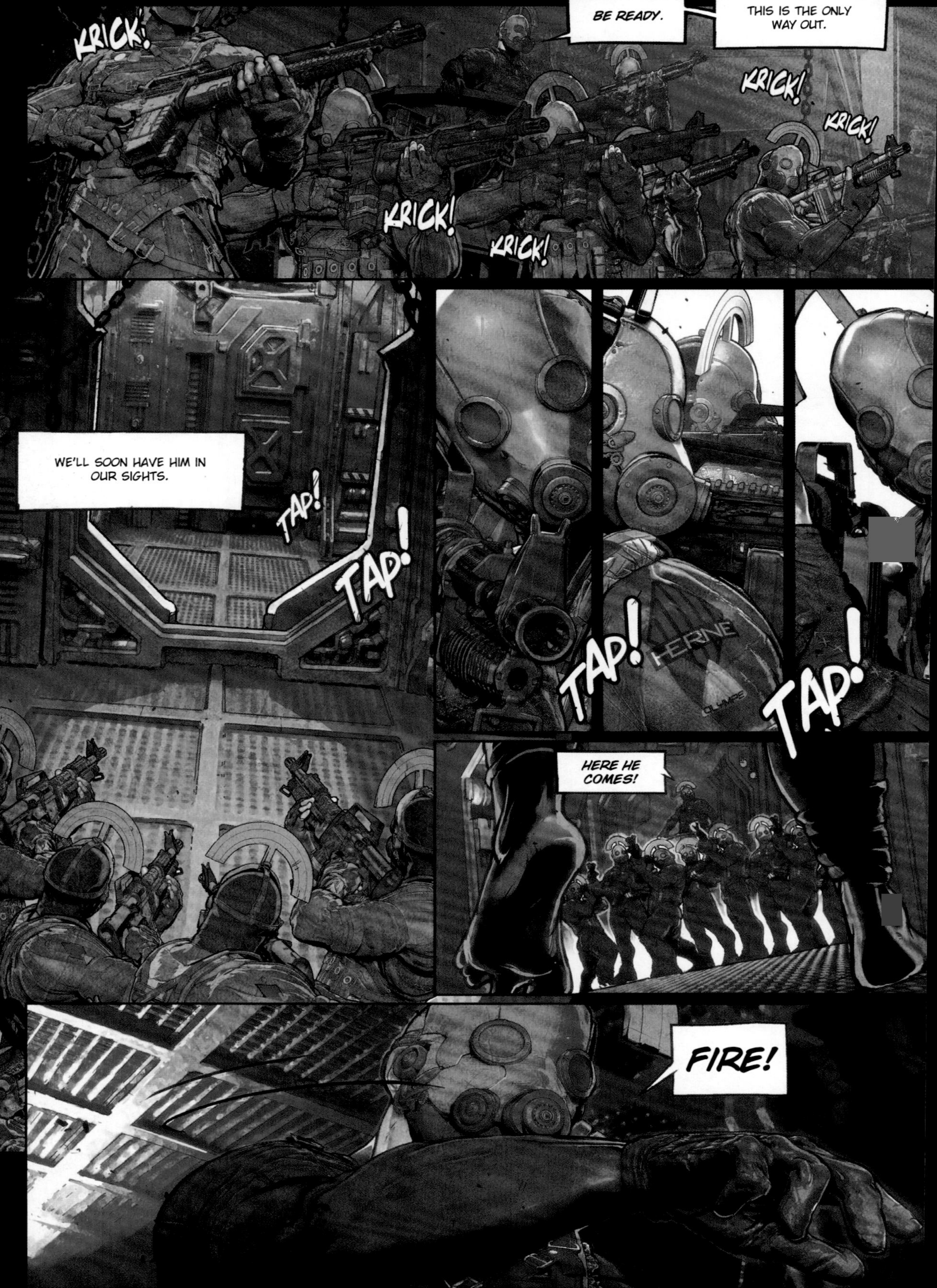

KRICK!
BE READY.
THIS IS THE ONLY WAY OUT.
KRICK!
KRICK!
KRICK!
KRICK!
WE'LL SOON HAVE HIM IN OUR SIGHTS.
TAP!
TAP!
TAP!
HERNE
OLYMPE
TAP!
HERE HE COMES!
FIRE!

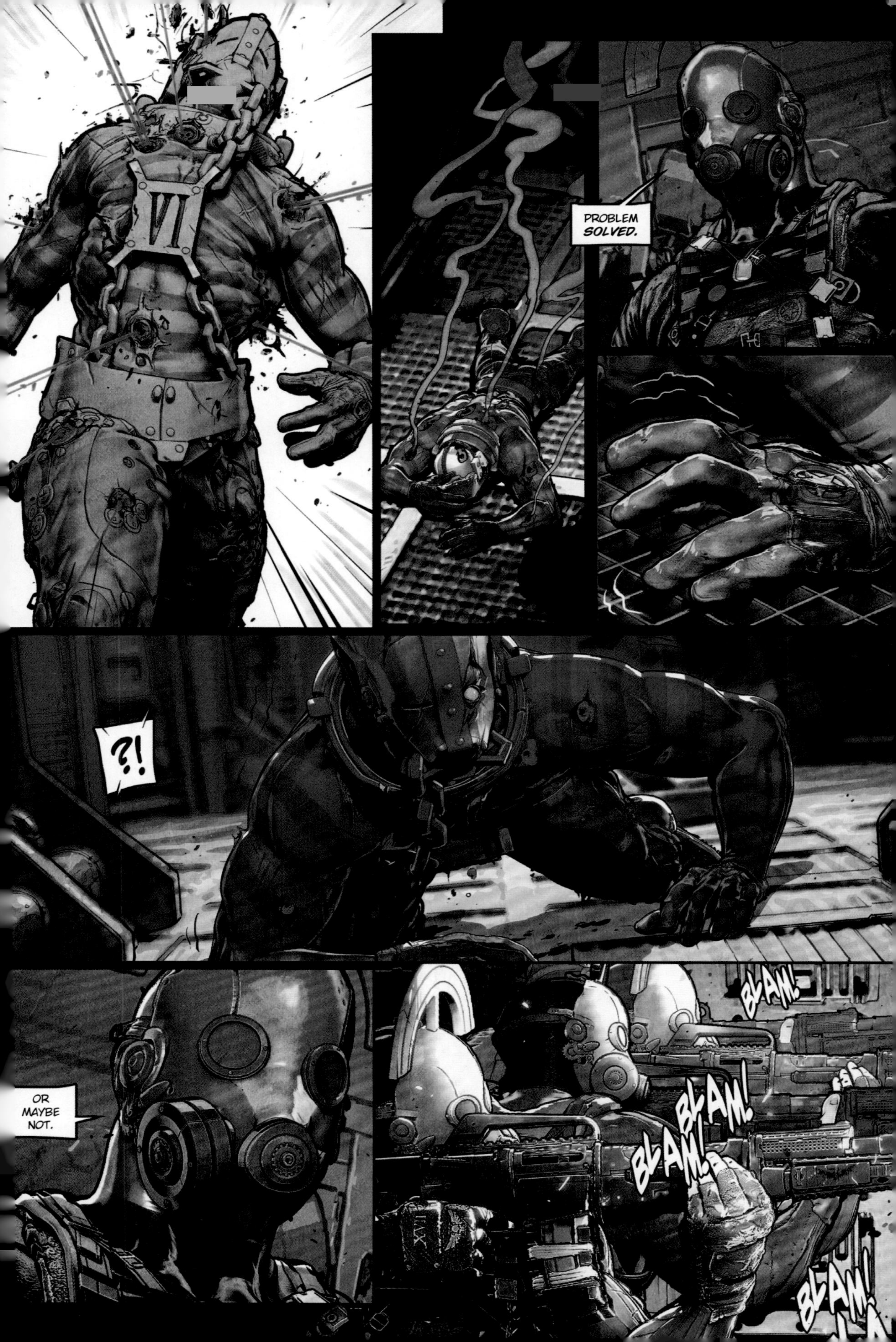

PROBLEM SOLVED.
?!
OR MAYBE NOT.
BLAM!
BLAM!
BLAM!
BLAM!
BLAM!

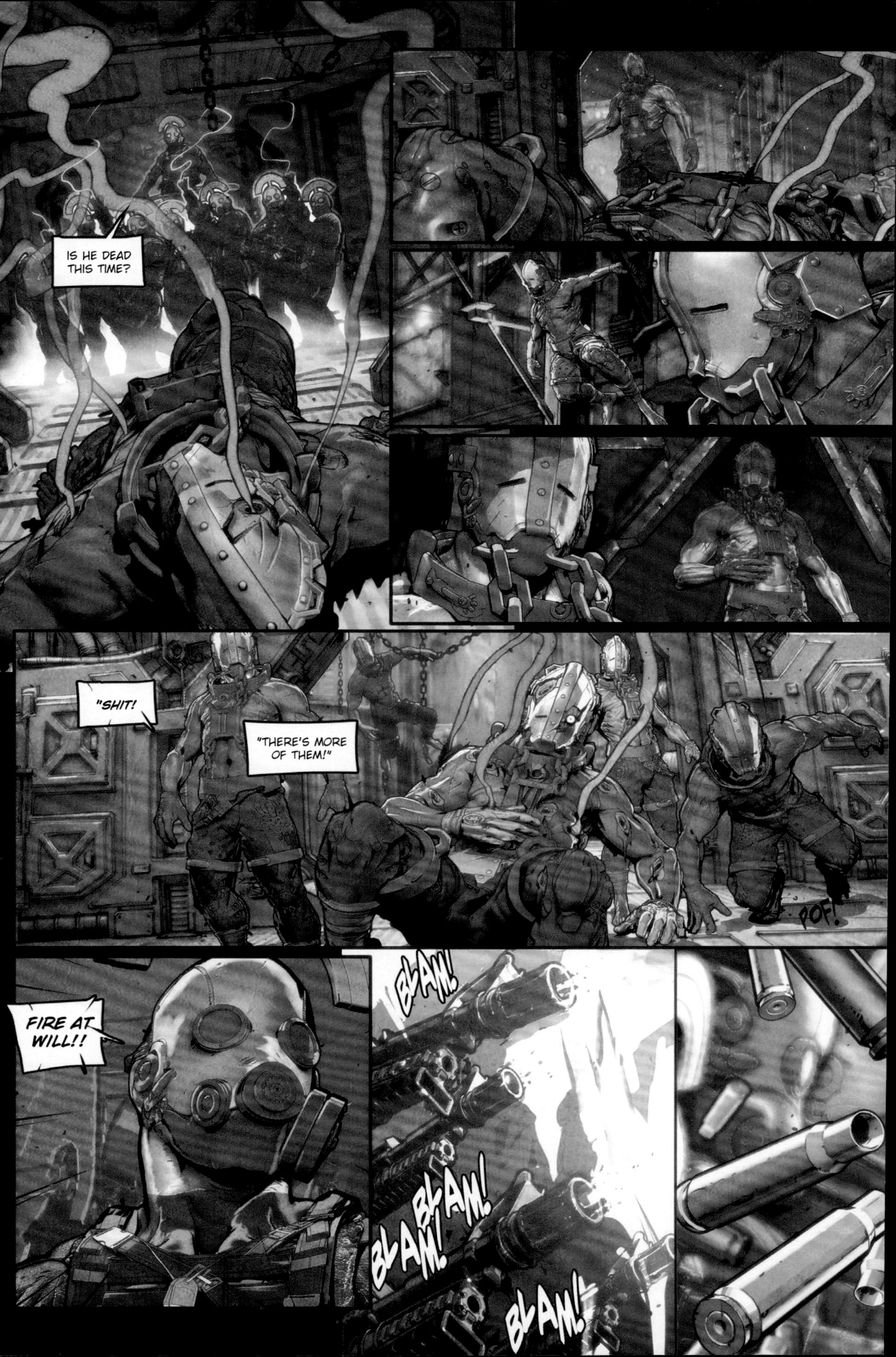
IS HE DEAD THIS TIME?
"SHIT!
"THERE'S MORE OF THEM!"
POF!
FIRE AT WILL!!
BLAM!
BLAM!
BLAM!
BLAM!

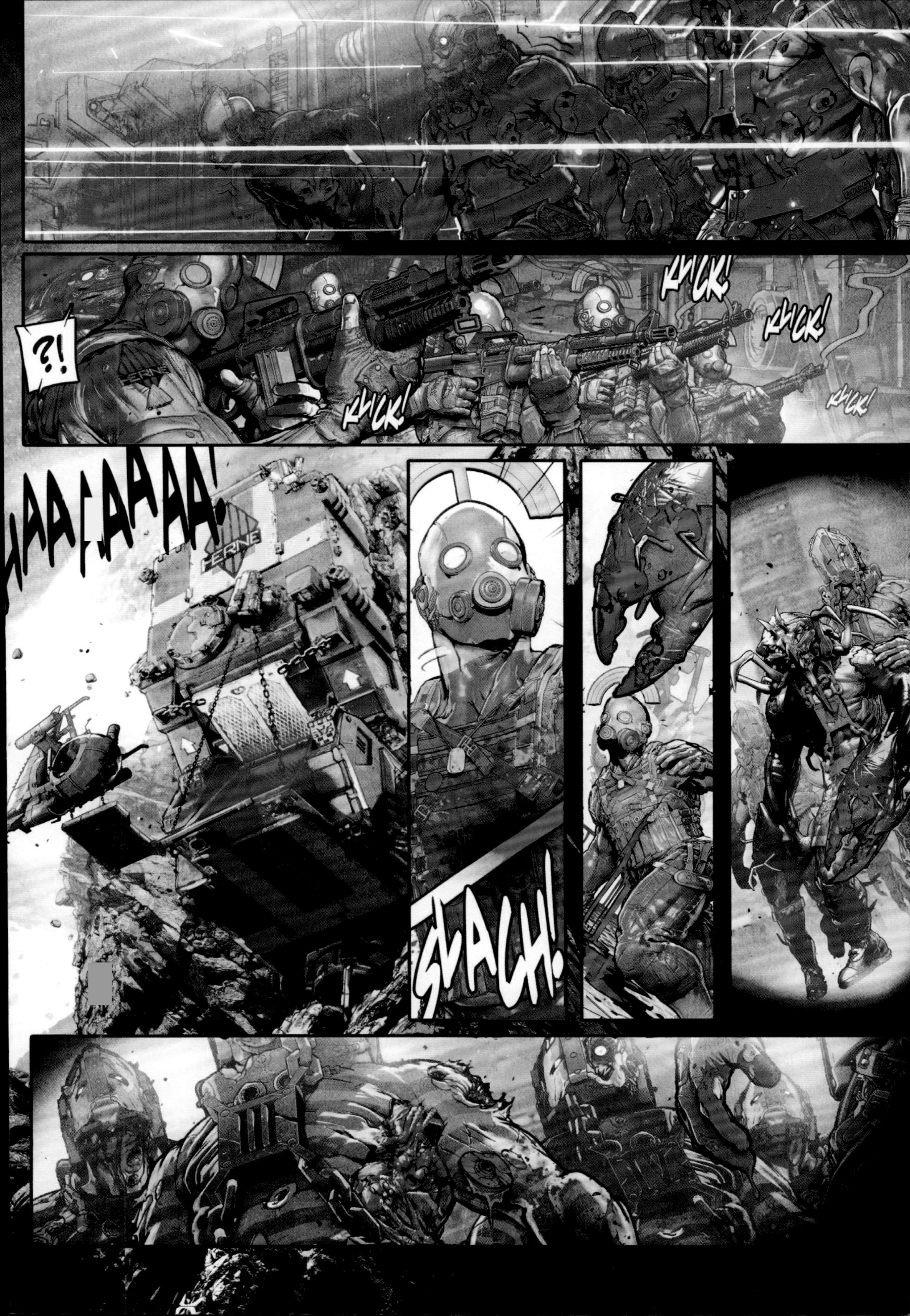
?!
KLICK!
KLICK!
KLICK!
KLICK!
AAAAAA!
SLACH!

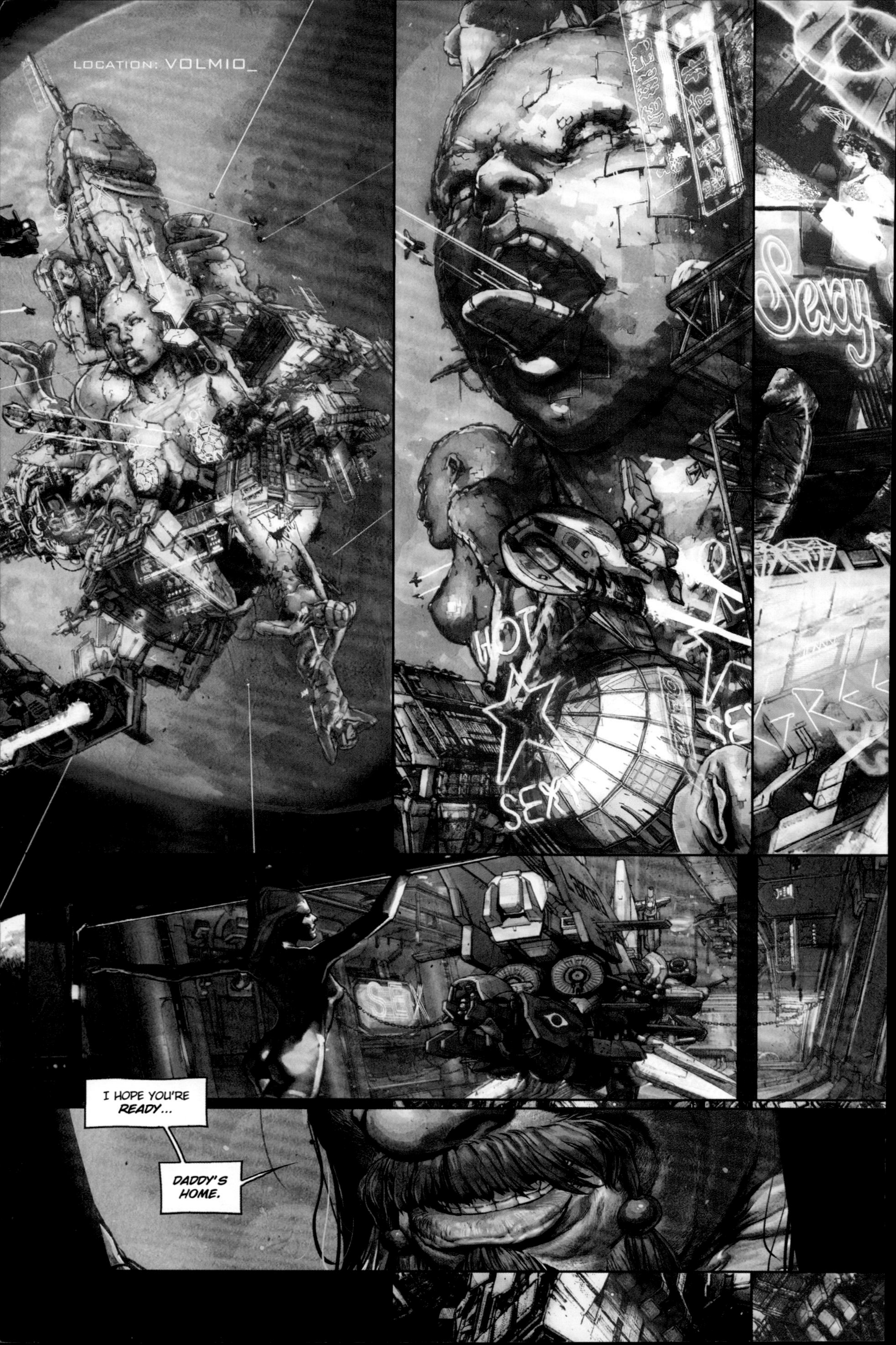
LOCATION: VOLMIO_
SEX
HOT
SEX
SEX
Sexy
SEX
I HOPE YOU'RE *READY*...
DADDY'S HOME.

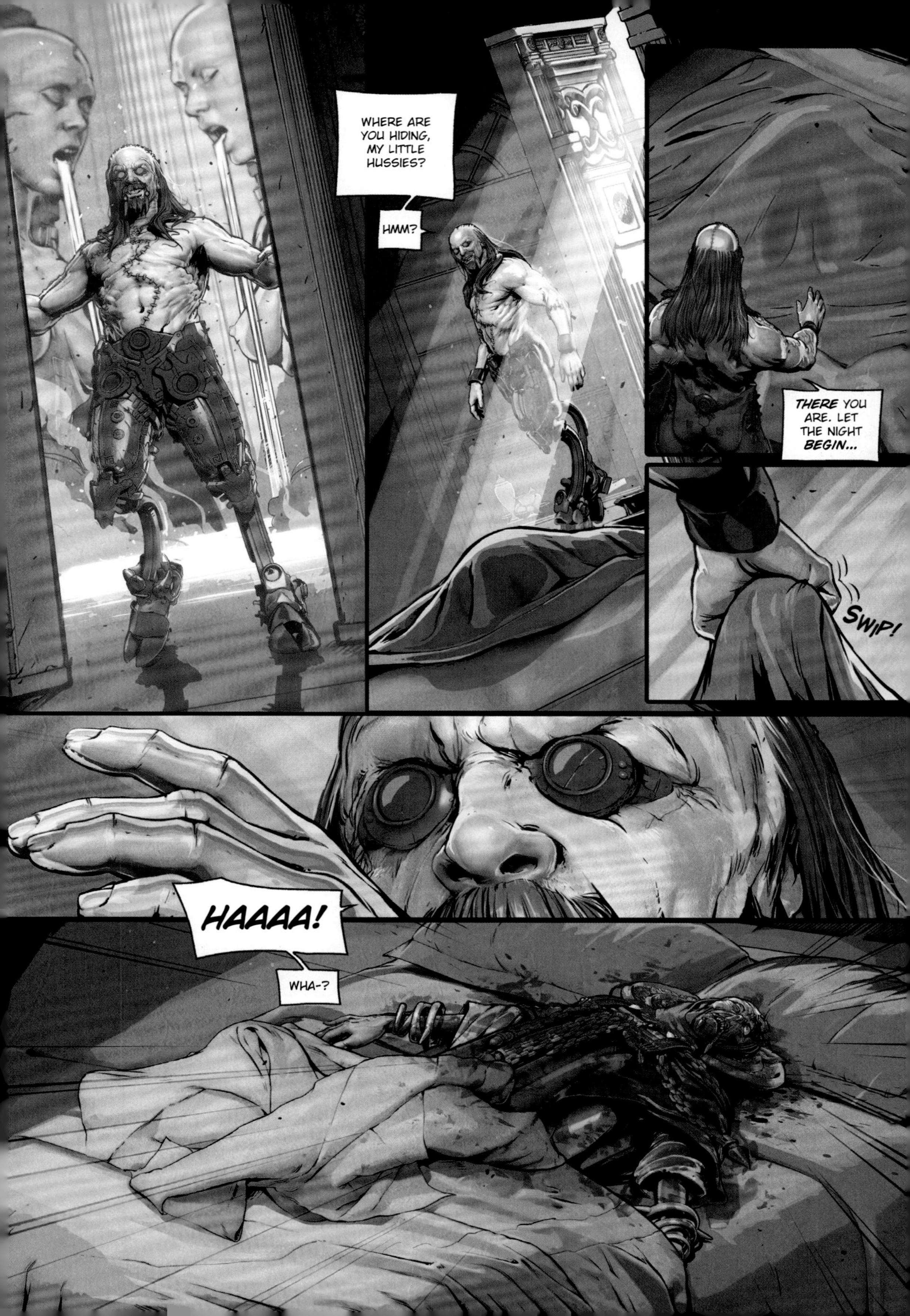
WHERE ARE YOU HIDING, MY LITTLE HUSSIES?
HMM?
THERE YOU ARE. LET THE NIGHT BEGIN...
SWIP!
HAAAA!
WHA-?

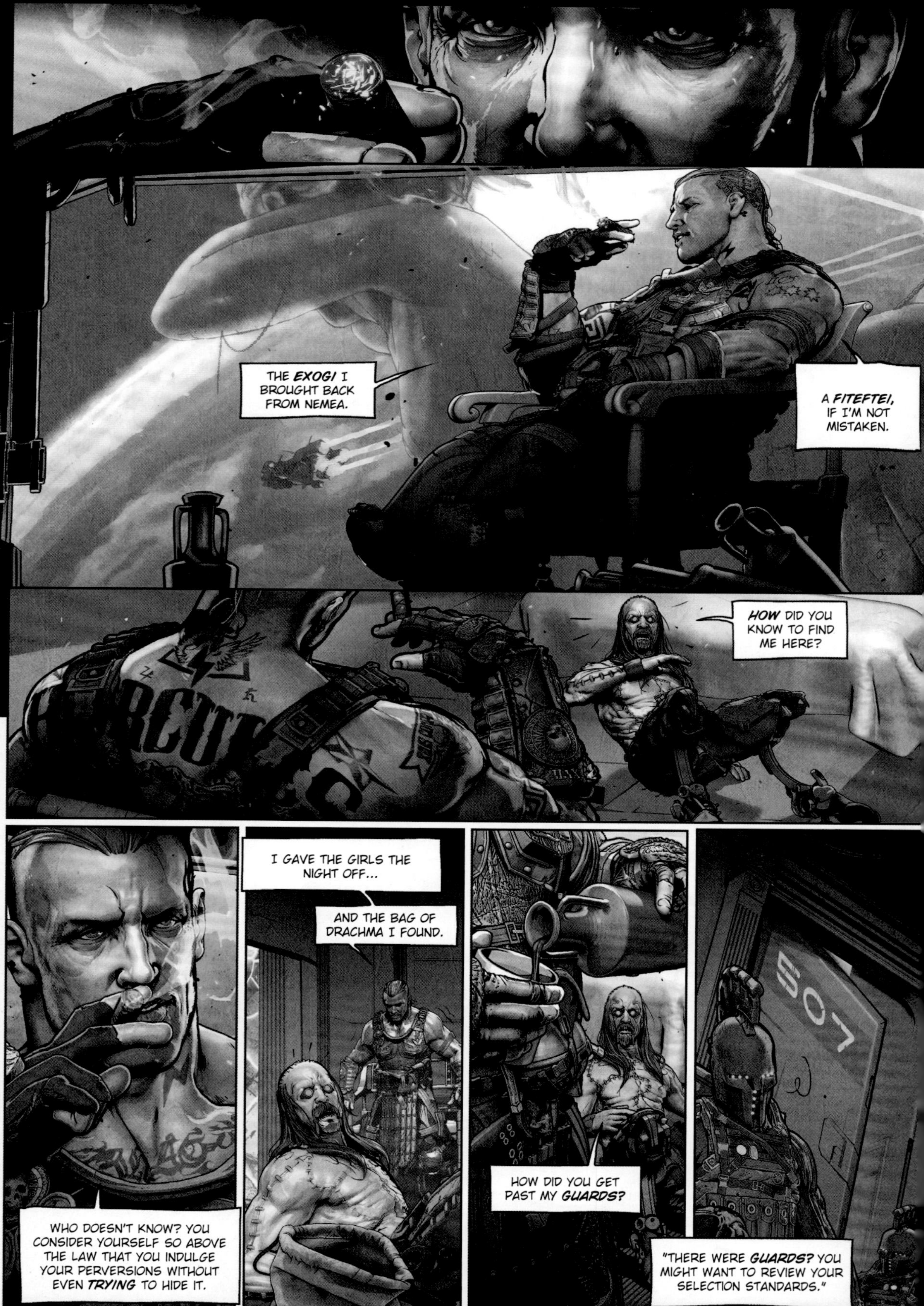
THE EXOGI I BROUGHT BACK FROM NEMEA.
A FITEFTEI, IF I'M NOT MISTAKEN.
HOW DID YOU KNOW TO FIND ME HERE?
WHO DOESN'T KNOW? YOU CONSIDER YOURSELF SO ABOVE THE LAW THAT YOU INDULGE YOUR PERVERSIONS WITHOUT EVEN TRYING TO HIDE IT.
I GAVE THE GIRLS THE NIGHT OFF...
AND THE BAG OF DRACHMA I FOUND.
HOW DID YOU GET PAST MY GUARDS?
"THERE WERE GUARDS? YOU MIGHT WANT TO REVIEW YOUR SELECTION STANDARDS."

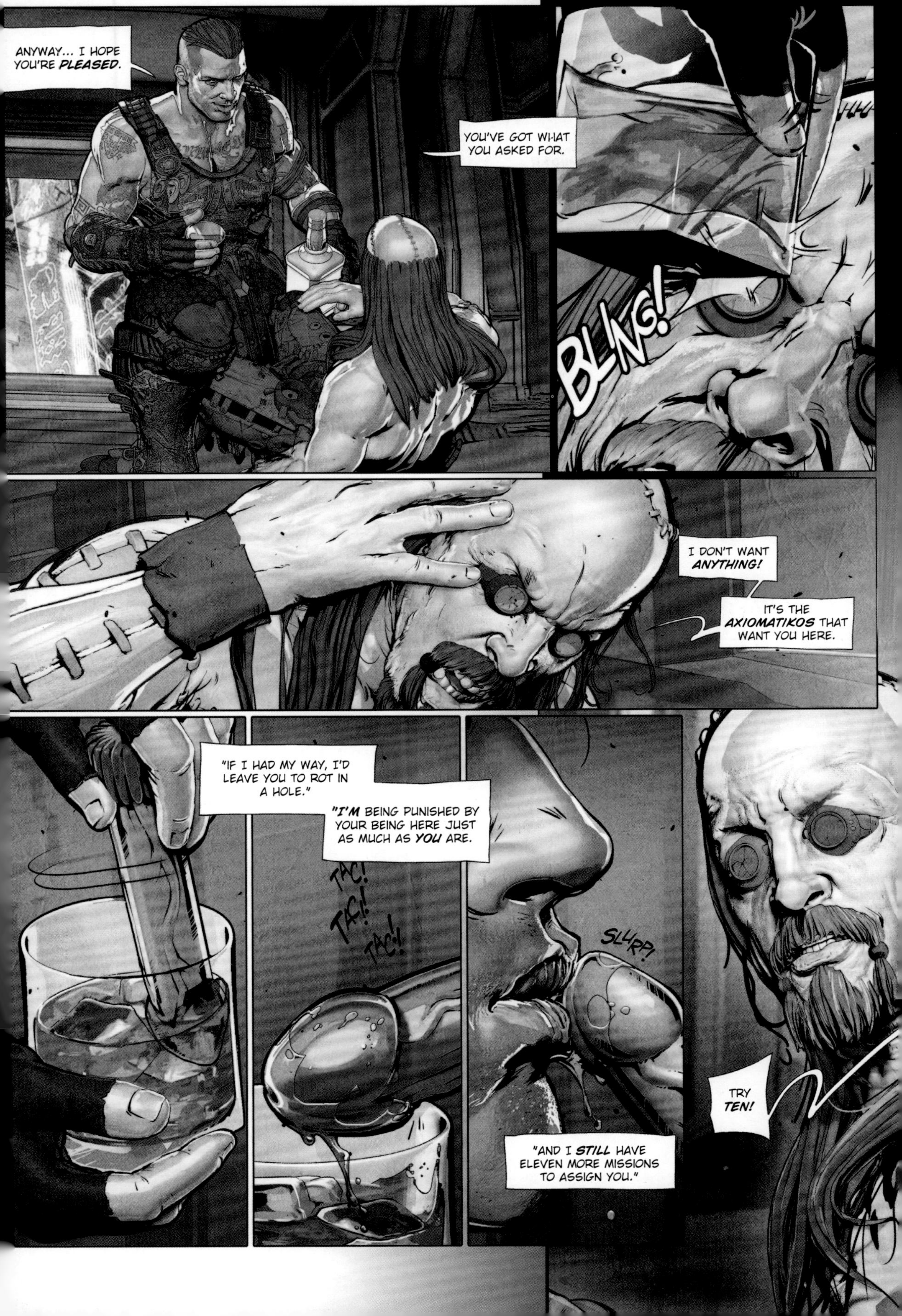
ANYWAY... I HOPE YOU'RE **PLEASED**.
YOU'VE GOT WHAT YOU ASKED FOR.
BLING!
I DON'T WANT **ANYTHING!**
IT'S THE **AXIOMATIKOS** THAT WANT YOU HERE.
"IF I HAD MY WAY, I'D LEAVE YOU TO ROT IN A HOLE."
"**I'M** BEING PUNISHED BY YOUR BEING HERE JUST AS MUCH AS **YOU** ARE.
TAC! TAC! TAC!
SLURP!
"AND I **STILL** HAVE ELEVEN MORE MISSIONS TO ASSIGN YOU."
TRY **TEN!**

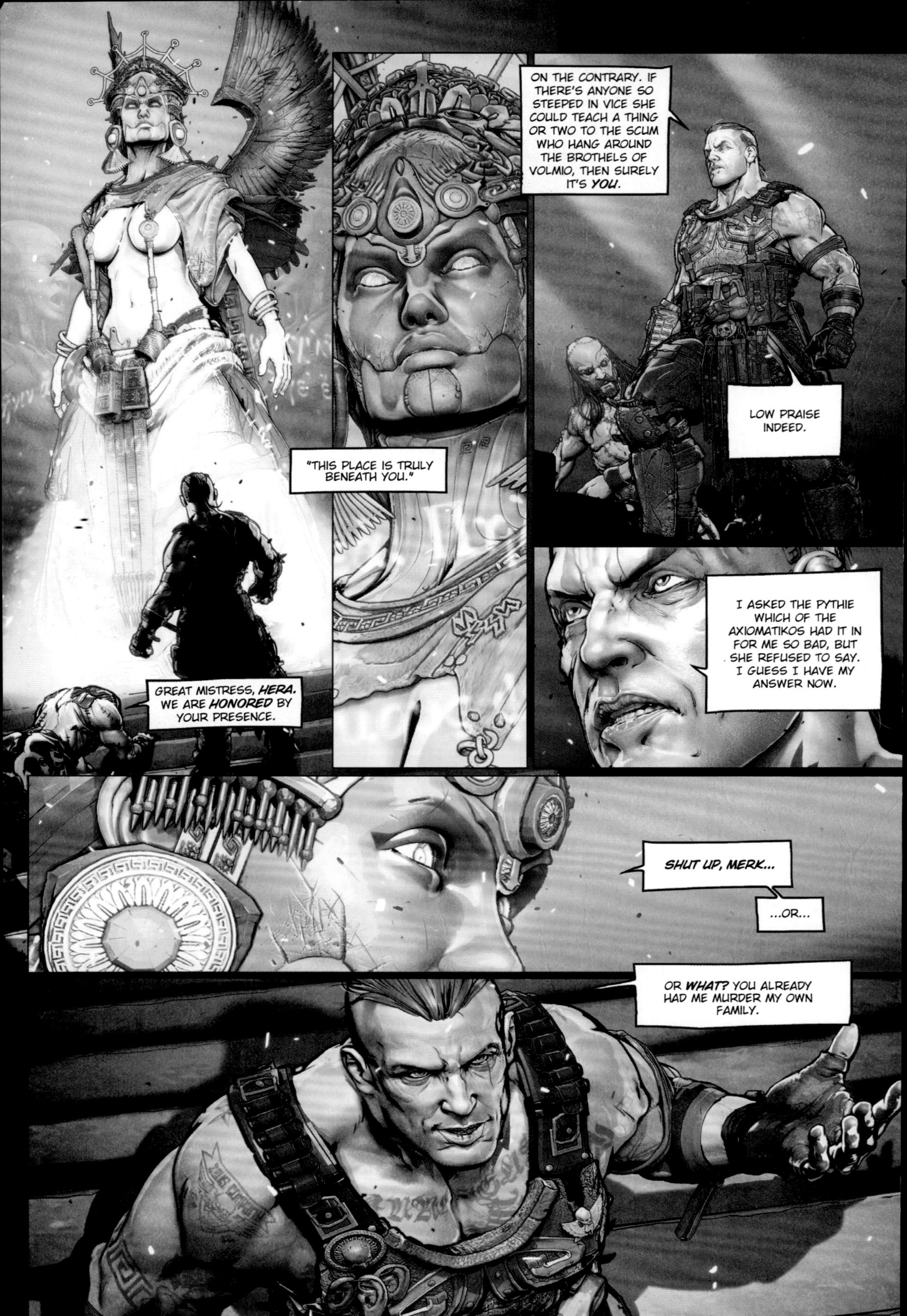
GREAT MISTRESS, HERA. WE ARE HONORED BY YOUR PRESENCE.
"THIS PLACE IS TRULY BENEATH YOU."
ON THE CONTRARY. IF THERE'S ANYONE SO STEEPED IN VICE SHE COULD TEACH A THING OR TWO TO THE SCUM WHO HANG AROUND THE BROTHELS OF VOLMIO, THEN SURELY IT'S YOU.
LOW PRAISE INDEED.
I ASKED THE PYTHIE WHICH OF THE AXIOMATIKOS HAD IT IN FOR ME SO BAD, BUT SHE REFUSED TO SAY. I GUESS I HAVE MY ANSWER NOW.
SHUT UP, MERK...
...OR...
OR WHAT? YOU ALREADY HAD ME MURDER MY OWN FAMILY.

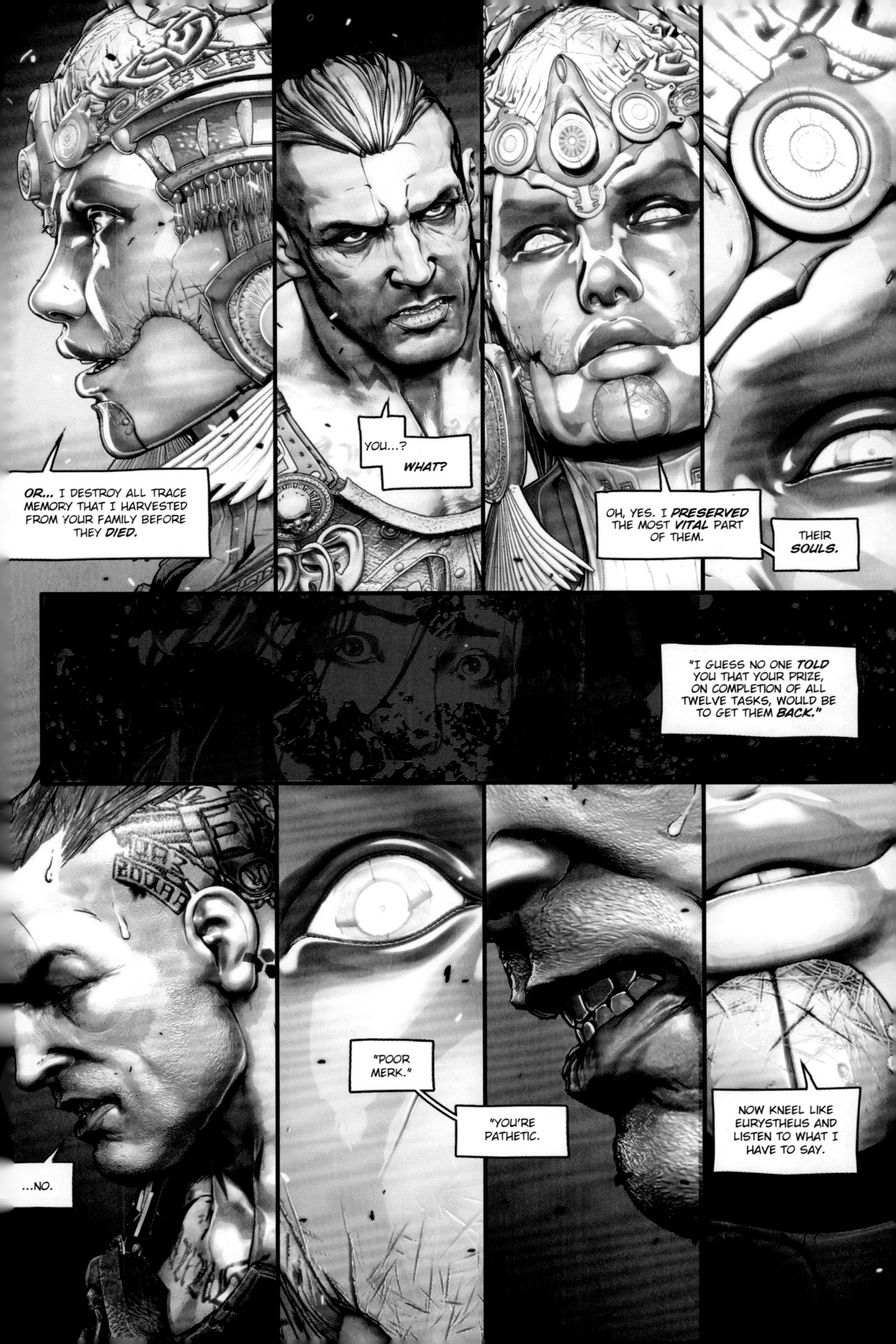
OR... I DESTROY ALL TRACE MEMORY THAT I HARVESTED FROM YOUR FAMILY BEFORE THEY DIED.
YOU...? WHAT?
OH, YES. I PRESERVED THE MOST VITAL PART OF THEM.
THEIR SOULS.
"I GUESS NO ONE TOLD YOU THAT YOUR PRIZE, ON COMPLETION OF ALL TWELVE TASKS, WOULD BE TO GET THEM BACK."
...NO.
"POOR MERK."
"YOU'RE PATHETIC.
NOW KNEEL LIKE EURYSTHEUS AND LISTEN TO WHAT I HAVE TO SAY.

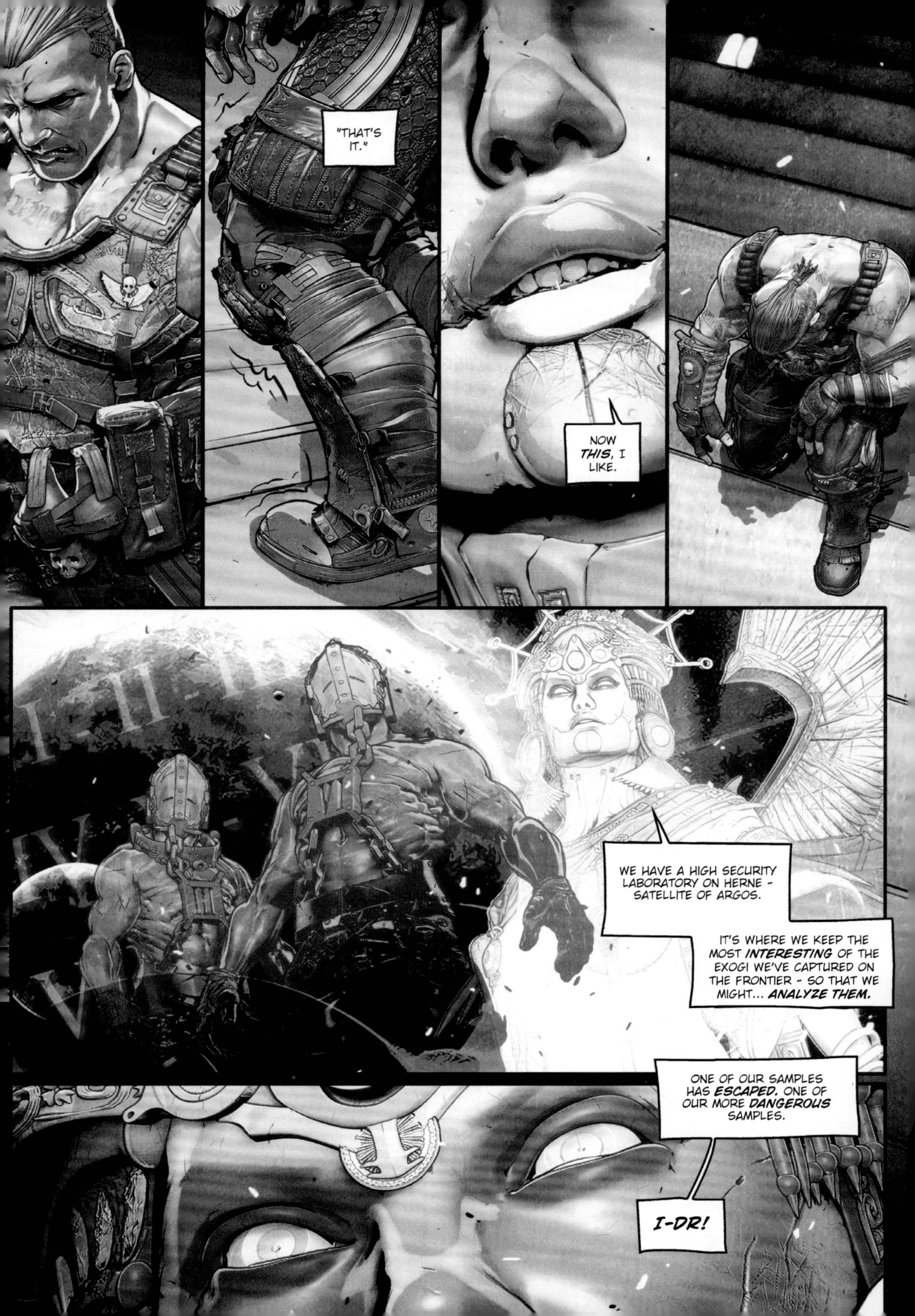
"THAT'S IT."
NOW *THIS*, I LIKE.
WE HAVE A HIGH SECURITY LABORATORY ON HERNE - SATELLITE OF ARGOS.
IT'S WHERE WE KEEP THE MOST ***INTERESTING*** OF THE EXOGI WE'VE CAPTURED ON THE FRONTIER - SO THAT WE MIGHT... ***ANALYZE THEM.***
ONE OF OUR SAMPLES HAS ***ESCAPED.*** ONE OF OUR MORE ***DANGEROUS*** SAMPLES.
I-DR!

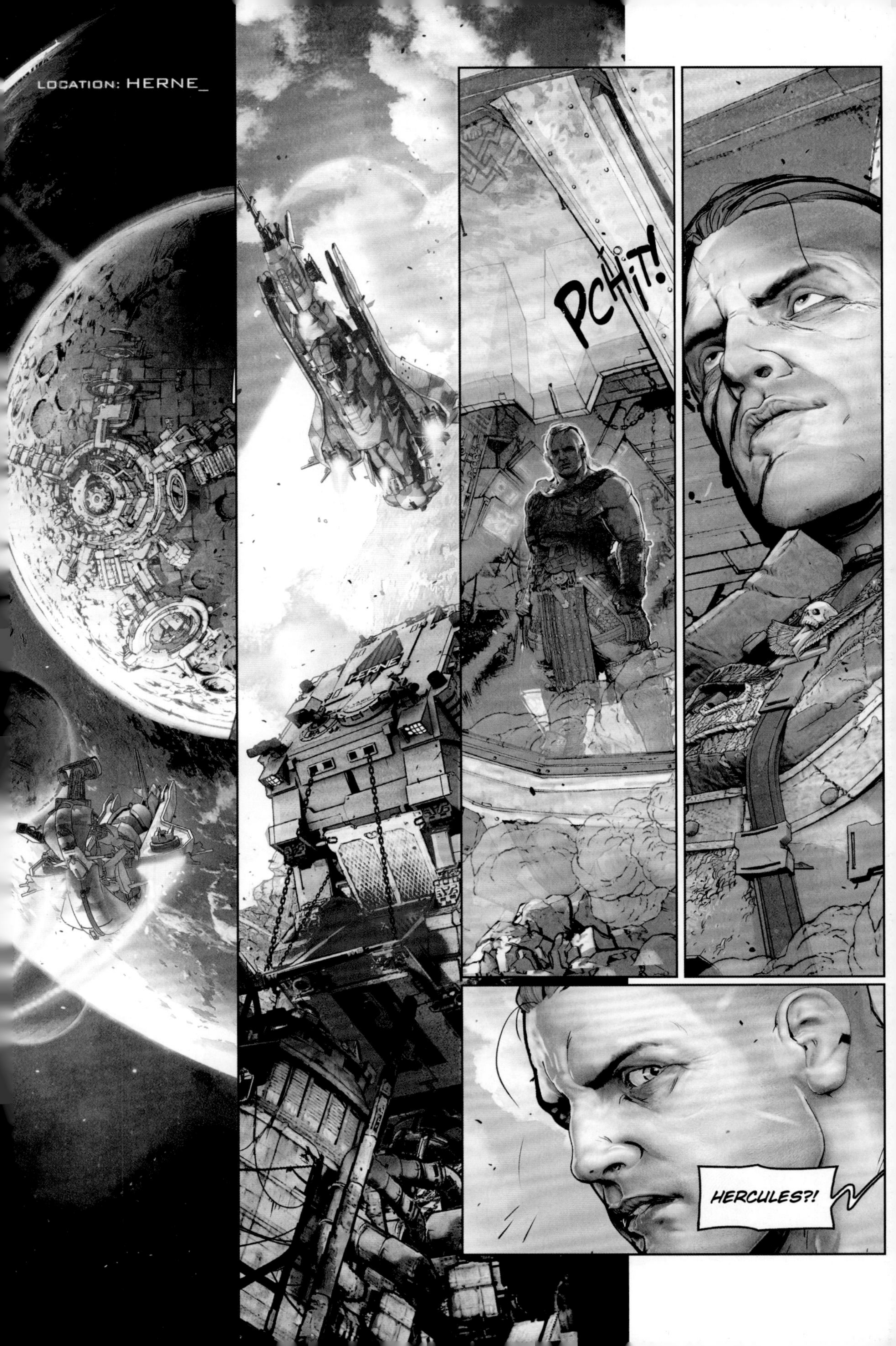
LOCATION: HERNE_
HERNE
PCHIT!
HERCULES?!

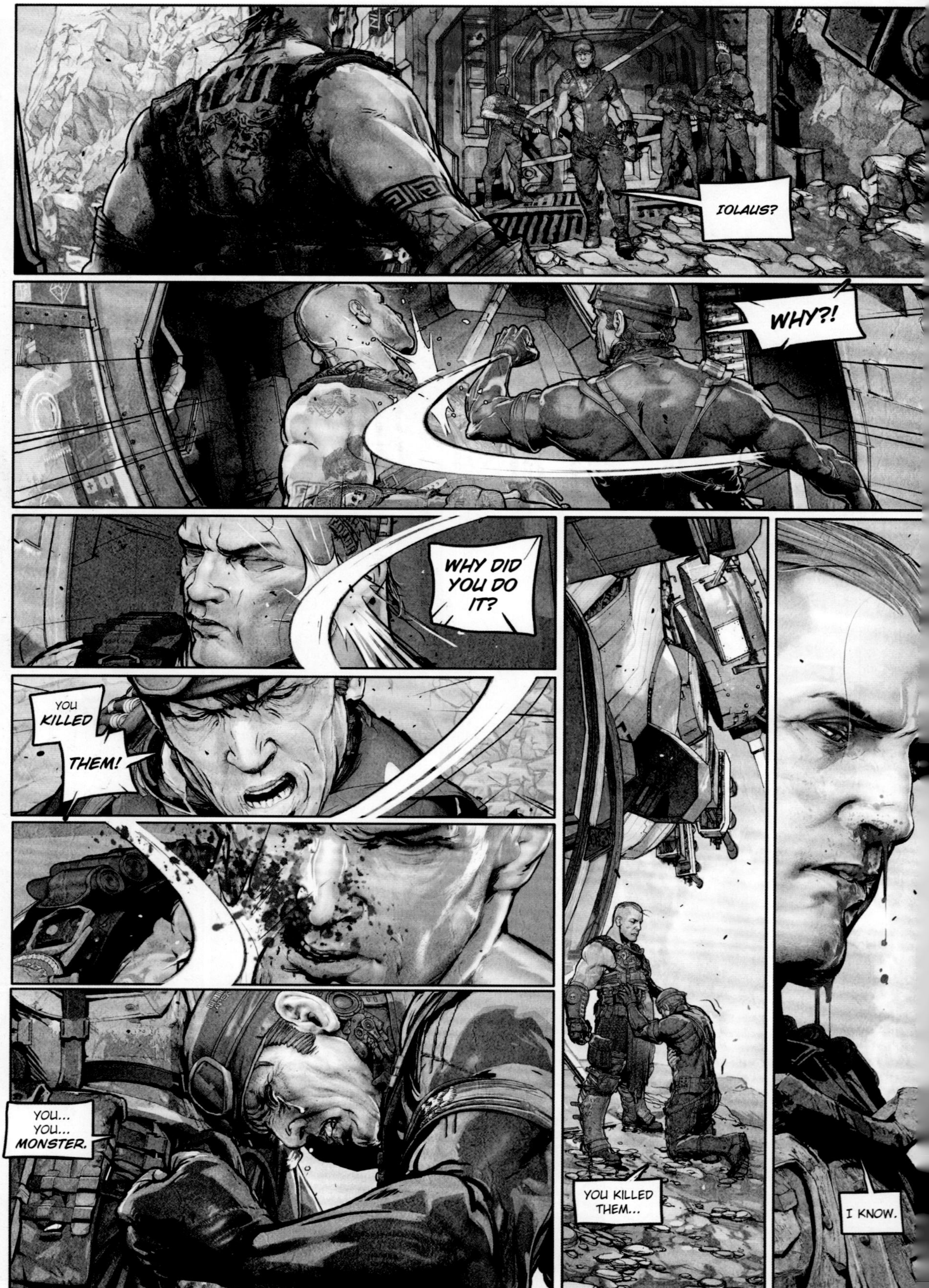
IOLAUS?
WHY?!
WHY DID YOU DO IT?
YOU KILLED
THEM!
YOU... YOU... MONSTER.
YOU KILLED THEM...
I KNOW.

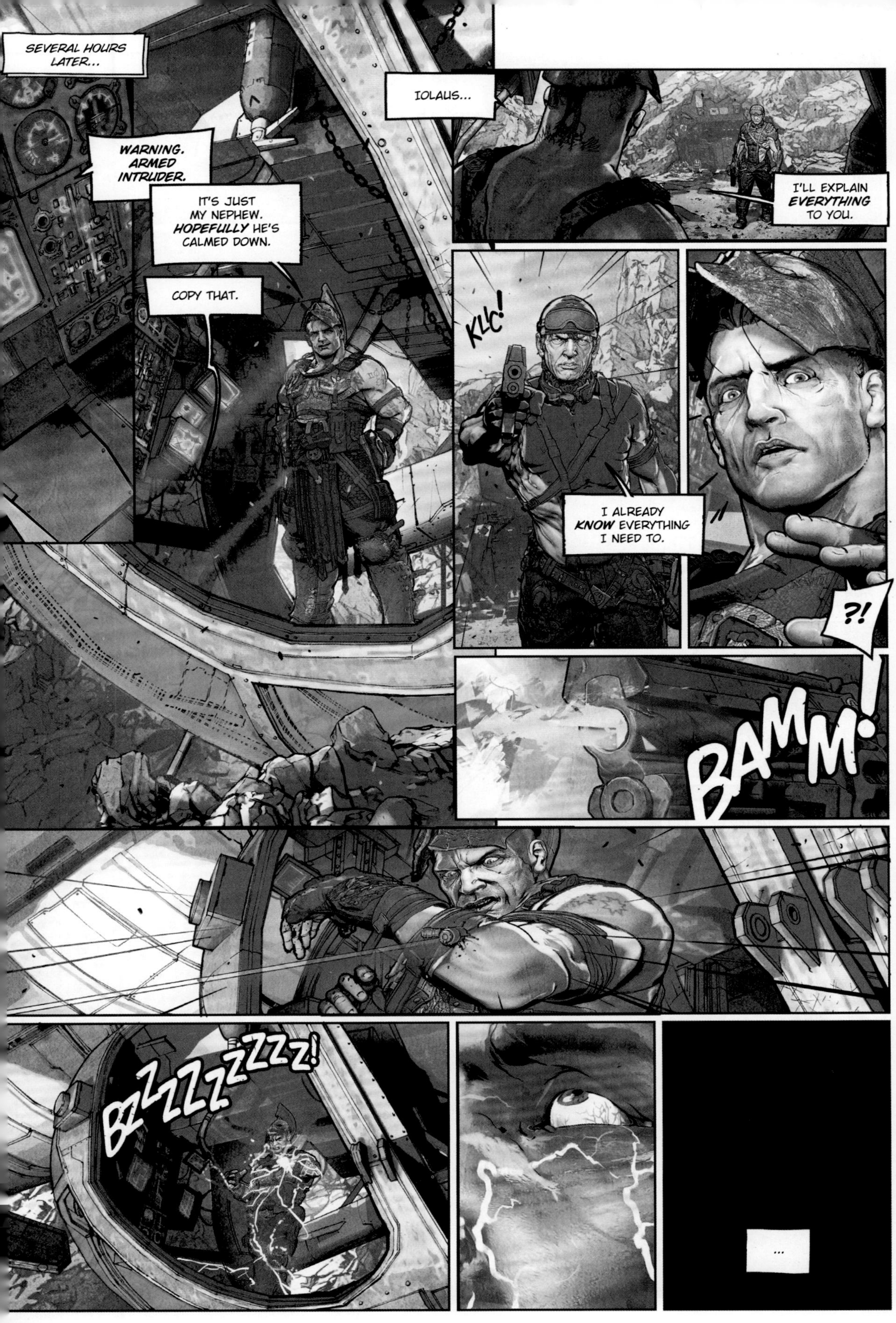
SEVERAL HOURS LATER...
WARNING. ARMED INTRUDER.
IT'S JUST MY NEPHEW. HOPEFULLY HE'S CALMED DOWN.
COPY THAT.
IOLAUS...
I'LL EXPLAIN EVERYTHING TO YOU.
KLIC!
I ALREADY KNOW EVERYTHING I NEED TO.
?!
BAMM!
BZZZZZZZZZ!
...

FROT!

FROT! FROT!

PERHAPS YOU'RE HOPING, DEEP INSIDE, THAT I AM GOING TO PUT YOU OUT OF YOUR MISERY.

BUT THAT'S NOT THE CASE.

ALL I'VE DONE IS DISABLE THE BUG THAT HERA INJECTED YOU WITH. SHE USES IT TO *MONITOR*...

AND *CONTROL* YOU.

FROT!

FROT!

FROT!

HOW DO YOU KNOW THAT?

" I WAS CONTACTED BY SOMEONE WHO EXPLAINED THE TRAP THAT'S BEEN SET FOR YOU."

SHE TOLD ME TO BRING YOU TO HER, BUT FIRST WE NEEDED TO TAKE HERA'S EYES AWAY.

SHE'S AN AXIOMATIKOS.

MEET YOUR GUARDIAN ANGEL.

TOO POWERFUL FOR OLYMPUS

ATHENA.

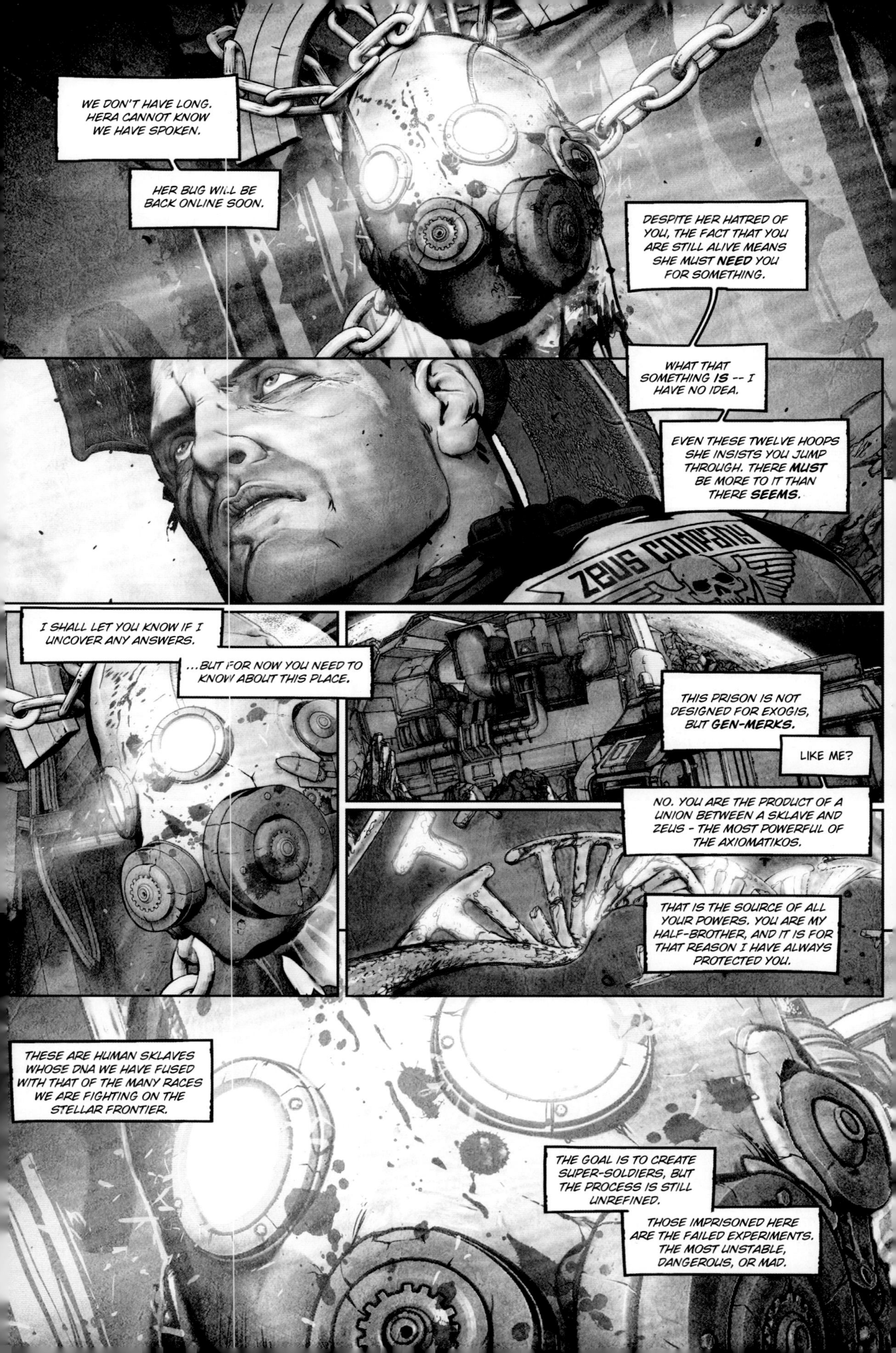
WE DON'T HAVE LONG. HERA CANNOT KNOW WE HAVE SPOKEN.
HER BUG WILL BE BACK ONLINE SOON.
DESPITE HER HATRED OF YOU, THE FACT THAT YOU ARE STILL ALIVE MEANS SHE MUST **NEED** YOU FOR SOMETHING.
WHAT THAT SOMETHING **IS** -- I HAVE NO IDEA.
EVEN THESE TWELVE HOOPS SHE INSISTS YOU JUMP THROUGH. THERE **MUST** BE MORE TO IT THAN THERE **SEEMS**.
ZEUS COMPANY
I SHALL LET YOU KNOW IF I UNCOVER ANY ANSWERS.
...BUT FOR NOW YOU NEED TO KNOW ABOUT THIS PLACE.
THIS PRISON IS NOT DESIGNED FOR EXOGIS, BUT **GEN-MERKS.**
LIKE ME?
NO. YOU ARE THE PRODUCT OF A UNION BETWEEN A SKLAVE AND ZEUS - THE MOST POWERFUL OF THE AXIOMATIKOS.
THAT IS THE SOURCE OF ALL YOUR POWERS. YOU ARE MY HALF-BROTHER, AND IT IS FOR THAT REASON I HAVE ALWAYS PROTECTED YOU.
THESE ARE HUMAN SKLAVES WHOSE DNA WE HAVE FUSED WITH THAT OF THE MANY RACES WE ARE FIGHTING ON THE STELLAR FRONTIER.
THE GOAL IS TO CREATE SUPER-SOLDIERS, BUT THE PROCESS IS STILL UNREFINED.
THOSE IMPRISONED HERE ARE THE FAILED EXPERIMENTS. THE MOST UNSTABLE, DANGEROUS, OR MAD.

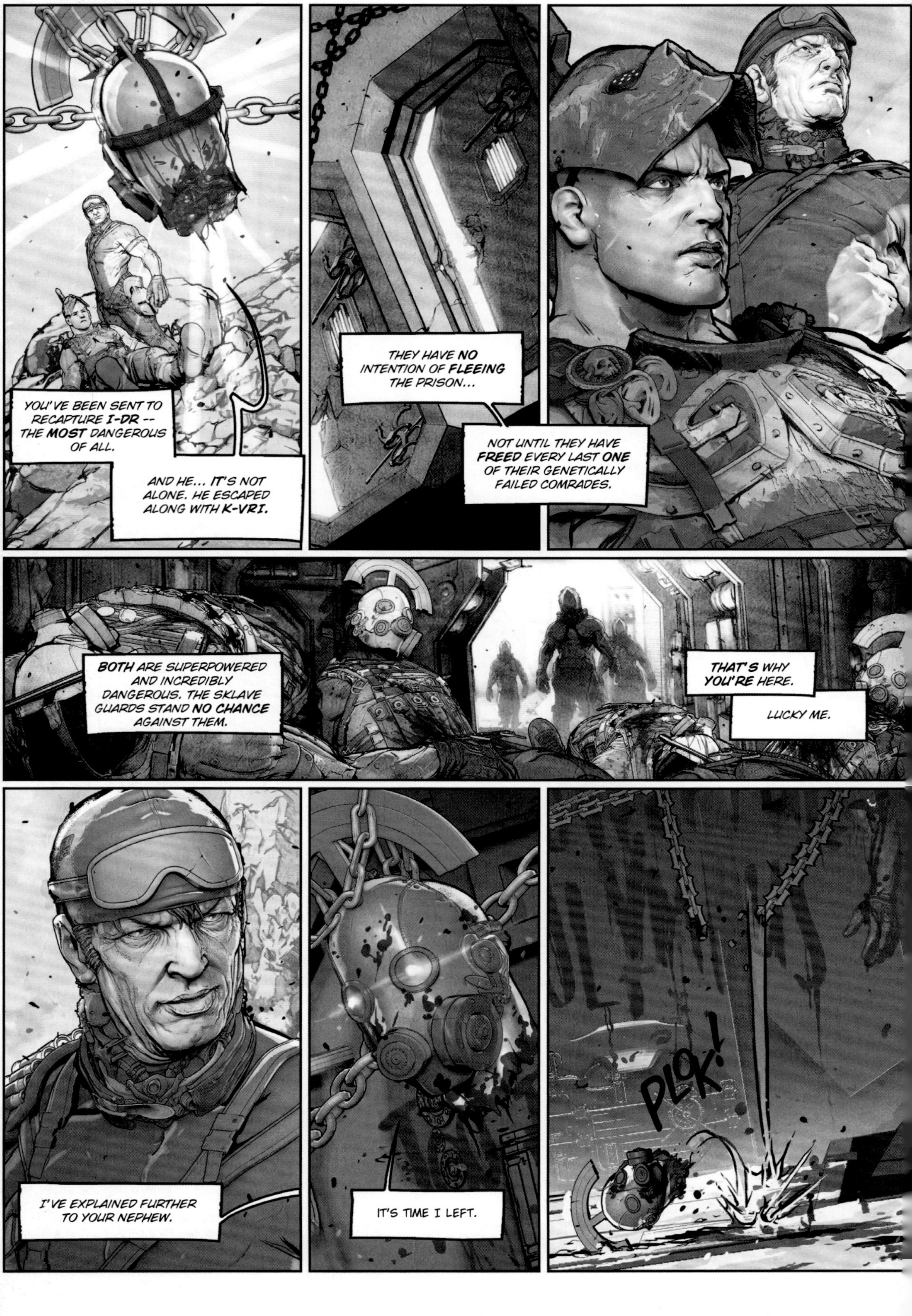
YOU'VE BEEN SENT TO RECAPTURE I-DR -- THE MOST DANGEROUS OF ALL.
AND HE... IT'S NOT ALONE. HE ESCAPED ALONG WITH K-VRI.
THEY HAVE NO INTENTION OF FLEEING THE PRISON...
NOT UNTIL THEY HAVE FREED EVERY LAST ONE OF THEIR GENETICALLY FAILED COMRADES.
BOTH ARE SUPERPOWERED AND INCREDIBLY DANGEROUS. THE SKLAVE GUARDS STAND NO CHANCE AGAINST THEM.
THAT'S WHY YOU'RE HERE.
LUCKY ME.
I'VE EXPLAINED FURTHER TO YOUR NEPHEW.
IT'S TIME I LEFT.
PLOK!

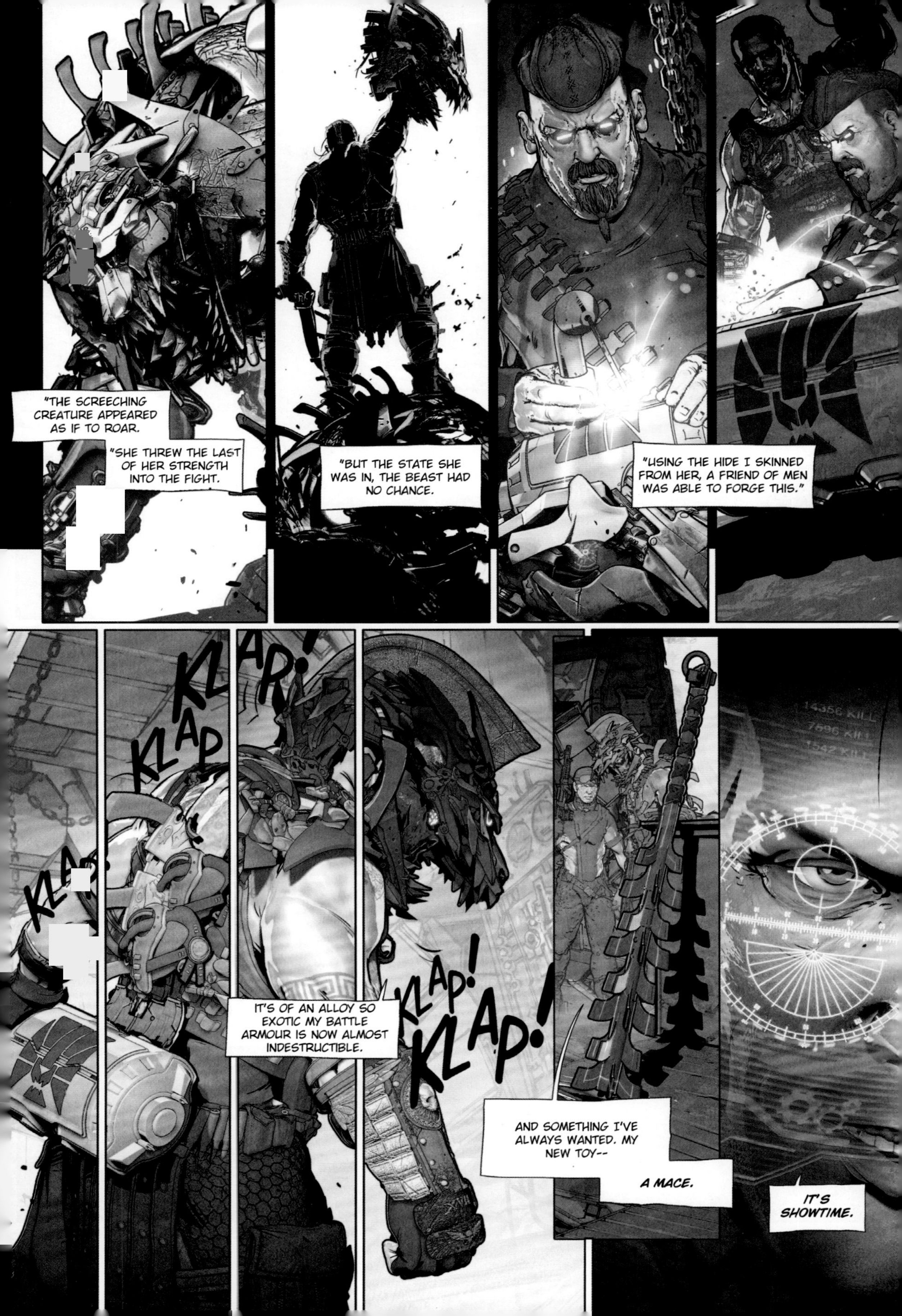
"THE SCREECHING CREATURE APPEARED AS IF TO ROAR.
"SHE THREW THE LAST OF HER STRENGTH INTO THE FIGHT.
"BUT THE STATE SHE WAS IN, THE BEAST HAD NO CHANCE.
"USING THE HIDE I SKINNED FROM HER, A FRIEND OF MEN WAS ABLE TO FORGE THIS."
KLAP
KLAP
KLAP!
KLAP!
IT'S OF AN ALLOY SO EXOTIC MY BATTLE ARMOUR IS NOW ALMOST INDESTRUCTIBLE.
KLAP!
KLAP!
AND SOMETHING I'VE ALWAYS WANTED. MY NEW TOY--
A MACE.
IT'S SHOWTIME.

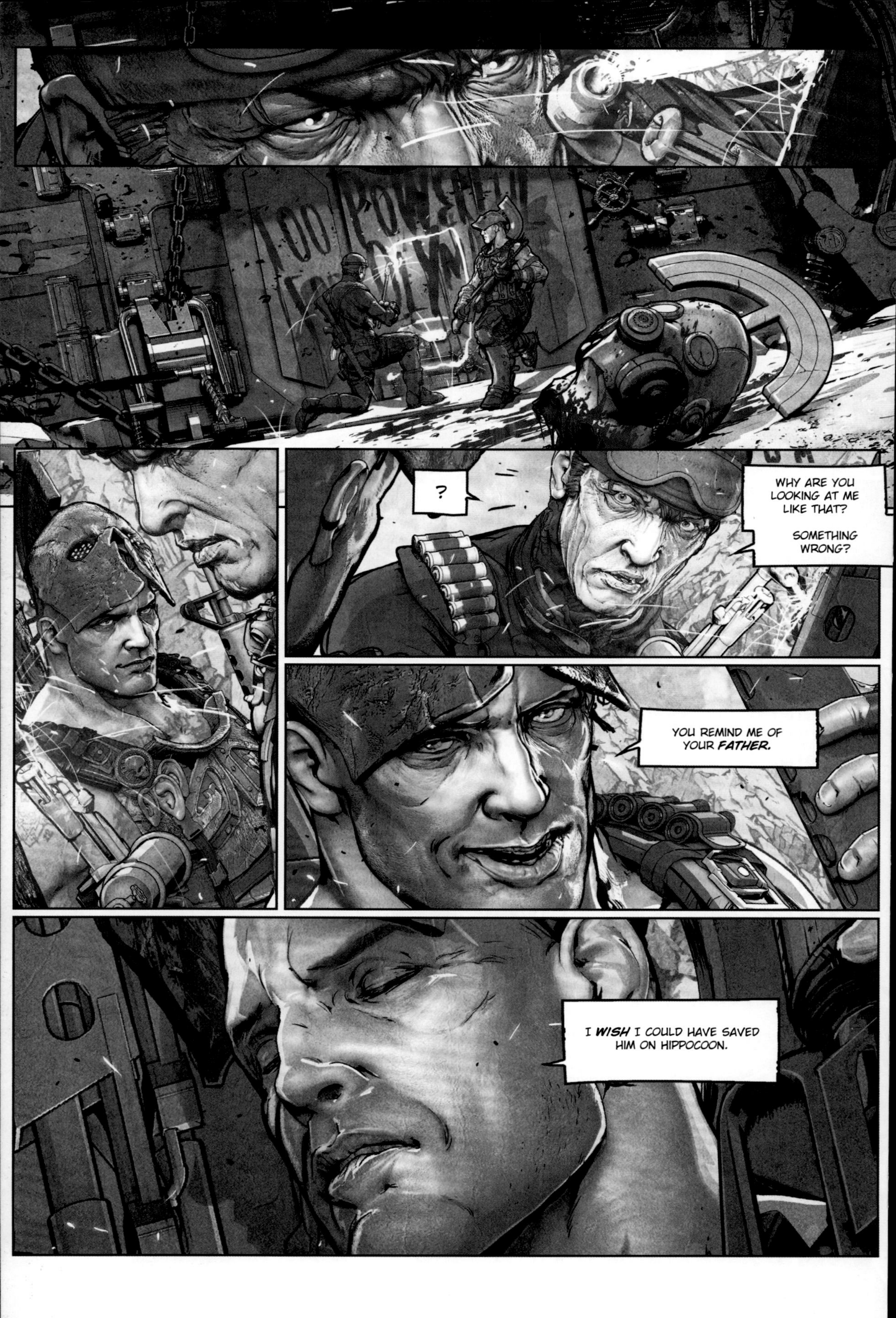
?
WHY ARE YOU LOOKING AT ME LIKE THAT?
SOMETHING WRONG?
YOU REMIND ME OF YOUR FATHER.
I WISH I COULD HAVE SAVED HIM ON HIPPOCOON.

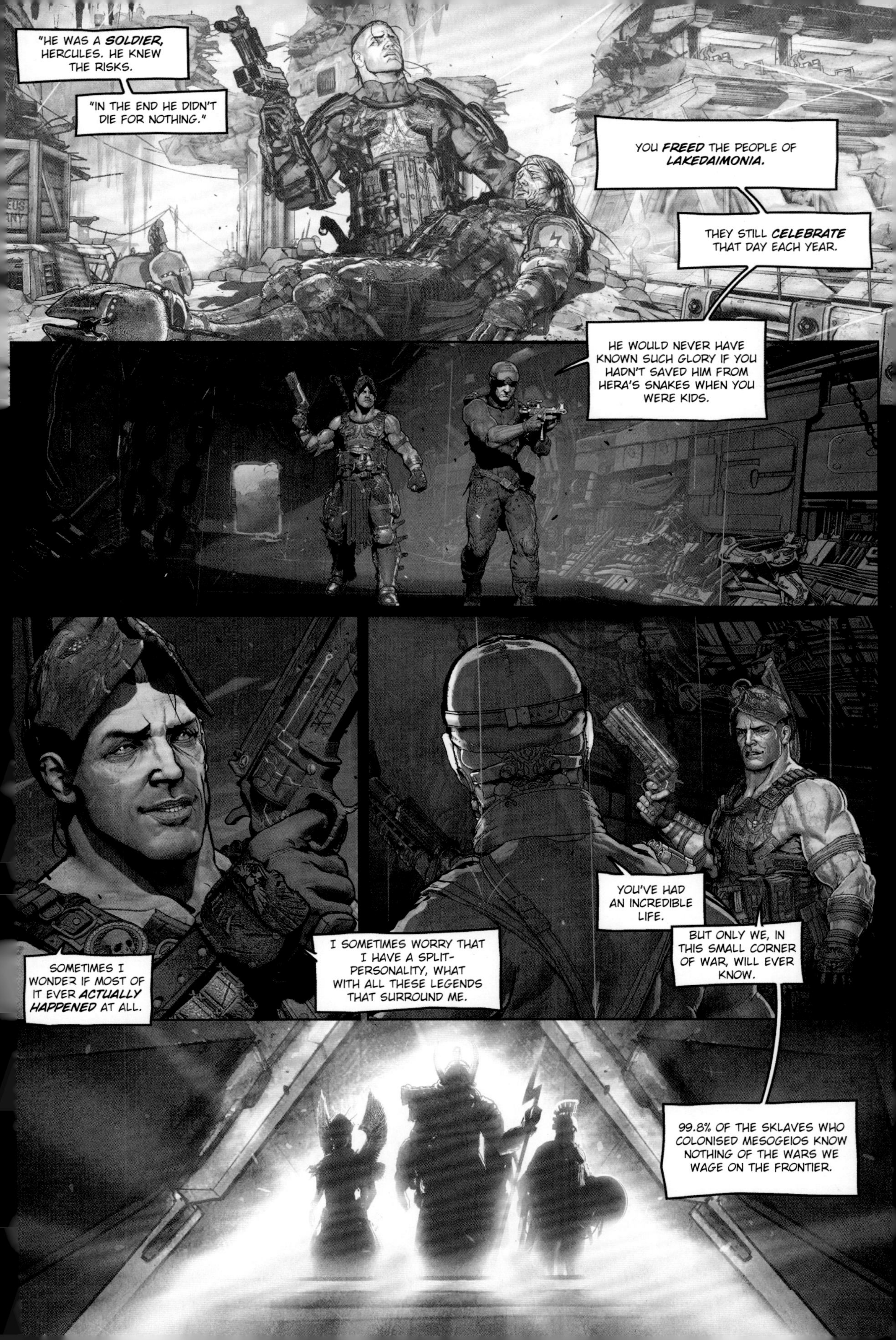
"HE WAS A SOLDIER, HERCULES. HE KNEW THE RISKS.
"IN THE END HE DIDN'T DIE FOR NOTHING."
YOU FREED THE PEOPLE OF LAKEDAIMONIA.
THEY STILL CELEBRATE THAT DAY EACH YEAR.
HE WOULD NEVER HAVE KNOWN SUCH GLORY IF YOU HADN'T SAVED HIM FROM HERA'S SNAKES WHEN YOU WERE KIDS.
SOMETIMES I WONDER IF MOST OF IT EVER ACTUALLY HAPPENED AT ALL.
I SOMETIMES WORRY THAT I HAVE A SPLIT-PERSONALITY, WHAT WITH ALL THESE LEGENDS THAT SURROUND ME.
YOU'VE HAD AN INCREDIBLE LIFE.
BUT ONLY WE, IN THIS SMALL CORNER OF WAR, WILL EVER KNOW.
99.8% OF THE SKLAVES WHO COLONISED MESOGEIOS KNOW NOTHING OF THE WARS WE WAGE ON THE FRONTIER.

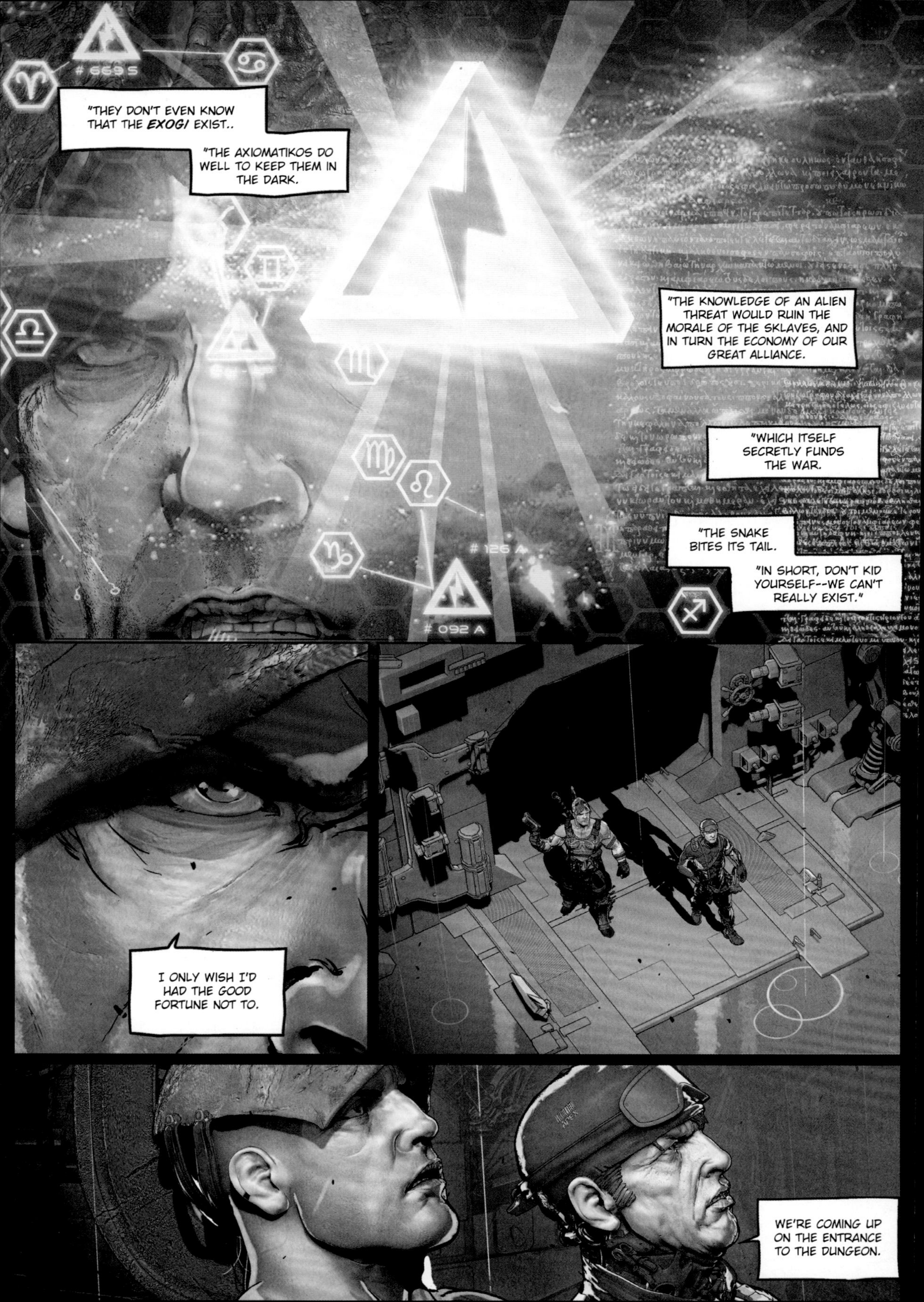

669 5
"THEY DON'T EVEN KNOW THAT THE *EXOGI* EXIST..
"THE AXIOMATIKOS DO WELL TO KEEP THEM IN THE DARK.
"THE KNOWLEDGE OF AN ALIEN THREAT WOULD RUIN THE MORALE OF THE SKLAVES, AND IN TURN THE ECONOMY OF OUR GREAT ALLIANCE.
"WHICH ITSELF SECRETLY FUNDS THE WAR.
"THE SNAKE BITES ITS TAIL.
"IN SHORT, DON'T KID YOURSELF--WE CAN'T REALLY EXIST."
126 A
092 A
I ONLY WISH I'D HAD THE GOOD FORTUNE NOT TO.
WE'RE COMING UP ON THE ENTRANCE TO THE DUNGEON.

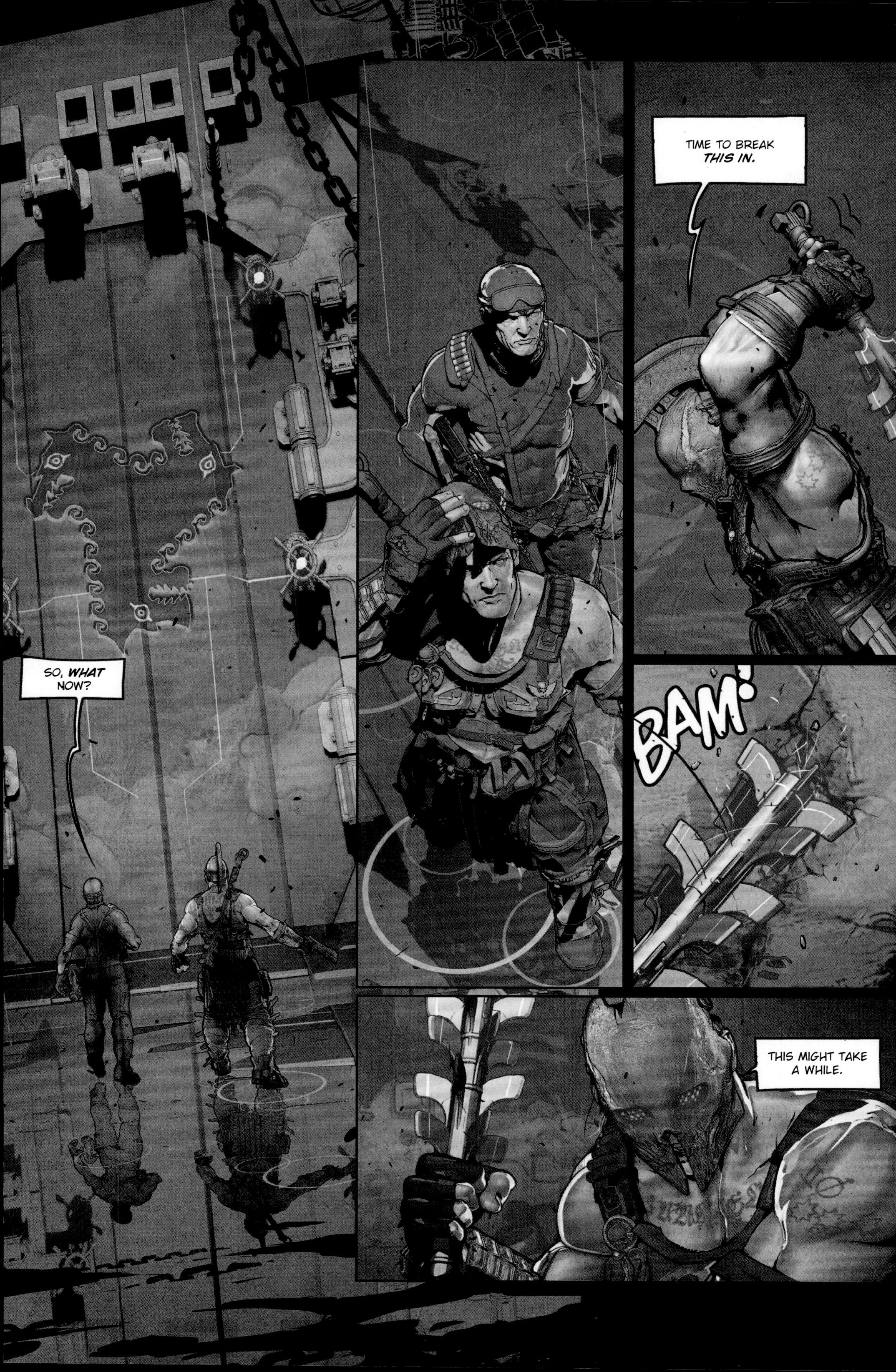
SO, *WHAT* NOW?
TIME TO BREAK *THIS IN.*
BAM!
THIS MIGHT TAKE A WHILE.

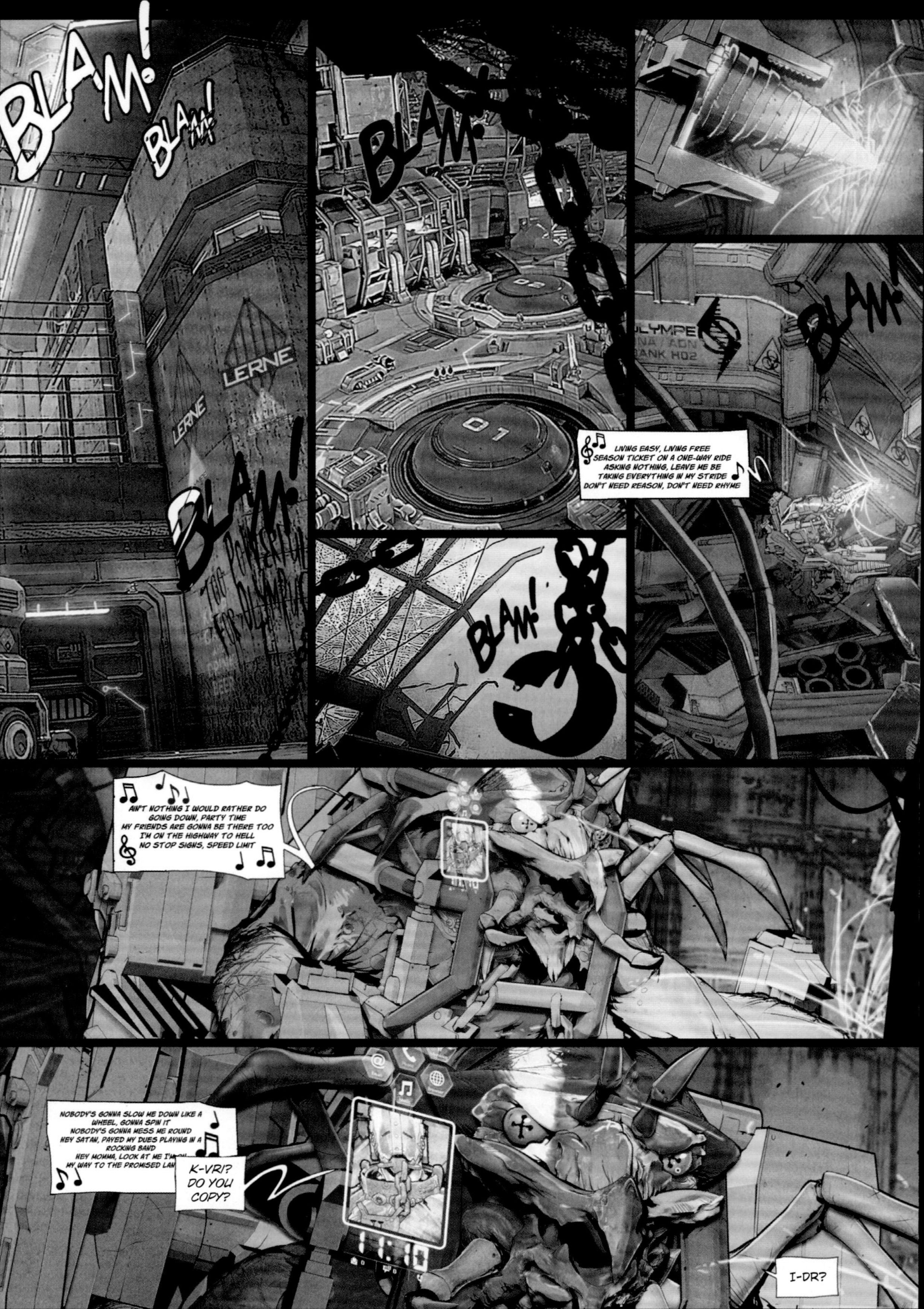
BLAM!
BLAM!
BLAM!
BLAM!
BLAM!
LERNE
LERNE
01
LIVING EASY, LIVING FREE
SEASON TICKET ON A ONE-WAY RIDE
ASKING NOTHING, LEAVE ME BE
TAKING EVERYTHING IN MY STRIDE
DON'T NEED REASON, DON'T NEED RHYME
BLAM!
BLAM!
AIN'T NOTHING I WOULD RATHER DO
GOING DOWN, PARTY TIME
MY FRIENDS ARE GONNA BE THERE TOO
I'M ON THE HIGHWAY TO HELL
NO STOP SIGNS, SPEED LIMIT
NOBODY'S GONNA SLOW ME DOWN LIKE A
WHEEL, GONNA SPIN IT
NOBODY'S GONNA MESS ME ROUND
HEY SATAN, PAYED MY DUES PLAYING IN A
ROCKING BAND
HEY MOMMA, LOOK AT ME I'M
MY WAY TO THE PROMISED LAN
K-VRI? DO YOU COPY?
11:10
I-DR?

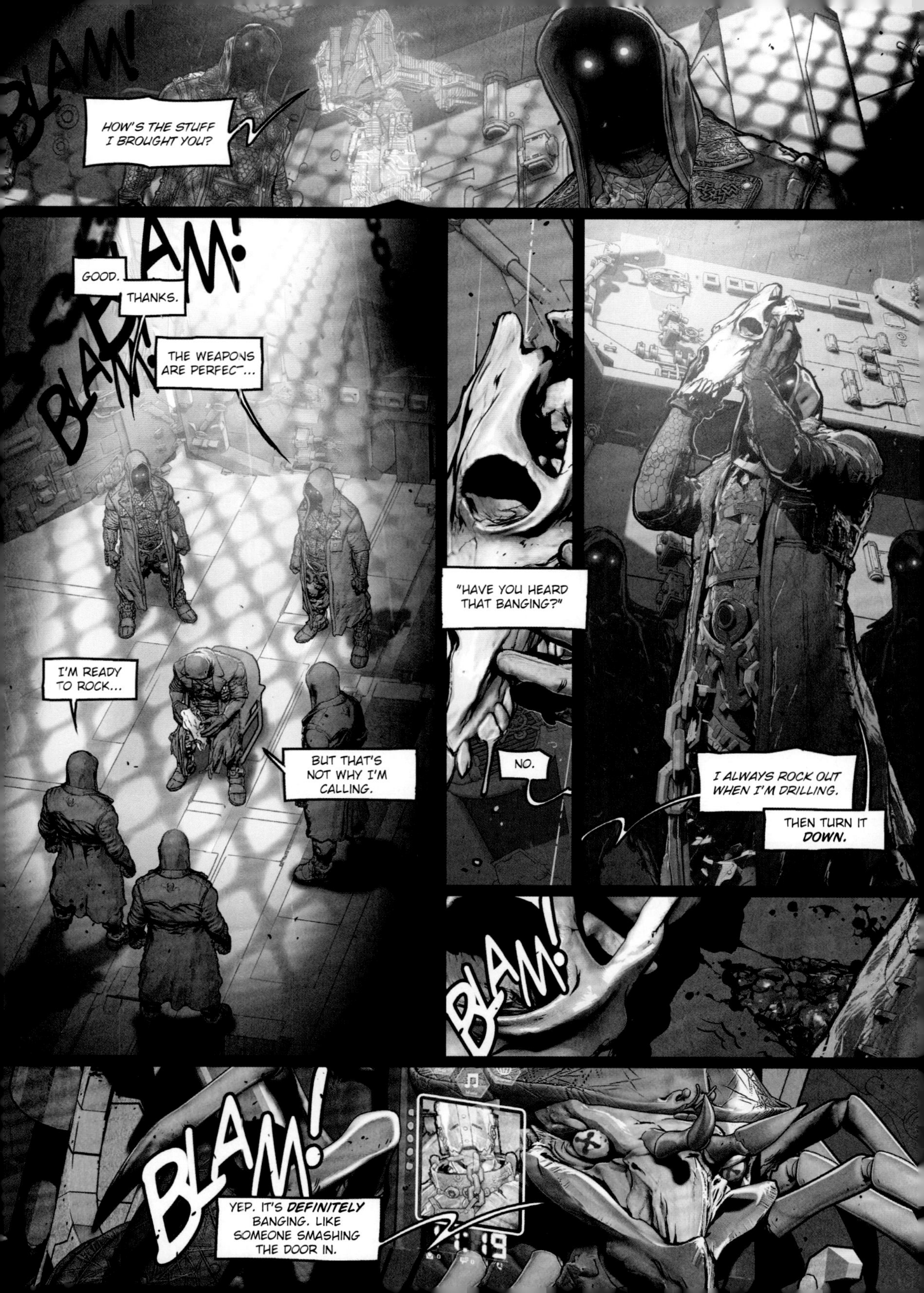
BLAM!
HOW'S THE STUFF I BROUGHT YOU?
BLAM!
GOOD.
THANKS.
BLAM!
THE WEAPONS ARE PERFECT...
I'M READY TO ROCK...
BUT THAT'S NOT WHY I'M CALLING.
"HAVE YOU HEARD THAT BANGING?"
NO.
I ALWAYS ROCK OUT WHEN I'M DRILLING.
THEN TURN IT ***DOWN.***
BLAM!
BLAM!
YEP. IT'S ***DEFINITELY*** BANGING. LIKE SOMEONE SMASHING THE DOOR IN.

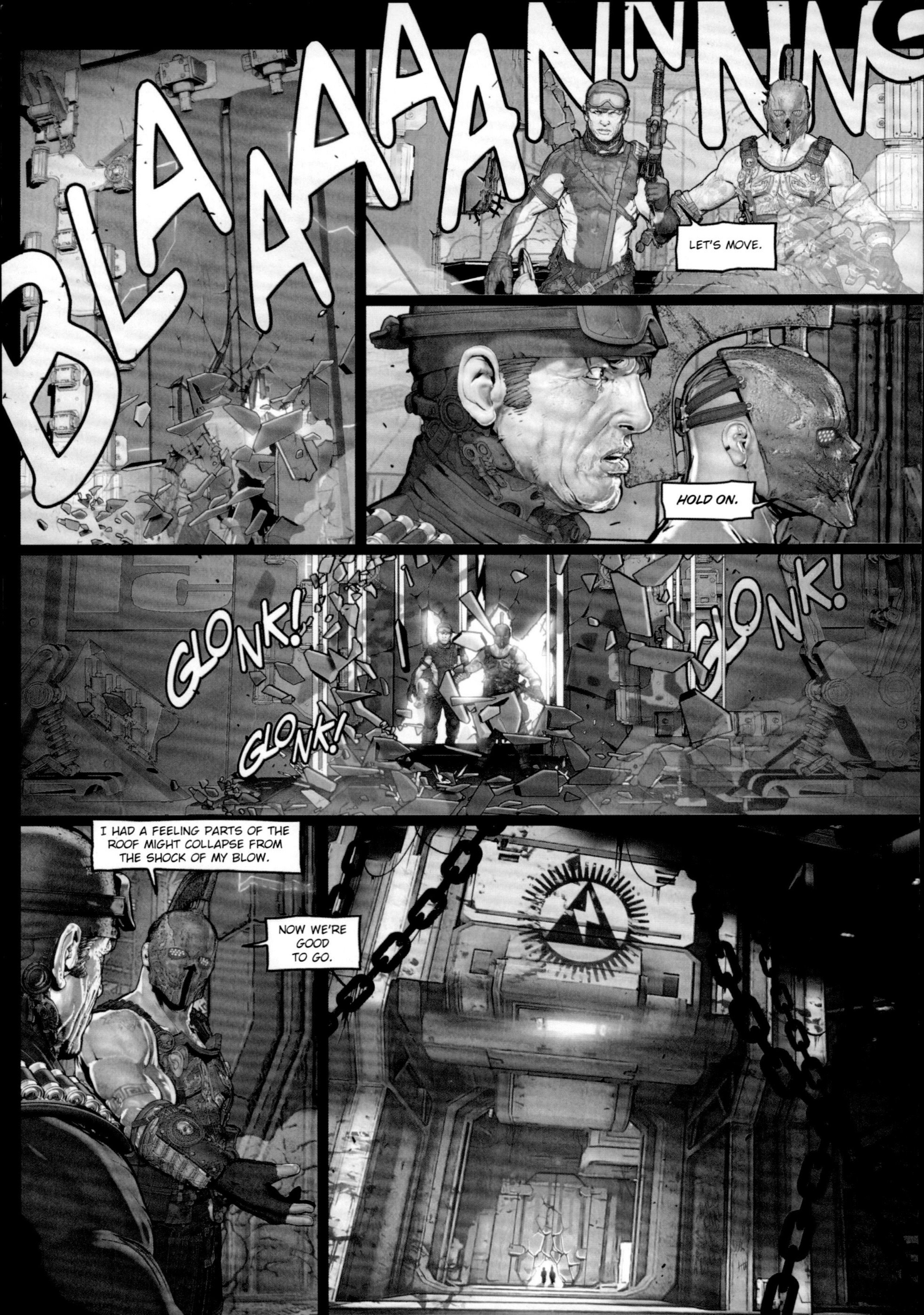
BLAAAANNNNG
LET'S MOVE.
HOLD ON.
GLONK!
GLONK!
GLONK!
I HAD A FEELING PARTS OF THE ROOF MIGHT COLLAPSE FROM THE SHOCK OF MY BLOW.
NOW WE'RE GOOD TO GO.

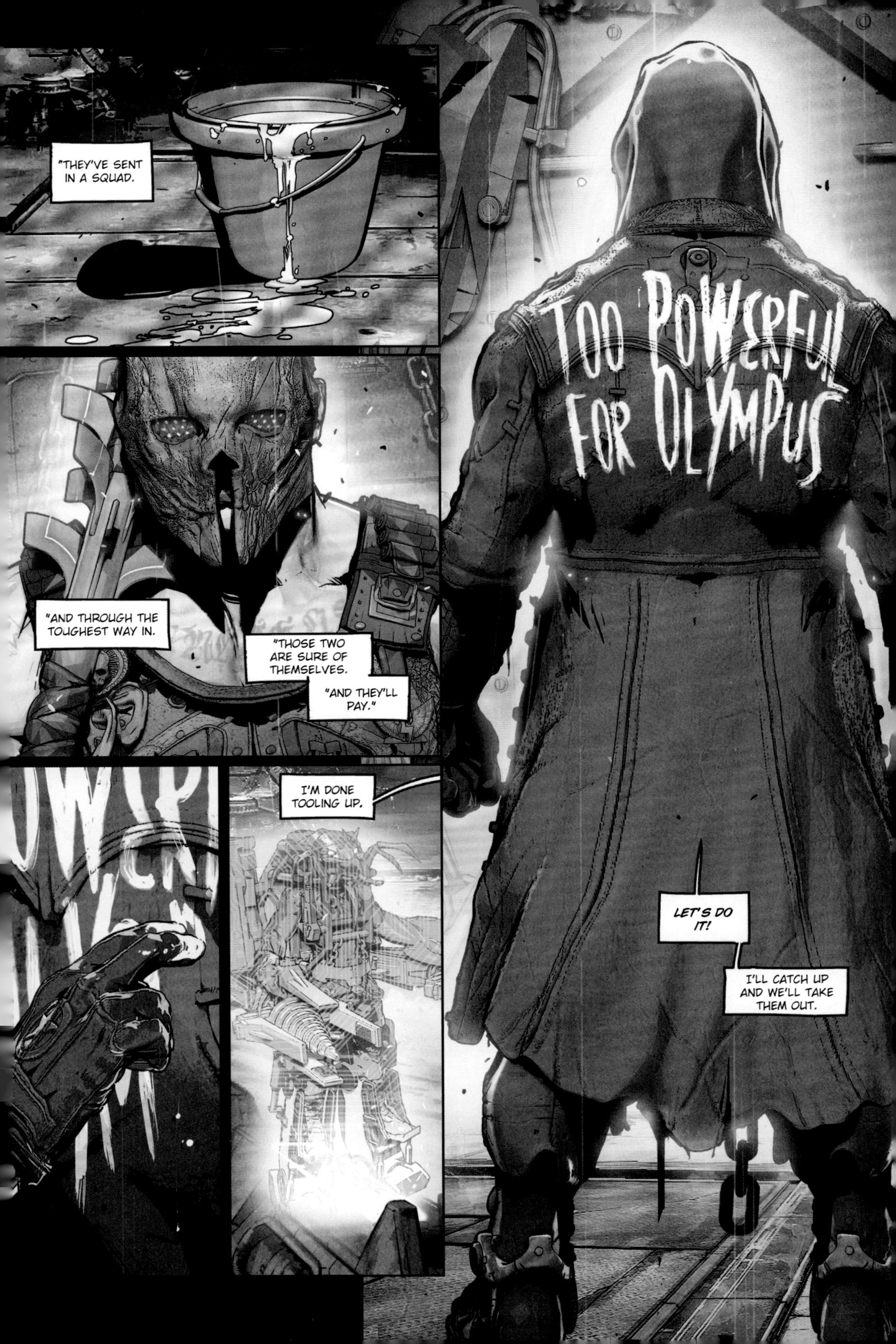
"THEY'VE SENT IN A SQUAD.
"AND THROUGH THE TOUGHEST WAY IN.
"THOSE TWO ARE SURE OF THEMSELVES.
"AND THEY'LL PAY."
I'M DONE TOOLING UP.
TOO POWERFUL FOR OLYMPUS
LET'S DO IT!
I'LL CATCH UP AND WE'LL TAKE THEM OUT.

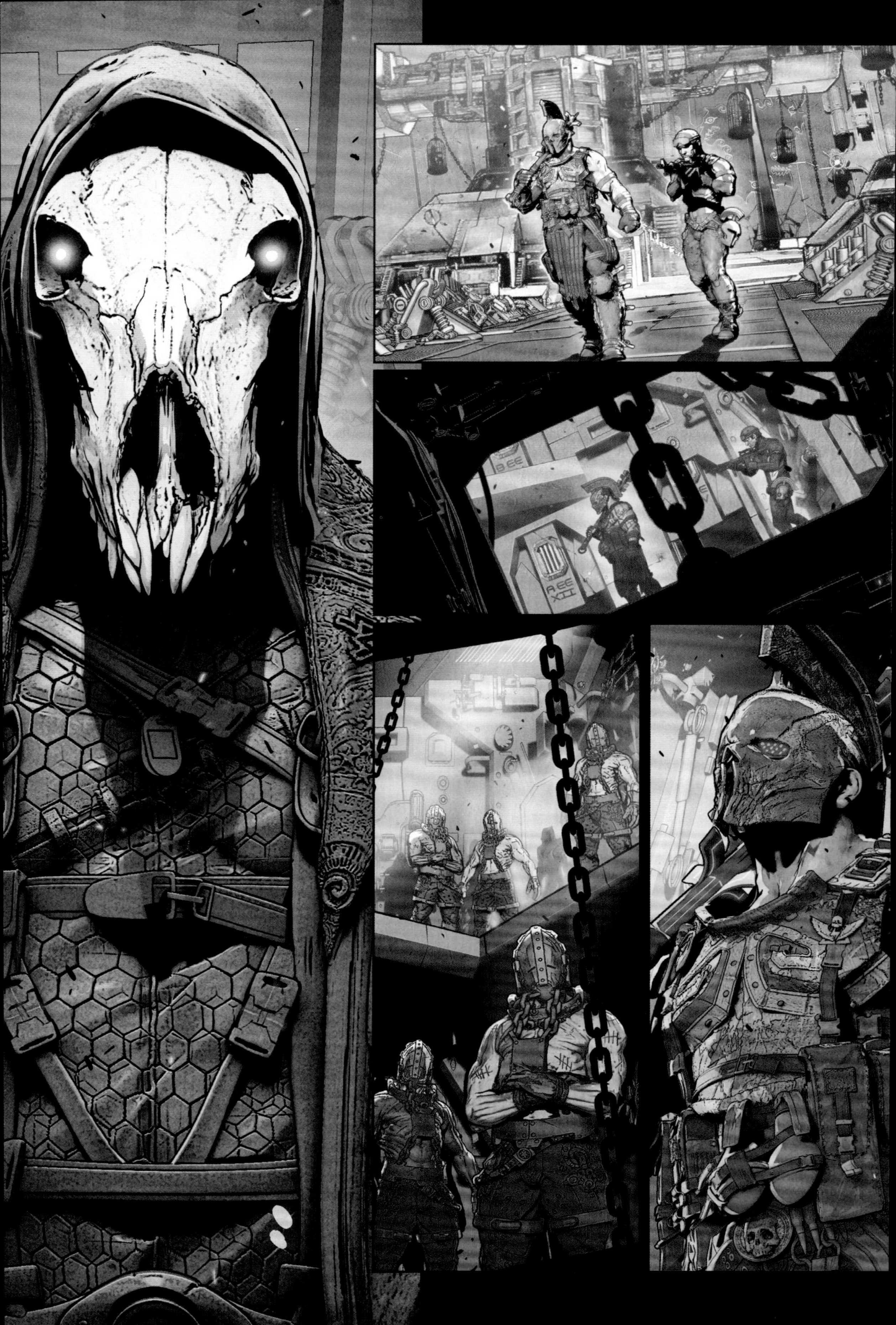

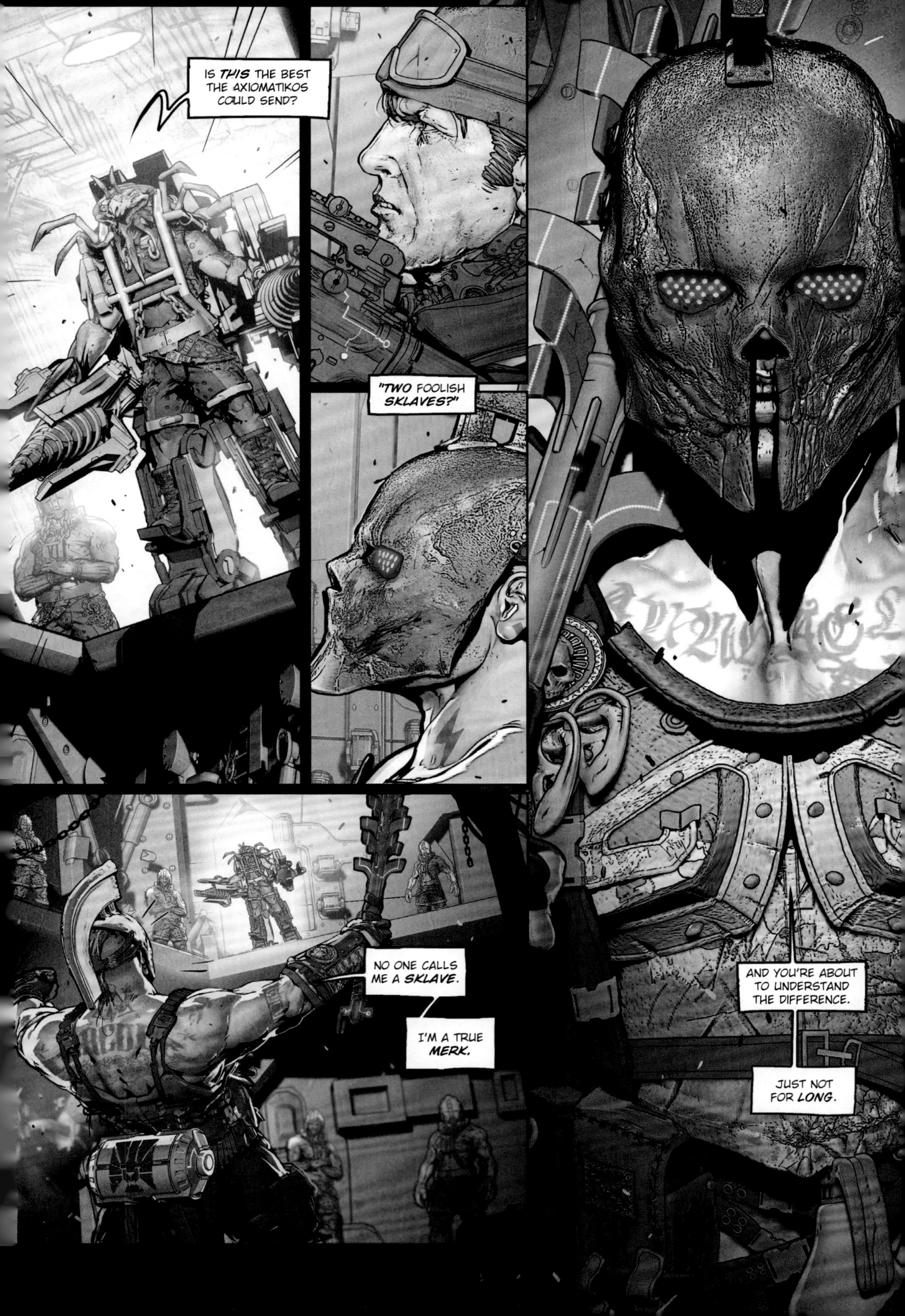
IS THIS THE BEST THE AXIOMATIKOS COULD SEND?
"TWO FOOLISH SKLAVES?"
NO ONE CALLS ME A SKLAVE.
I'M A TRUE MERK.
AND YOU'RE ABOUT TO UNDERSTAND THE DIFFERENCE.
JUST NOT FOR LONG.

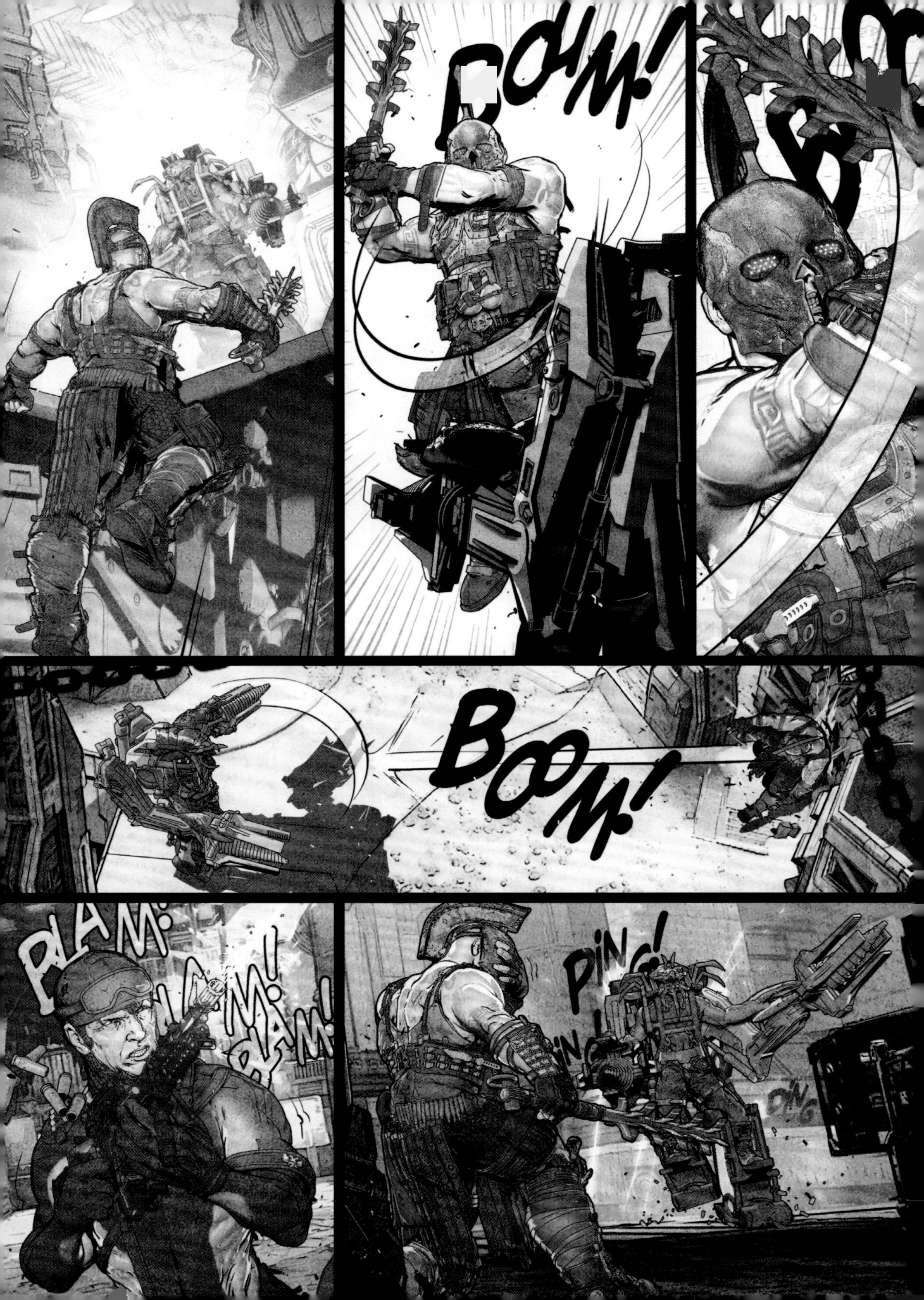

BOOM!
BOOM!
BLAM!
PING!
PING

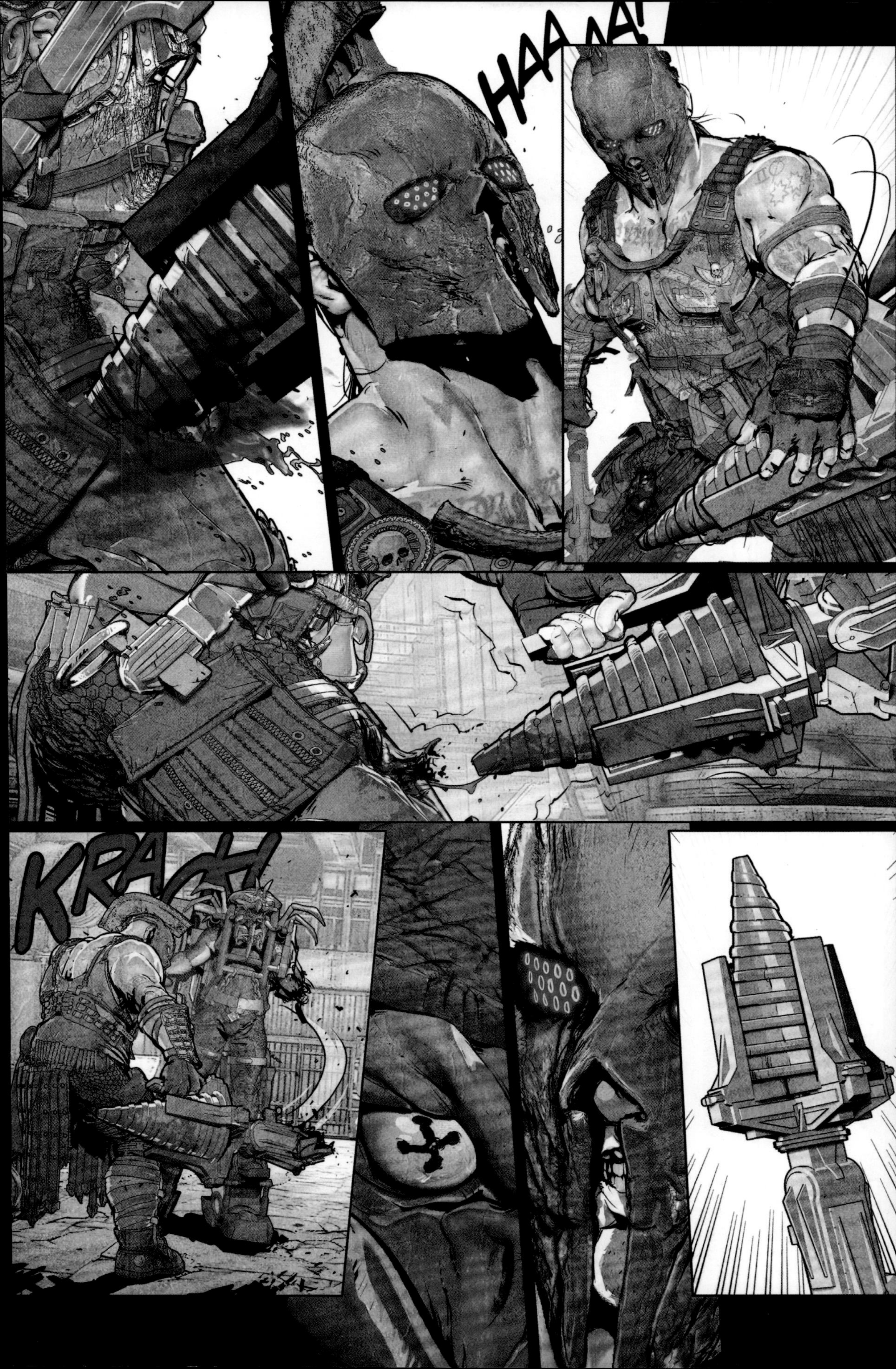
HAAAA!
KRACH

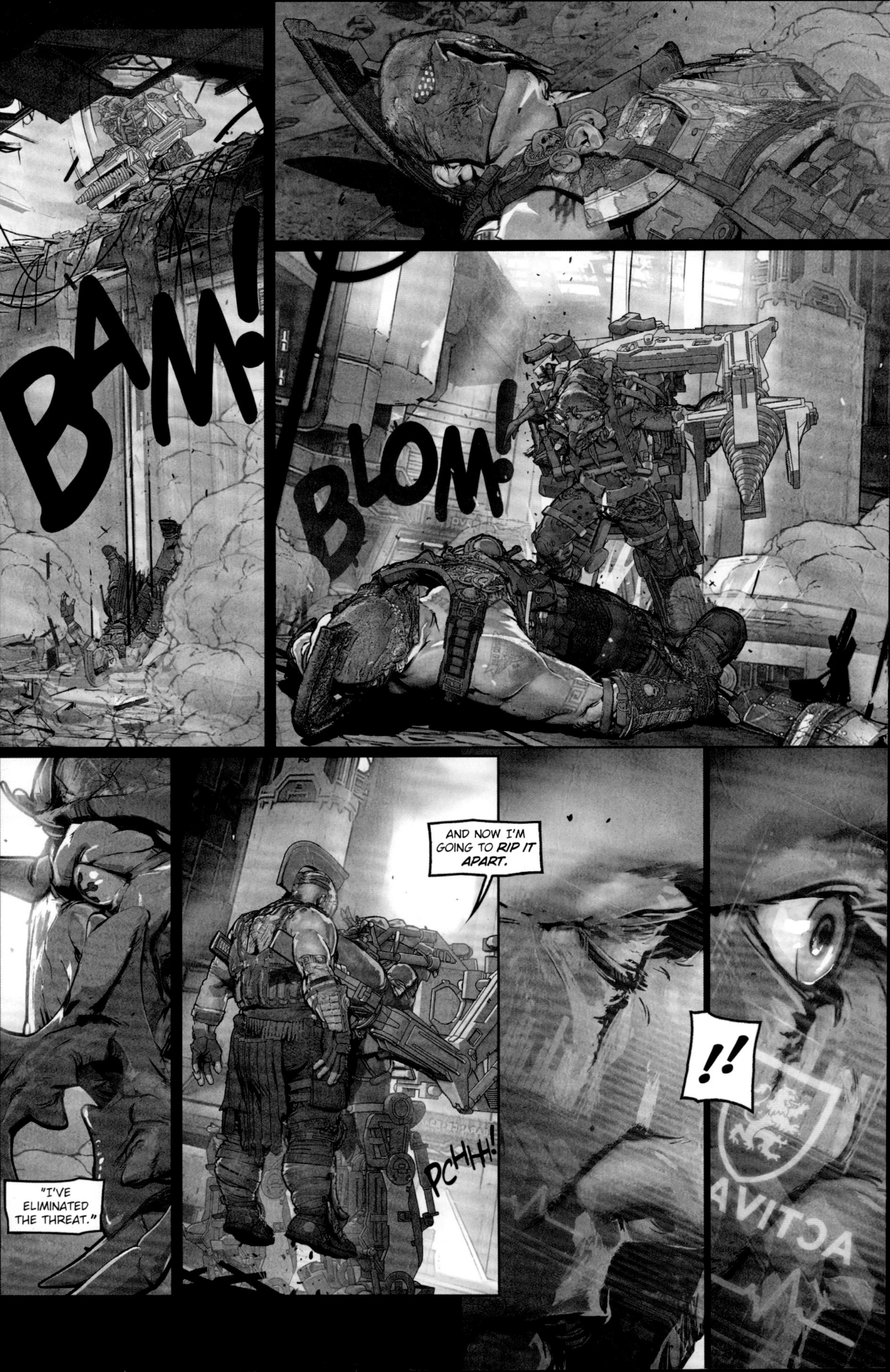
BAM!
BLOM!
"I'VE ELIMINATED THE THREAT."
AND NOW I'M GOING TO *RIP IT APART.*
PCHHH!
!!

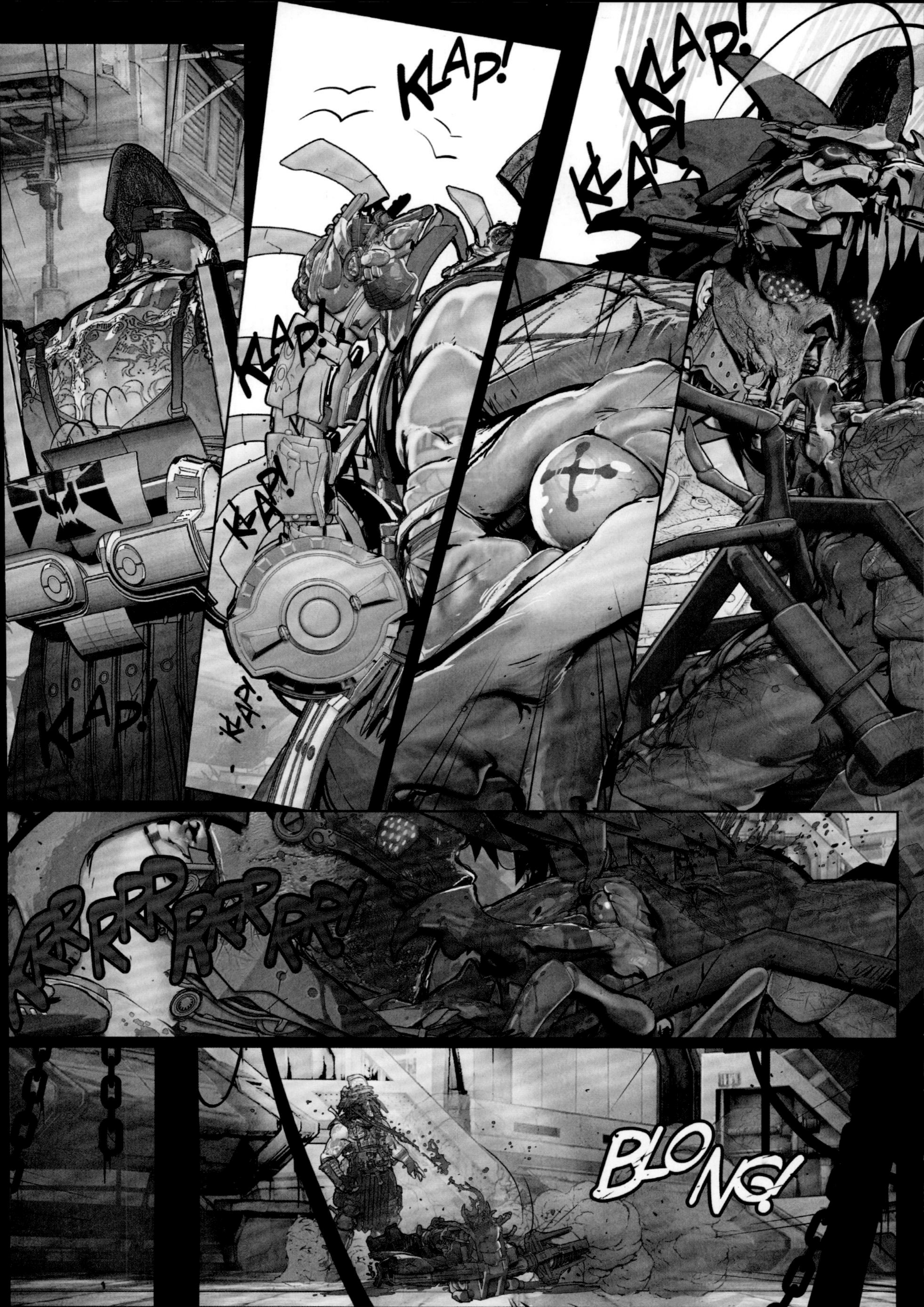
KLAP!
KLAP!
KLAP!
KLAP!
KLAP!
KLAR!
KLAP!
RRRRRRRRRRR!
BLONG!

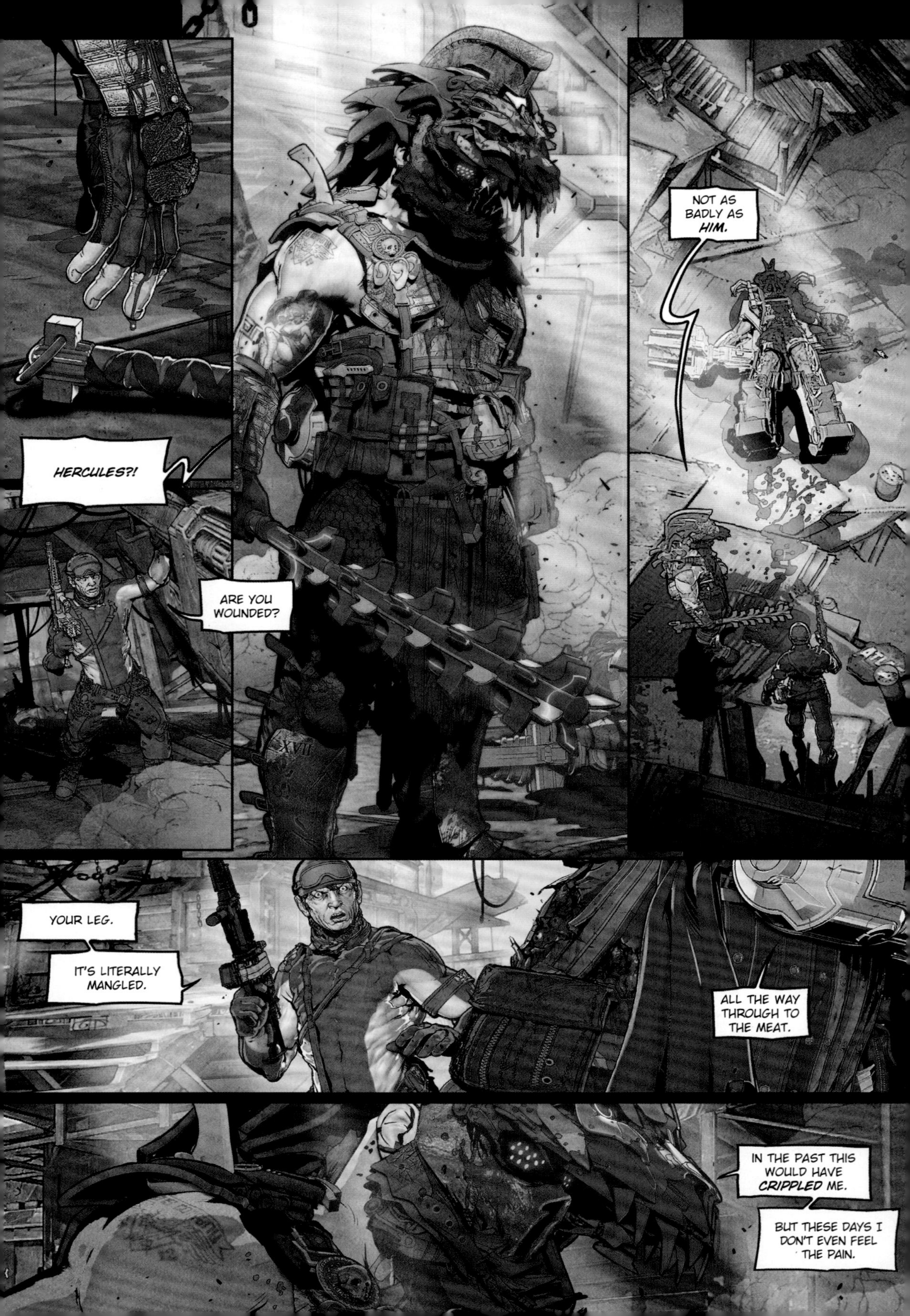
HERCULES?!
ARE YOU WOUNDED?
NOT AS BADLY AS *HIM.*
YOUR LEG.
IT'S LITERALLY MANGLED.
ALL THE WAY THROUGH TO THE MEAT.
IN THE PAST THIS WOULD HAVE *CRIPPLED* ME.
BUT THESE DAYS I DON'T EVEN FEEL THE PAIN.

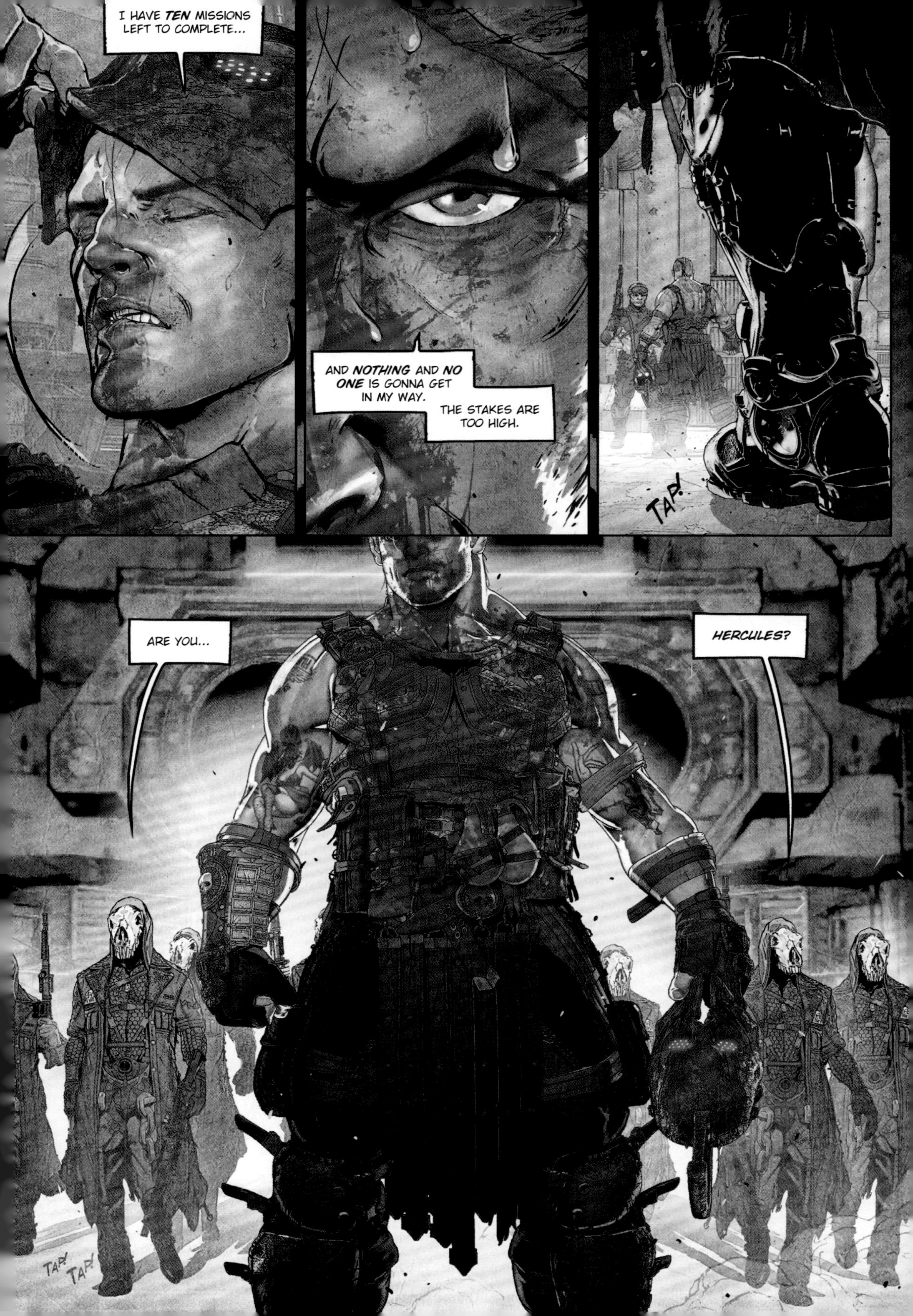
I HAVE **TEN** MISSIONS LEFT TO COMPLETE...
AND **NOTHING** AND **NO ONE** IS GONNA GET IN MY WAY.
THE STAKES ARE TOO HIGH.
TAP!
ARE YOU...
HERCULES?
TAP! TAP!

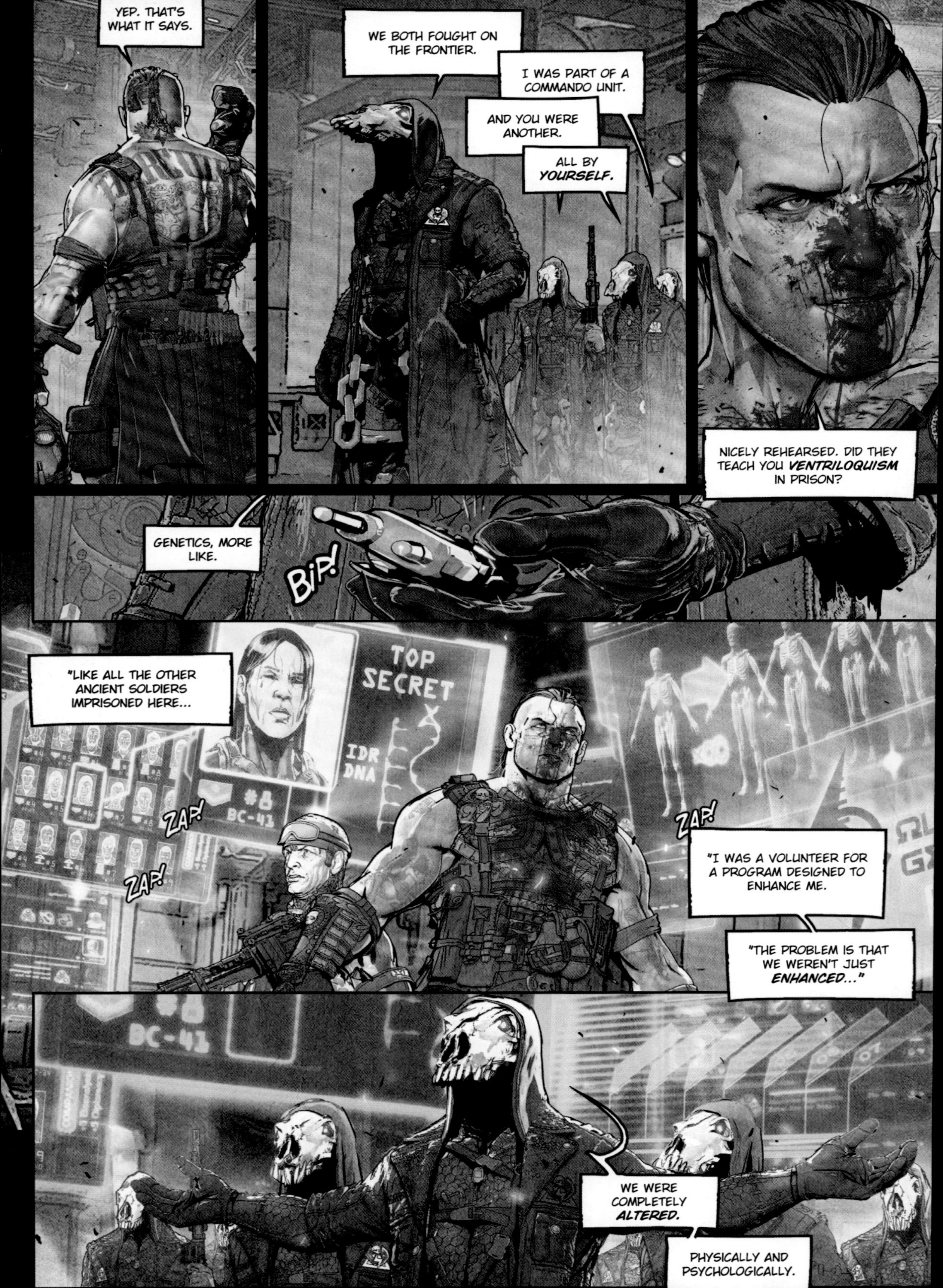

YEP. THAT'S WHAT IT SAYS.
WE BOTH FOUGHT ON THE FRONTIER.
I WAS PART OF A COMMANDO UNIT.
AND YOU WERE ANOTHER.
ALL BY ***YOURSELF.***
NICELY REHEARSED. DID THEY TEACH YOU ***VENTRILOQUISM*** IN PRISON?
GENETICS, MORE LIKE.
BIP!
"LIKE ALL THE OTHER ANCIENT SOLDIERS IMPRISONED HERE...
TOP SECRET
IDR DNA
#8 BC-41
ZAP!
ZAP!
ZAP!
"I WAS A VOLUNTEER FOR A PROGRAM DESIGNED TO ENHANCE ME.
"THE PROBLEM IS THAT WE WEREN'T JUST ***ENHANCED...***"
#8 BC-41
WE WERE COMPLETELY ***ALTERED.***
PHYSICALLY AND PSYCHOLOGICALLY.

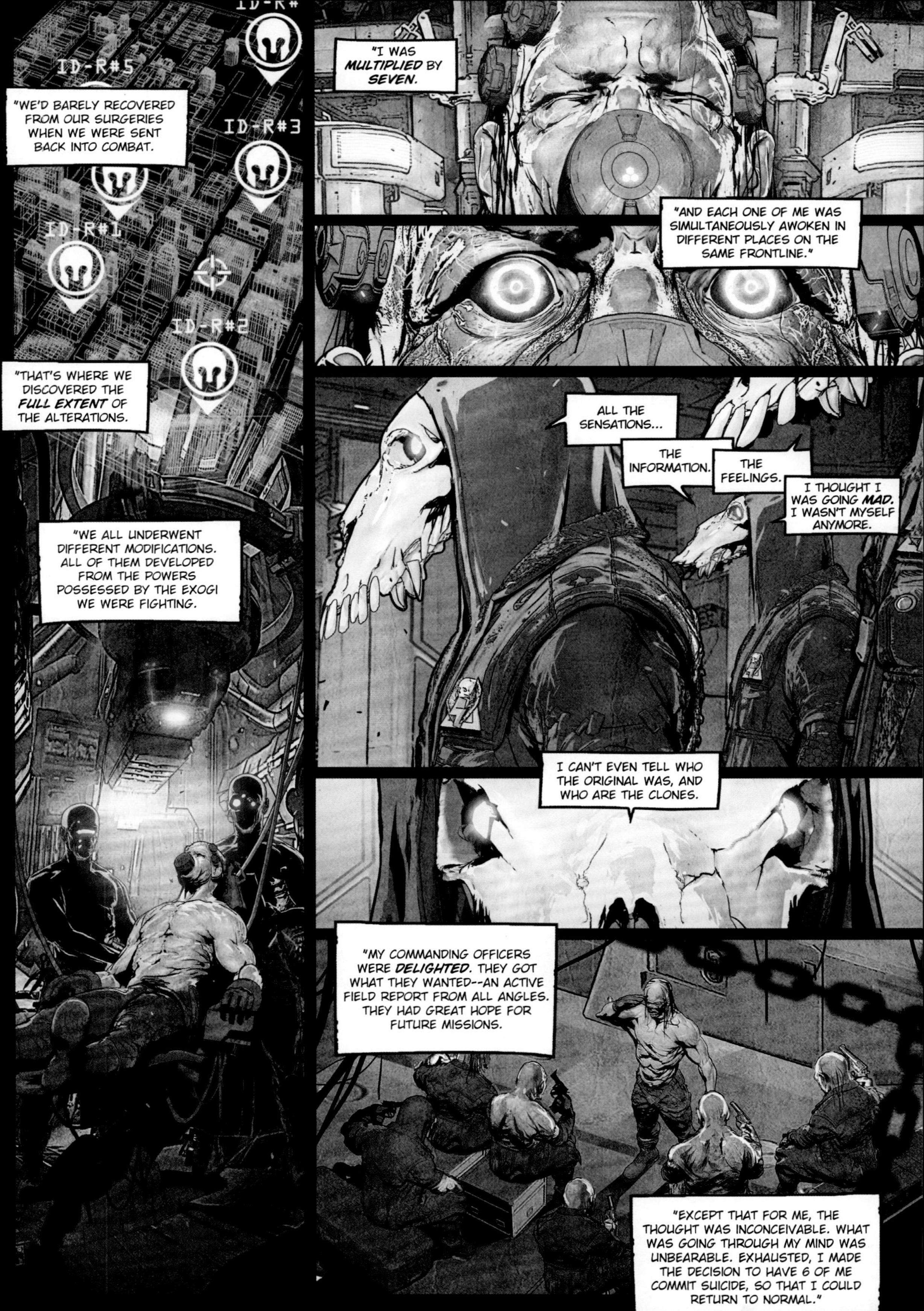
ID-R#
ID-R#5
"WE'D BARELY RECOVERED FROM OUR SURGERIES WHEN WE WERE SENT BACK INTO COMBAT.
ID-R#3
ID-R#1
ID-R#2
"THAT'S WHERE WE DISCOVERED THE FULL EXTENT OF THE ALTERATIONS.
"WE ALL UNDERWENT DIFFERENT MODIFICATIONS. ALL OF THEM DEVELOPED FROM THE POWERS POSSESSED BY THE EXOGI WE WERE FIGHTING.
"I WAS MULTIPLIED BY SEVEN.
"AND EACH ONE OF ME WAS SIMULTANEOUSLY AWOKEN IN DIFFERENT PLACES ON THE SAME FRONTLINE."
ALL THE SENSATIONS...
THE INFORMATION.
THE FEELINGS.
I THOUGHT I WAS GOING MAD. I WASN'T MYSELF ANYMORE.
I CAN'T EVEN TELL WHO THE ORIGINAL WAS, AND WHO ARE THE CLONES.
"MY COMMANDING OFFICERS WERE DELIGHTED. THEY GOT WHAT THEY WANTED--AN ACTIVE FIELD REPORT FROM ALL ANGLES. THEY HAD GREAT HOPE FOR FUTURE MISSIONS.
"EXCEPT THAT FOR ME, THE THOUGHT WAS INCONCEIVABLE. WHAT WAS GOING THROUGH MY MIND WAS UNBEARABLE. EXHAUSTED, I MADE THE DECISION TO HAVE 6 OF ME COMMIT SUICIDE, SO THAT I COULD RETURN TO NORMAL."

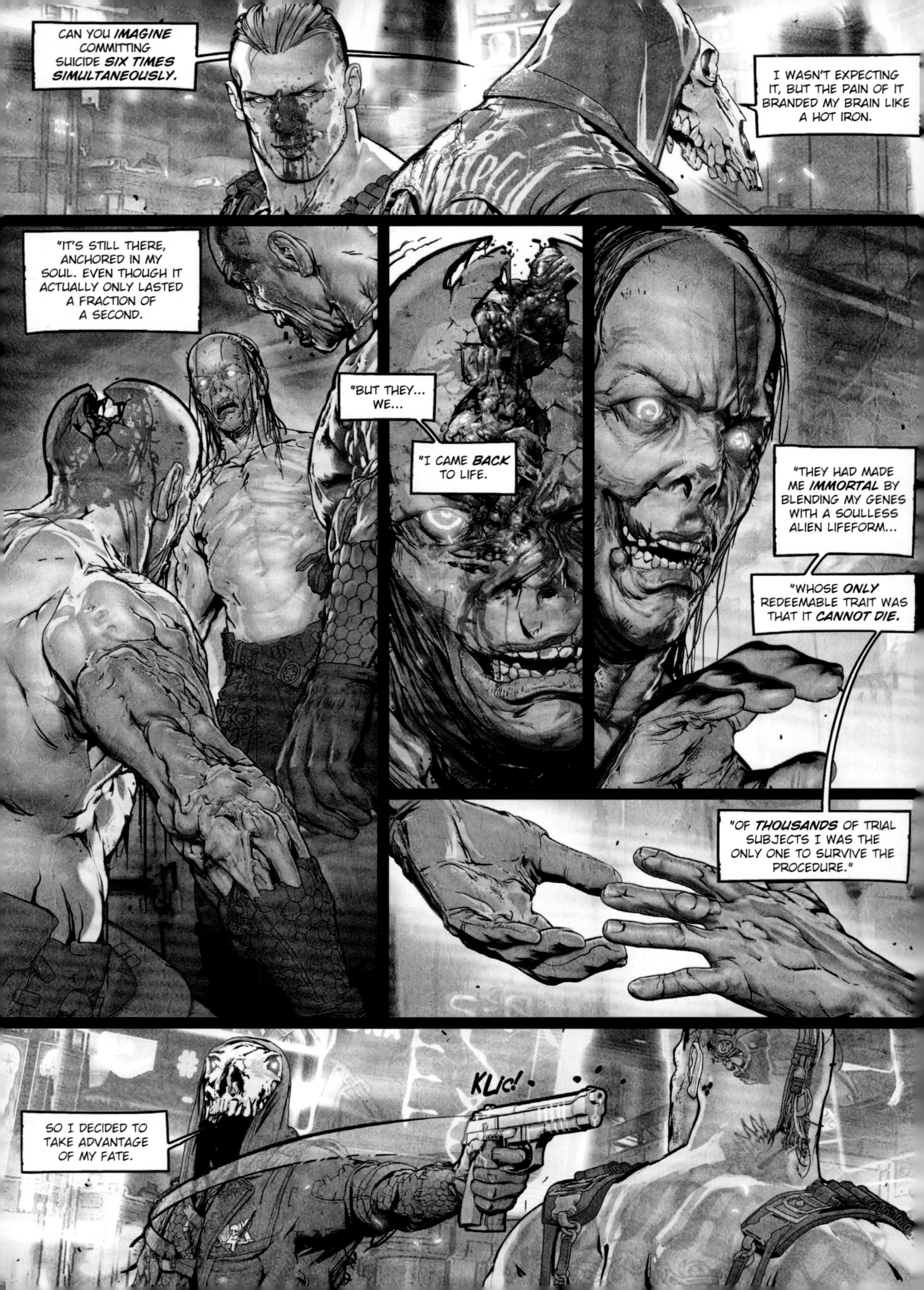
CAN YOU *IMAGINE* COMMITTING SUICIDE *SIX TIMES SIMULTANEOUSLY.*
I WASN'T EXPECTING IT, BUT THE PAIN OF IT BRANDED MY BRAIN LIKE A HOT IRON.
"IT'S STILL THERE, ANCHORED IN MY SOUL. EVEN THOUGH IT ACTUALLY ONLY LASTED A FRACTION OF A SECOND.
"BUT THEY... WE...
"I CAME *BACK* TO LIFE.
"THEY HAD MADE ME *IMMORTAL* BY BLENDING MY GENES WITH A SOULLESS ALIEN LIFEFORM...
"WHOSE *ONLY* REDEEMABLE TRAIT WAS THAT IT *CANNOT DIE.*
"OF *THOUSANDS* OF TRIAL SUBJECTS I WAS THE ONLY ONE TO SURVIVE THE PROCEDURE."
KLIC!
SO I DECIDED TO TAKE ADVANTAGE OF MY FATE.

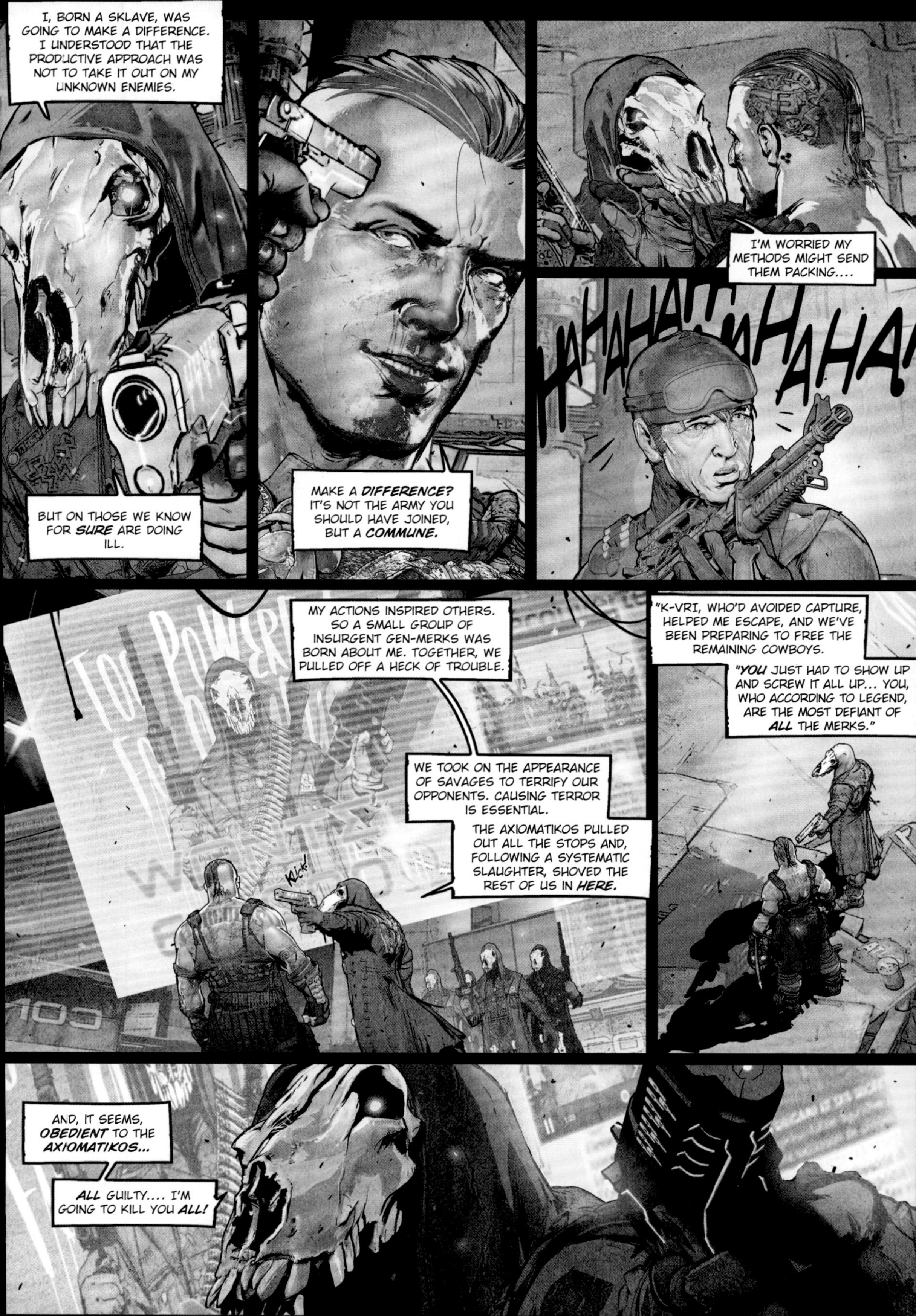
I, BORN A SKLAVE, WAS GOING TO MAKE A DIFFERENCE. I UNDERSTOOD THAT THE PRODUCTIVE APPROACH WAS NOT TO TAKE IT OUT ON MY UNKNOWN ENEMIES.
BUT ON THOSE WE KNOW FOR *SURE* ARE DOING ILL.
MAKE A *DIFFERENCE?* IT'S NOT THE ARMY YOU SHOULD HAVE JOINED, BUT A *COMMUNE.*
I'M WORRIED MY METHODS MIGHT SEND THEM PACKING....
HAHAHAHAHAHAHAHA!
MY ACTIONS INSPIRED OTHERS. SO A SMALL GROUP OF INSURGENT GEN-MERKS WAS BORN ABOUT ME. TOGETHER, WE PULLED OFF A HECK OF TROUBLE.
WE TOOK ON THE APPEARANCE OF SAVAGES TO TERRIFY OUR OPPONENTS. CAUSING TERROR IS ESSENTIAL.
THE AXIOMATIKOS PULLED OUT ALL THE STOPS AND, FOLLOWING A SYSTEMATIC SLAUGHTER, SHOVED THE REST OF US IN *HERE.*
KLICK!
"K-VRI, WHO'D AVOIDED CAPTURE, HELPED ME ESCAPE, AND WE'VE BEEN PREPARING TO FREE THE REMAINING COWBOYS.
"*YOU* JUST HAD TO SHOW UP AND SCREW IT ALL UP... YOU, WHO ACCORDING TO LEGEND, ARE THE MOST DEFIANT OF *ALL* THE MERKS."
AND, IT SEEMS, *OBEDIENT* TO THE *AXIOMATIKOS...*
ALL GUILTY.... I'M GOING TO KILL YOU *ALL!*

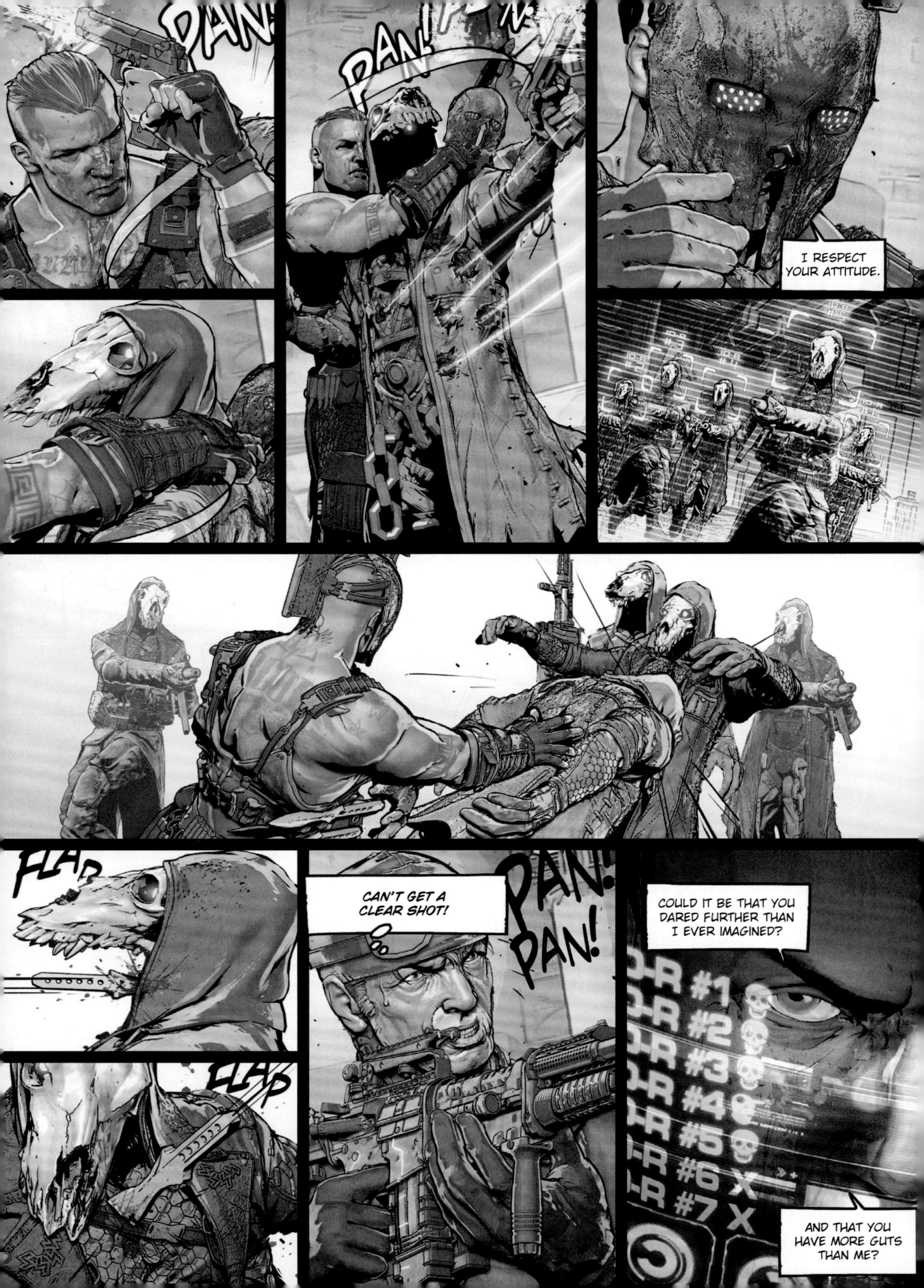
PAN!
PAN! PAN!
I RESPECT YOUR ATTITUDE.
FLAP
CAN'T GET A CLEAR SHOT!
PAN! PAN!
COULD IT BE THAT YOU DARED FURTHER THAN I EVER IMAGINED?
ID-R #1
ID-R #2
ID-R #3
ID-R #4
ID-R #5
ID-R #6 X
ID-R #7 X
FLAP
AND THAT YOU HAVE MORE GUTS THAN ME?

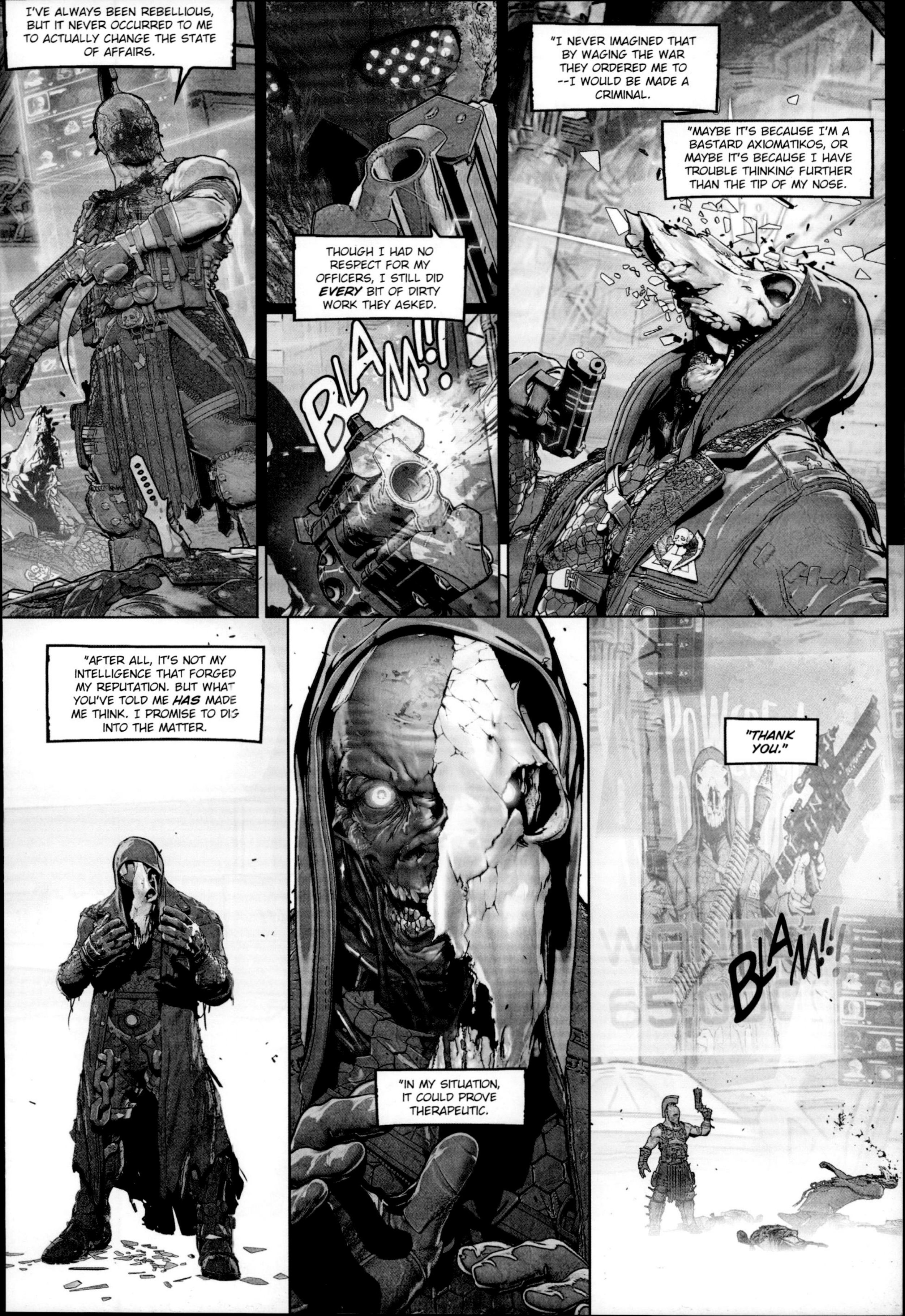
I'VE ALWAYS BEEN REBELLIOUS, BUT IT NEVER OCCURRED TO ME TO ACTUALLY CHANGE THE STATE OF AFFAIRS.
THOUGH I HAD NO RESPECT FOR MY OFFICERS, I STILL DID EVERY BIT OF DIRTY WORK THEY ASKED.
BLAM!!
"I NEVER IMAGINED THAT BY WAGING THE WAR THEY ORDERED ME TO --I WOULD BE MADE A CRIMINAL.
"MAYBE IT'S BECAUSE I'M A BASTARD AXIOMATIKOS, OR MAYBE IT'S BECAUSE I HAVE TROUBLE THINKING FURTHER THAN THE TIP OF MY NOSE.
"AFTER ALL, IT'S NOT MY INTELLIGENCE THAT FORGED MY REPUTATION. BUT WHAT YOU'VE TOLD ME HAS MADE ME THINK. I PROMISE TO DIG INTO THE MATTER.
"IN MY SITUATION, IT COULD PROVE THERAPEUTIC.
"THANK YOU."
BLAM!!

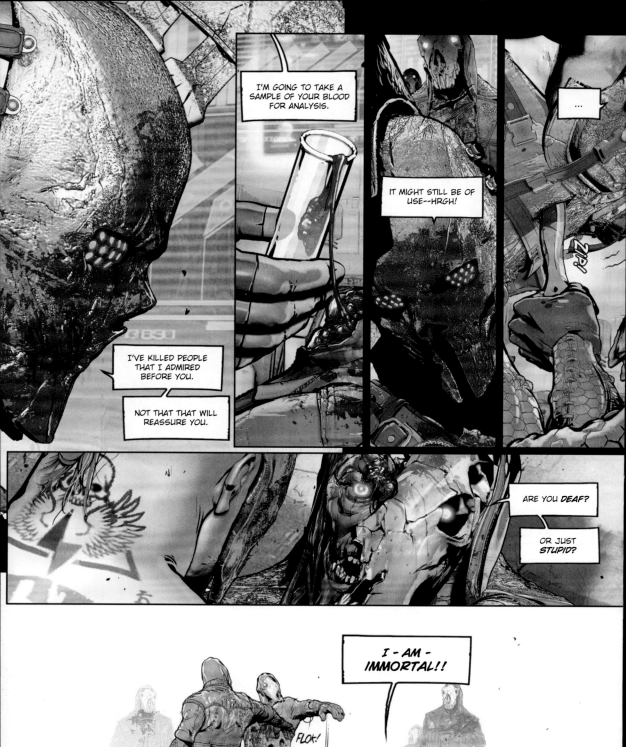

I'M GOING TO TAKE A SAMPLE OF YOUR BLOOD FOR ANALYSIS.

IT MIGHT STILL BE OF USE--HRGH!

...

I'VE KILLED PEOPLE THAT I ADMIRED BEFORE YOU.

NOT THAT THAT WILL REASSURE YOU.

ARE YOU *DEAF*? OR JUST *STUPID*?

I - AM - IMMORTAL!!

FLOK!

FLOK!

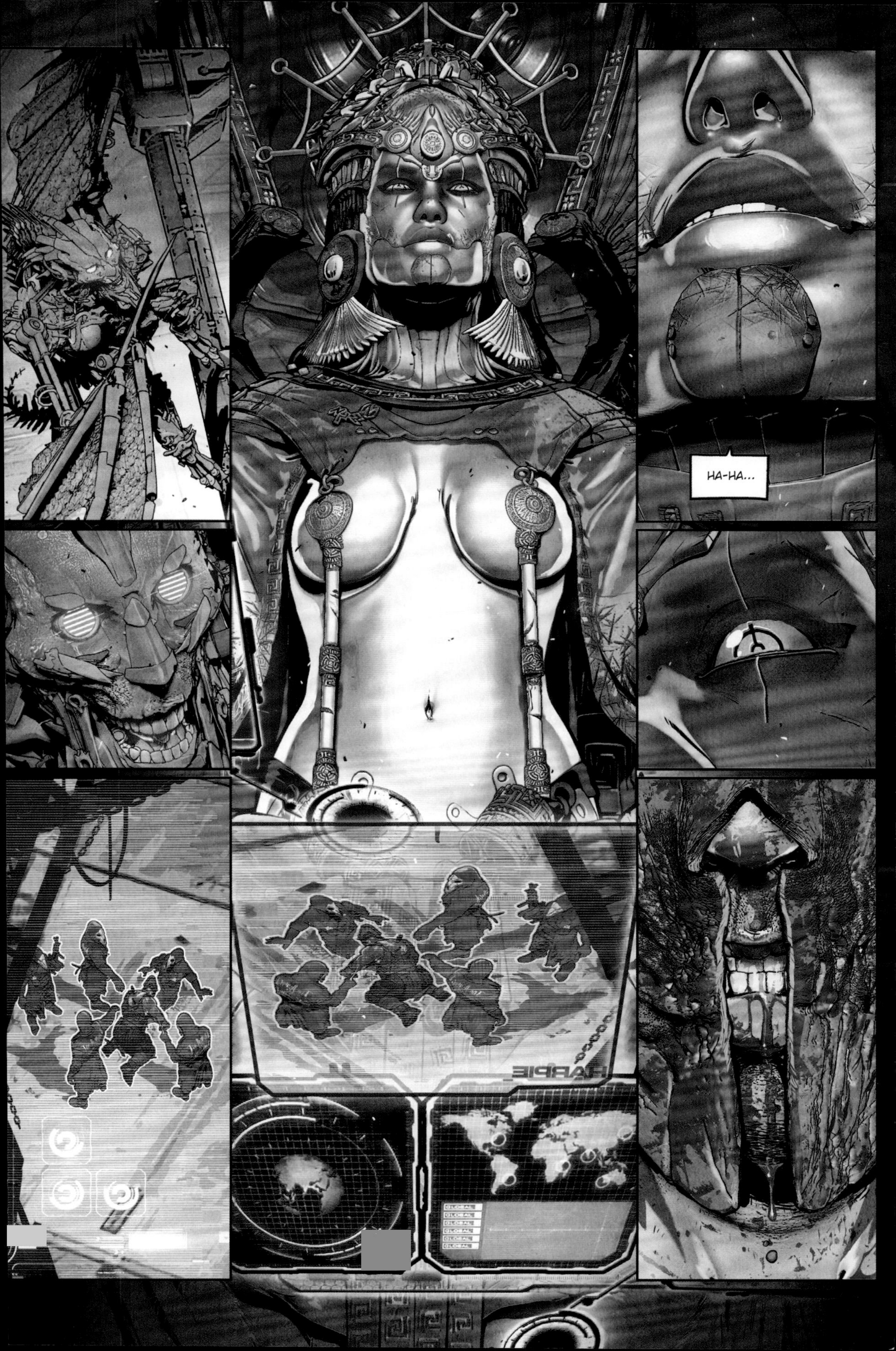
HA-HA...

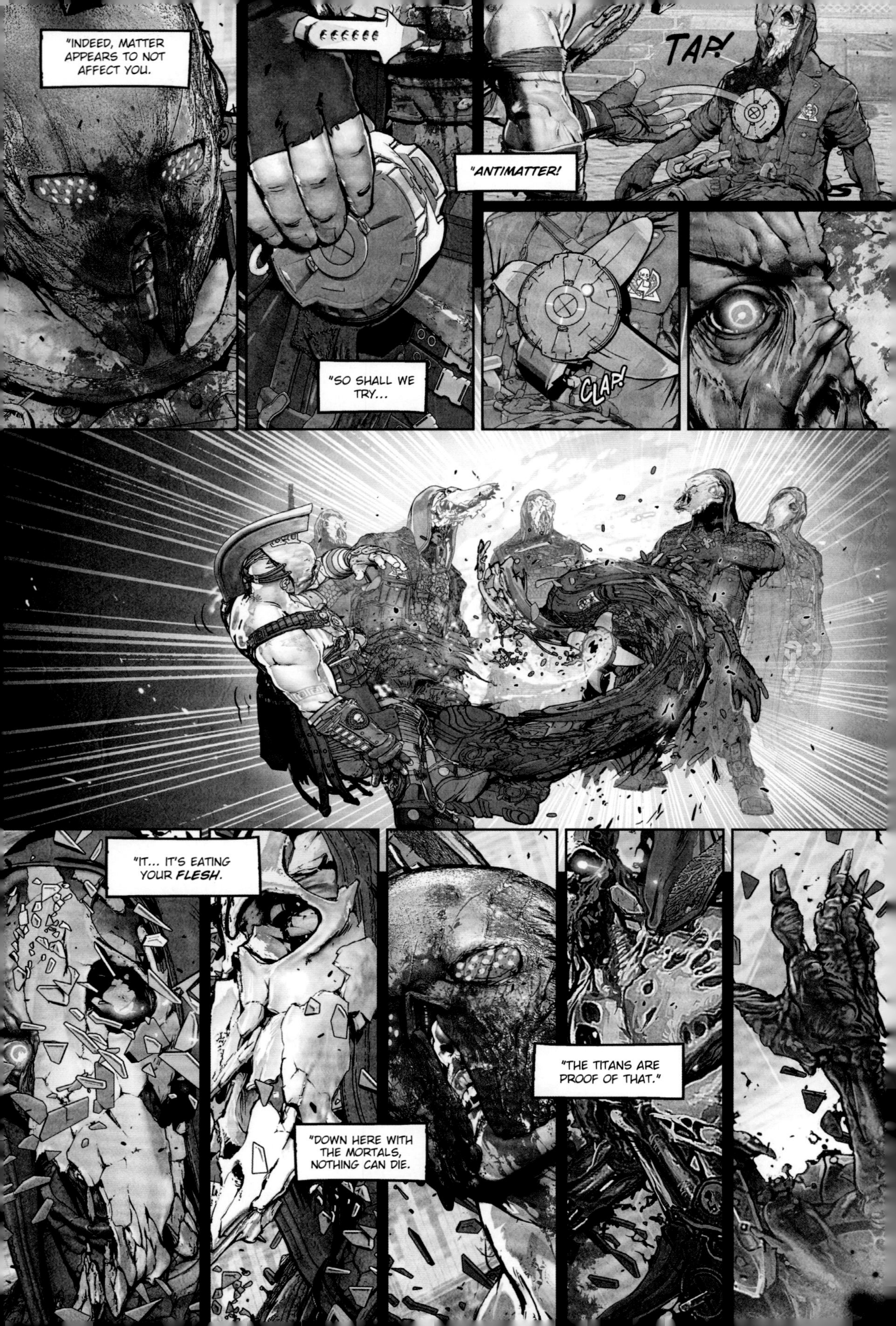
"INDEED, MATTER APPEARS TO NOT AFFECT YOU.
"SO SHALL WE TRY...
"ANTIMATTER!
TAP!
CLAP!
"IT... IT'S EATING YOUR FLESH.
"DOWN HERE WITH THE MORTALS, NOTHING CAN DIE.
"THE TITANS ARE PROOF OF THAT."

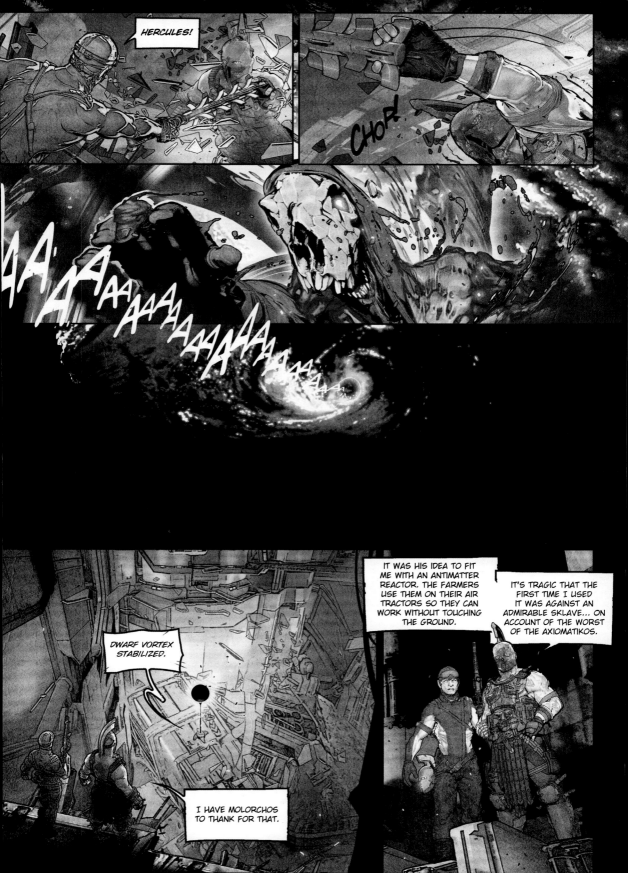

HERCULES!

CHOR!

AAAAAAAAAAAAAAAAAAAAAAAAAAAA

IT WAS HIS IDEA TO FIT ME WITH AN ANTIMATTER REACTOR. THE FARMERS USE THEM ON THEIR AIR TRACTORS SO THEY CAN WORK WITHOUT TOUCHING THE GROUND.

IT'S TRAGIC THAT THE FIRST TIME I USED IT WAS AGAINST AN ADMIRABLE SKLAVE... ON ACCOUNT OF THE WORST OF THE AXIOMATIKOS.

DWARF VORTEX STABILIZED.

I HAVE MOLORCHOS TO THANK FOR THAT.

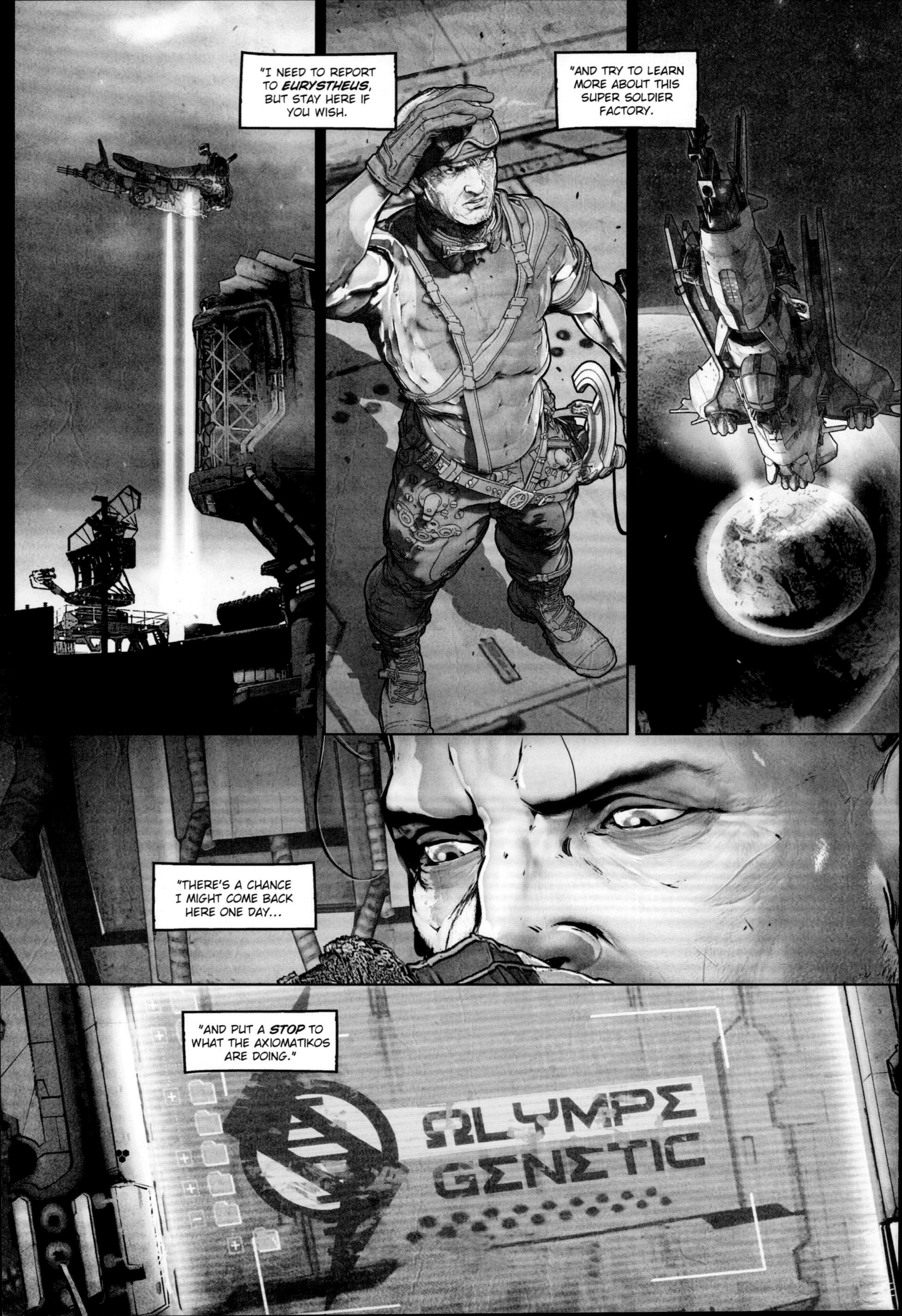
"I NEED TO REPORT TO *EURYSTHEUS*, BUT STAY HERE IF YOU WISH.
"AND TRY TO LEARN MORE ABOUT THIS SUPER SOLDIER FACTORY.
"THERE'S A CHANCE I MIGHT COME BACK HERE ONE DAY...
"AND PUT A *STOP* TO WHAT THE AXIOMATIKOS ARE DOING."
ΩLYMPΣ GΣNΣTIC

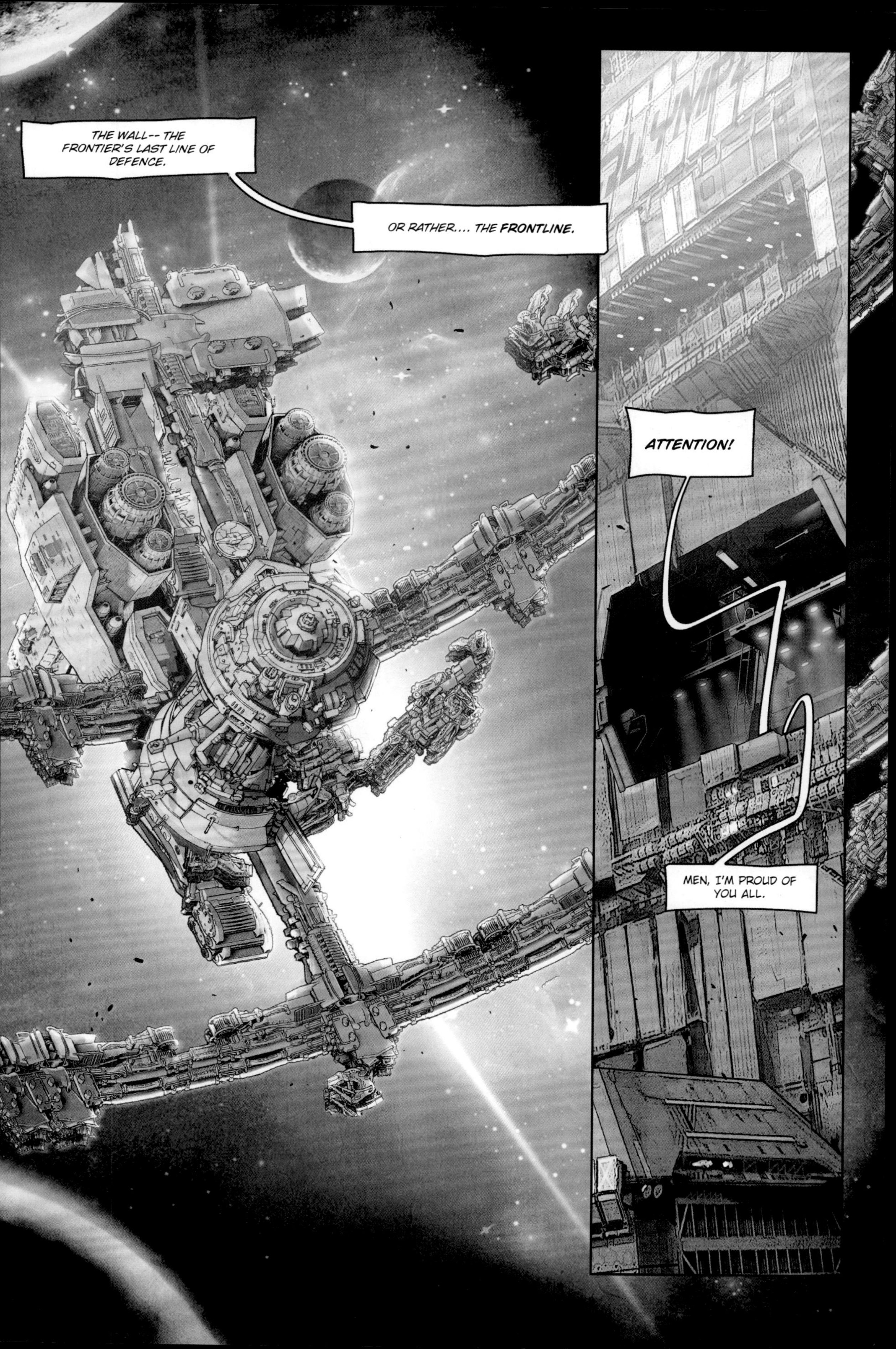
THE WALL-- THE FRONTIER'S LAST LINE OF DEFENCE.
OR RATHER.... THE **FRONTLINE.**
ATTENTION!
MEN, I'M PROUD OF YOU ALL.

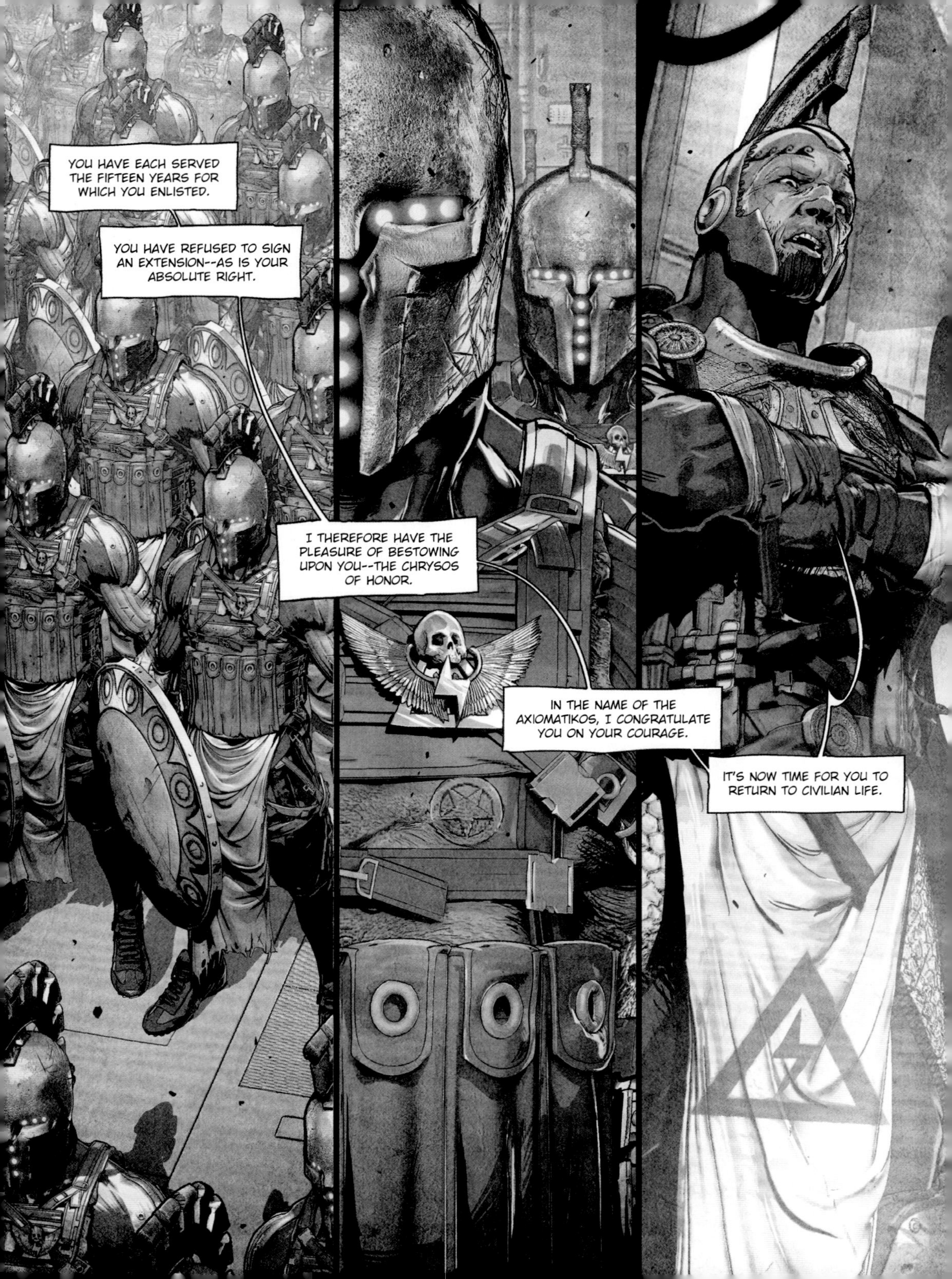
YOU HAVE EACH SERVED THE FIFTEEN YEARS FOR WHICH YOU ENLISTED.
YOU HAVE REFUSED TO SIGN AN EXTENSION--AS IS YOUR ABSOLUTE RIGHT.
I THEREFORE HAVE THE PLEASURE OF BESTOWING UPON YOU--THE CHRYSOS OF HONOR.
IN THE NAME OF THE AXIOMATIKOS, I CONGRATULATE YOU ON YOUR COURAGE.
IT'S NOW TIME FOR YOU TO RETURN TO CIVILIAN LIFE.

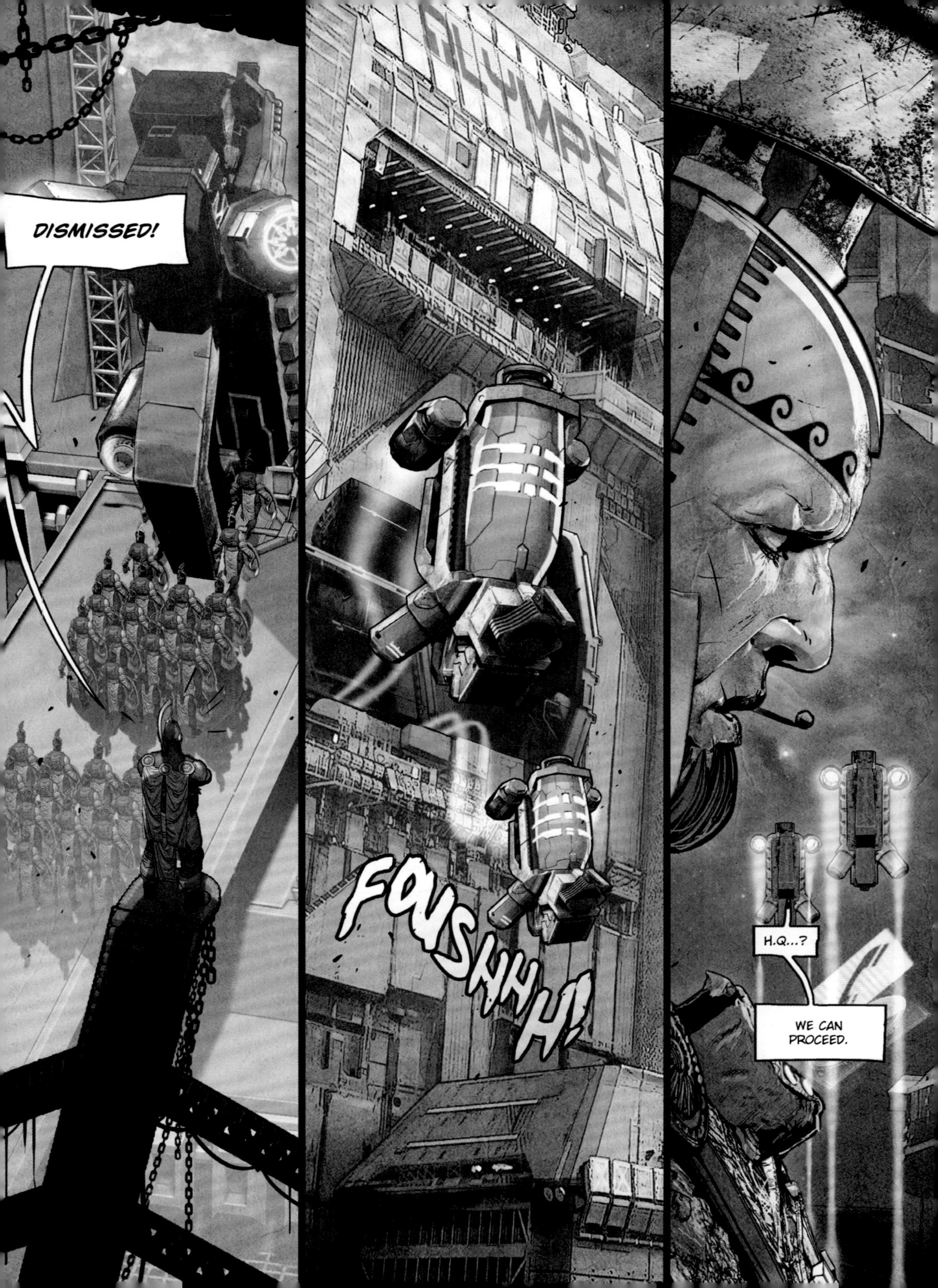
DISMISSED!
FOUSHHH!
H.Q...?
WE CAN PROCEED.

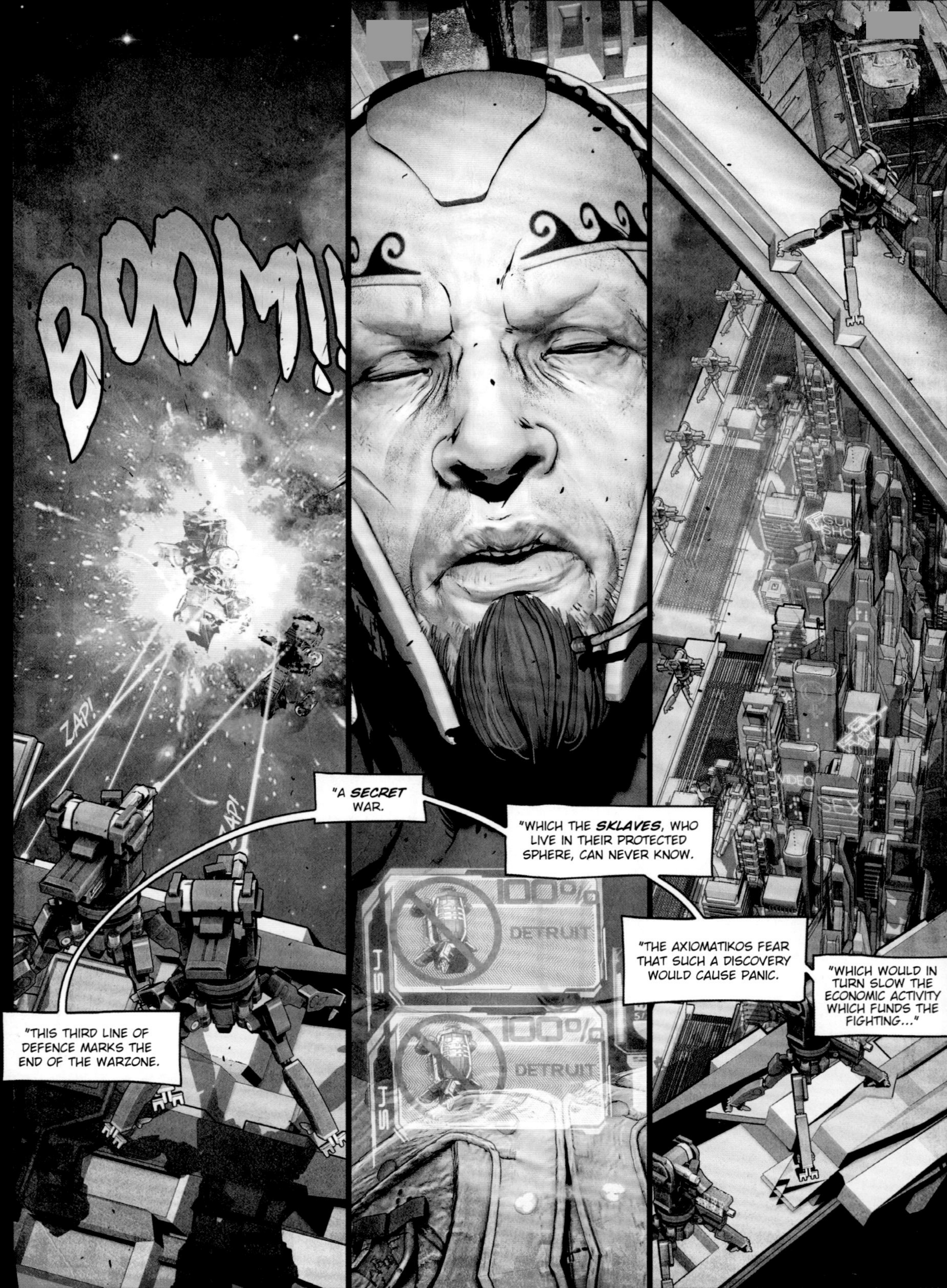
BOOM!!
ZAP!
ZAP!
"A SECRET WAR.
"WHICH THE SKLAVES, WHO LIVE IN THEIR PROTECTED SPHERE, CAN NEVER KNOW.
"THE AXIOMATIKOS FEAR THAT SUCH A DISCOVERY WOULD CAUSE PANIC.
"WHICH WOULD IN TURN SLOW THE ECONOMIC ACTIVITY WHICH FUNDS THE FIGHTING..."
"THIS THIRD LINE OF DEFENCE MARKS THE END OF THE WARZONE.
100%
DETRUIT
100%
DETRUIT

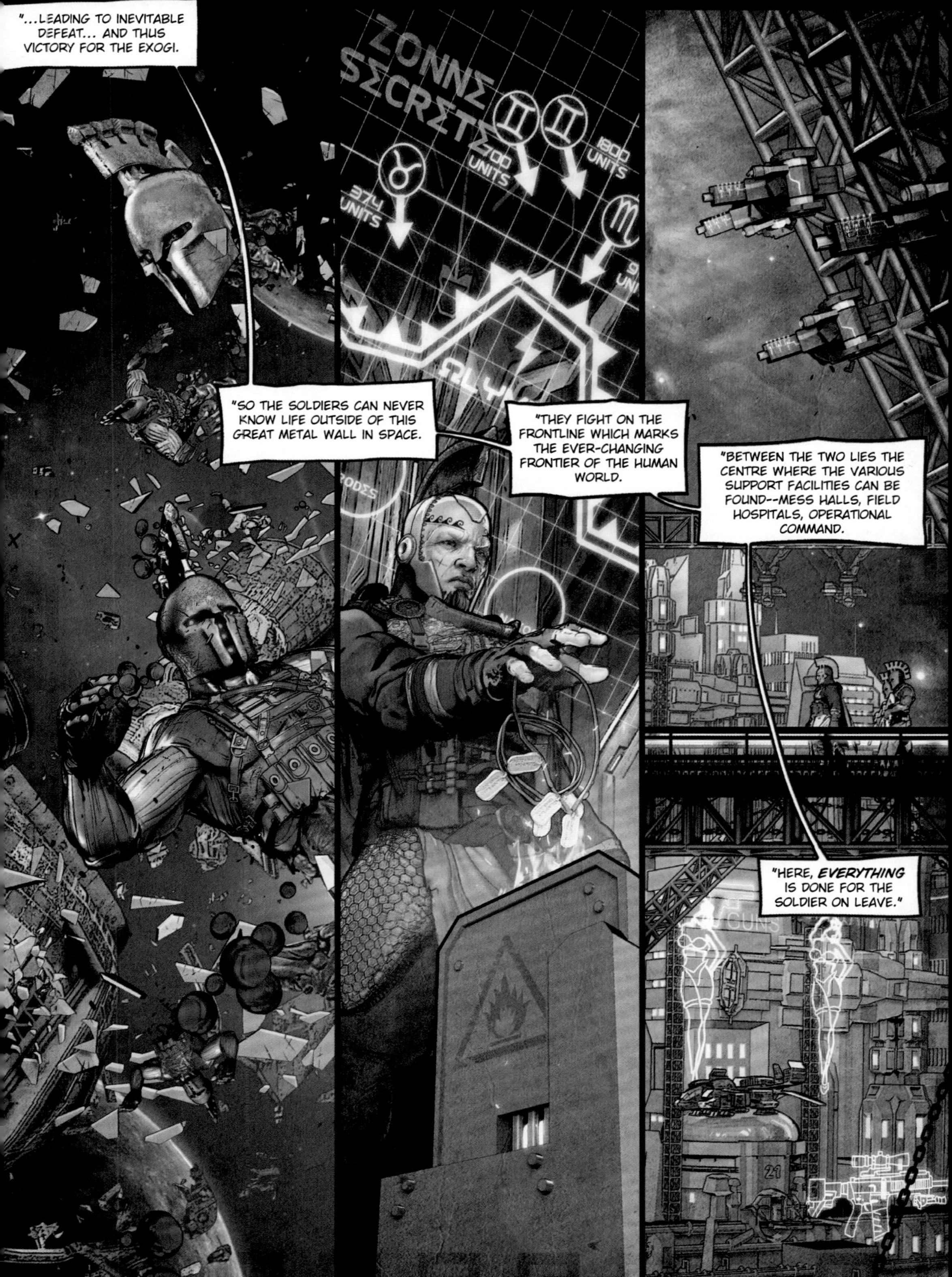
"...LEADING TO INEVITABLE DEFEAT... AND THUS VICTORY FOR THE EXOGI.
"SO THE SOLDIERS CAN NEVER KNOW LIFE OUTSIDE OF THIS GREAT METAL WALL IN SPACE.
ZONNE SECRETE
374 UNITS
1800 UNITS
"THEY FIGHT ON THE FRONTLINE WHICH MARKS THE EVER-CHANGING FRONTIER OF THE HUMAN WORLD.
"BETWEEN THE TWO LIES THE CENTRE WHERE THE VARIOUS SUPPORT FACILITIES CAN BE FOUND--MESS HALLS, FIELD HOSPITALS, OPERATIONAL COMMAND.
"HERE, ***EVERYTHING*** IS DONE FOR THE SOLDIER ON LEAVE."

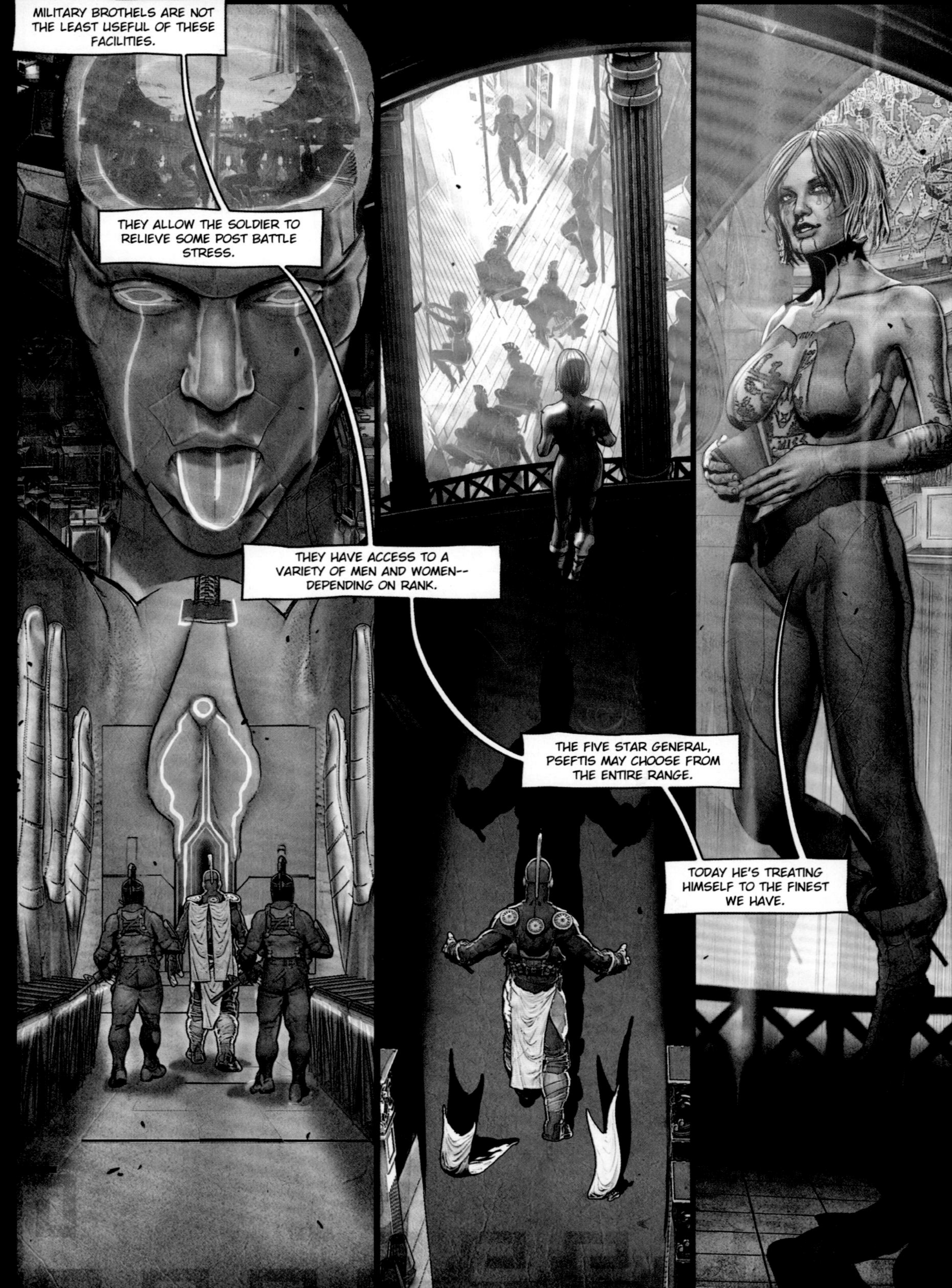
MILITARY BROTHELS ARE NOT THE LEAST USEFUL OF THESE FACILITIES.
THEY ALLOW THE SOLDIER TO RELIEVE SOME POST BATTLE STRESS.
THEY HAVE ACCESS TO A VARIETY OF MEN AND WOMEN-- DEPENDING ON RANK.
THE FIVE STAR GENERAL, PSEFTIS MAY CHOOSE FROM THE ENTIRE RANGE.
TODAY HE'S TREATING HIMSELF TO THE FINEST WE HAVE.

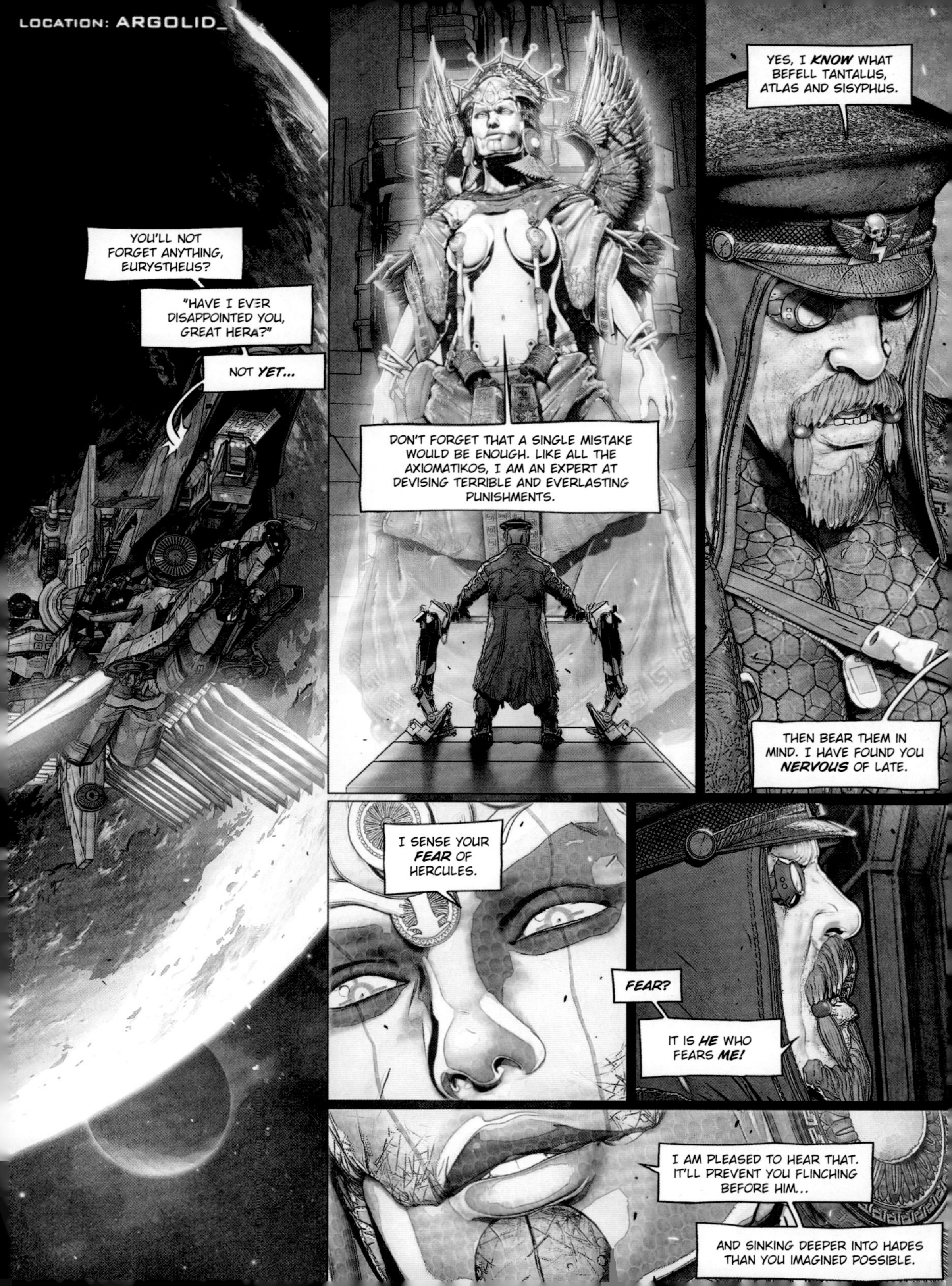
LOCATION: ARGOLID_
YOU'LL NOT FORGET ANYTHING, EURYSTHEUS?
"HAVE I EVER DISAPPOINTED YOU, GREAT HERA?"
NOT YET...
DON'T FORGET THAT A SINGLE MISTAKE WOULD BE ENOUGH. LIKE ALL THE AXIOMATIKOS, I AM AN EXPERT AT DEVISING TERRIBLE AND EVERLASTING PUNISHMENTS.
YES, I KNOW WHAT BEFELL TANTALUS, ATLAS AND SISYPHUS.
THEN BEAR THEM IN MIND. I HAVE FOUND YOU NERVOUS OF LATE.
I SENSE YOUR FEAR OF HERCULES.
FEAR?
IT IS HE WHO FEARS ME!
I AM PLEASED TO HEAR THAT. IT'LL PREVENT YOU FLINCHING BEFORE HIM..
AND SINKING DEEPER INTO HADES THAN YOU IMAGINED POSSIBLE.

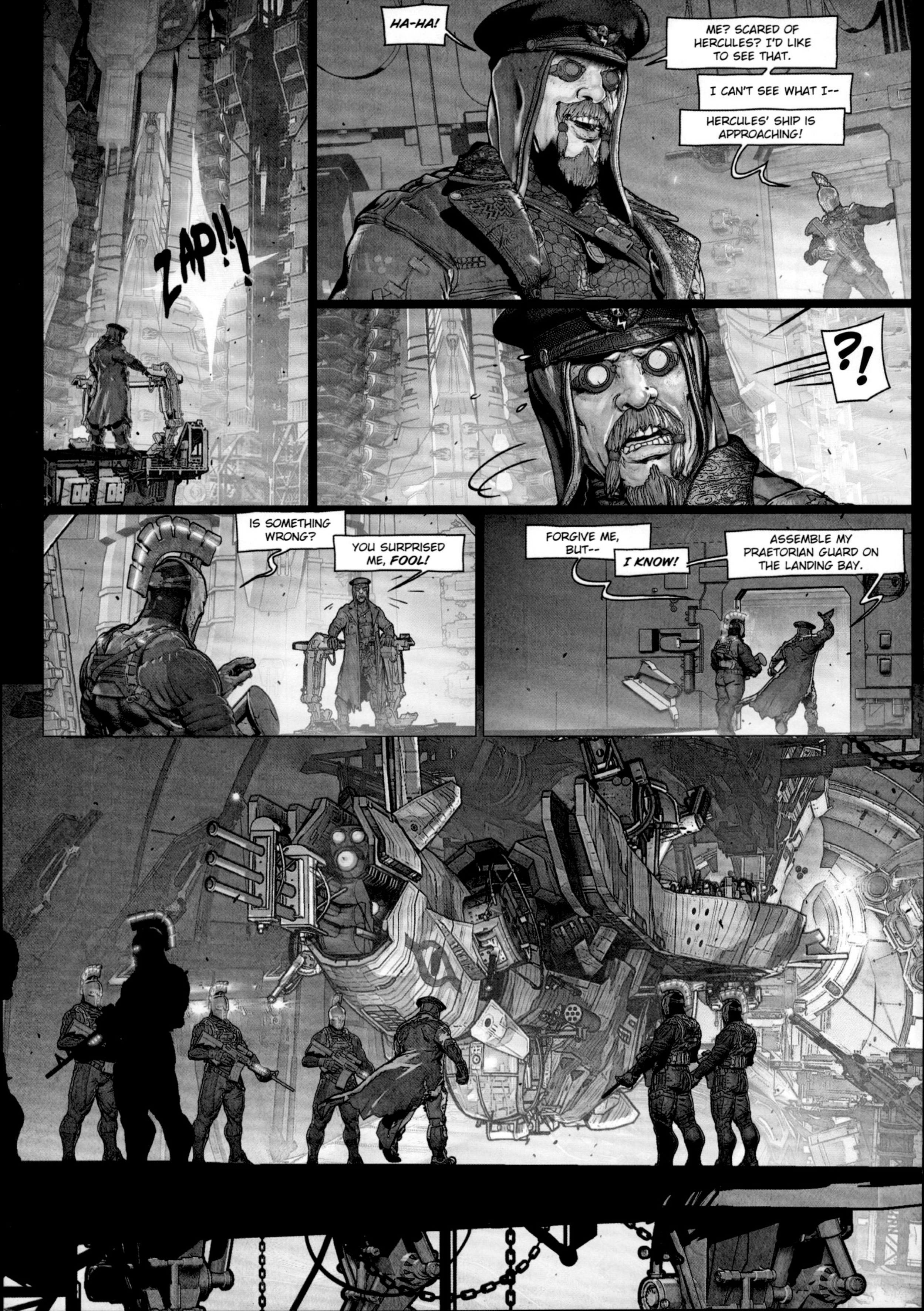
ZAP!!
HA-HA!
ME? SCARED OF HERCULES? I'D LIKE TO SEE THAT.
I CAN'T SEE WHAT I--
HERCULES' SHIP IS APPROACHING!
?!
IS SOMETHING WRONG?
YOU SURPRISED ME, FOOL!
FORGIVE ME, BUT--
I KNOW!
ASSEMBLE MY PRAETORIAN GUARD ON THE LANDING BAY.

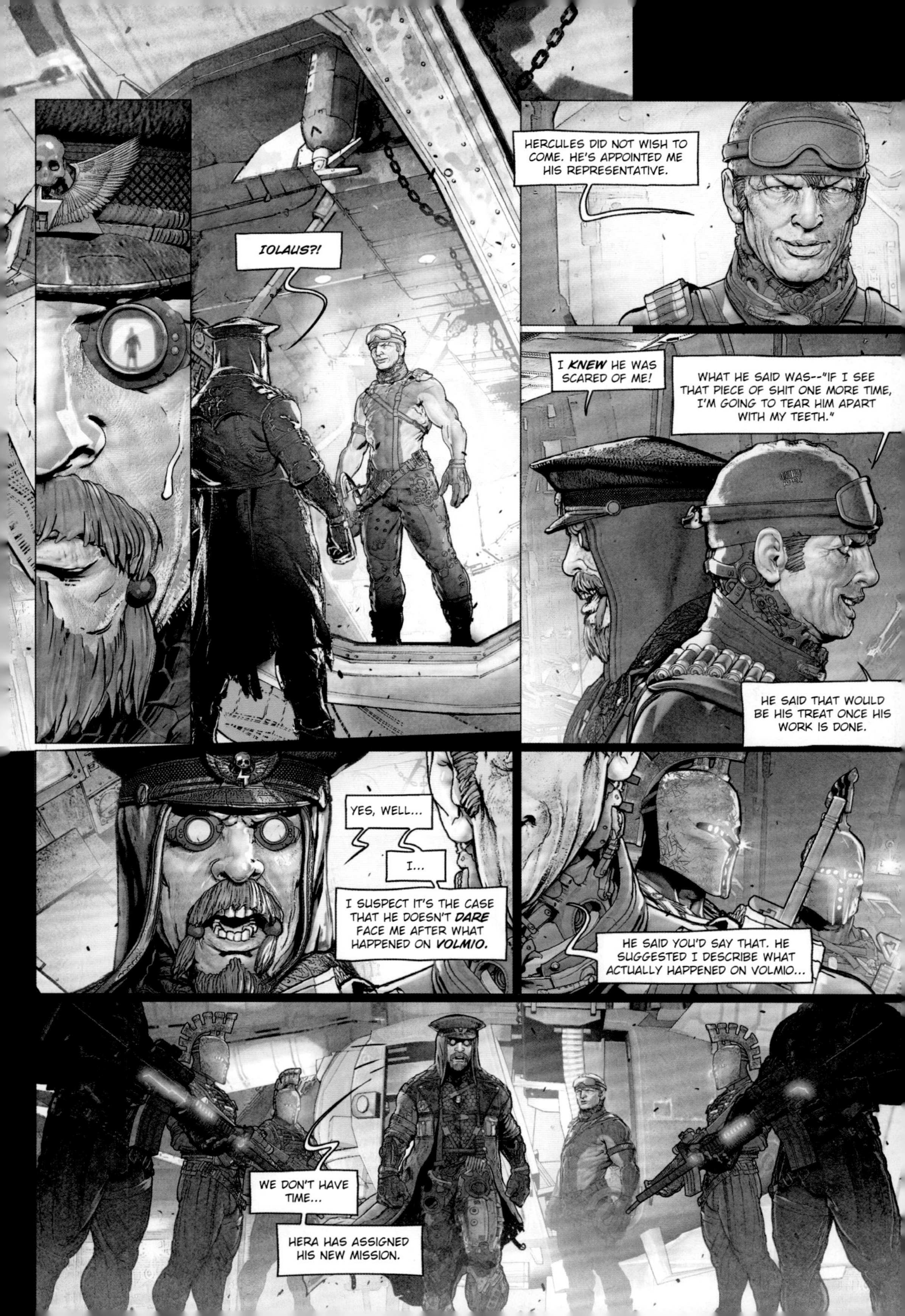
IOLAUS?!
HERCULES DID NOT WISH TO COME. HE'S APPOINTED ME HIS REPRESENTATIVE.
I KNEW HE WAS SCARED OF ME!
WHAT HE SAID WAS--"IF I SEE THAT PIECE OF SHIT ONE MORE TIME, I'M GOING TO TEAR HIM APART WITH MY TEETH."
HE SAID THAT WOULD BE HIS TREAT ONCE HIS WORK IS DONE.
YES, WELL...
I...
I SUSPECT IT'S THE CASE THAT HE DOESN'T DARE FACE ME AFTER WHAT HAPPENED ON VOLMIO.
HE SAID YOU'D SAY THAT. HE SUGGESTED I DESCRIBE WHAT ACTUALLY HAPPENED ON VOLMIO...
WE DON'T HAVE TIME...
HERA HAS ASSIGNED HIS NEW MISSION.

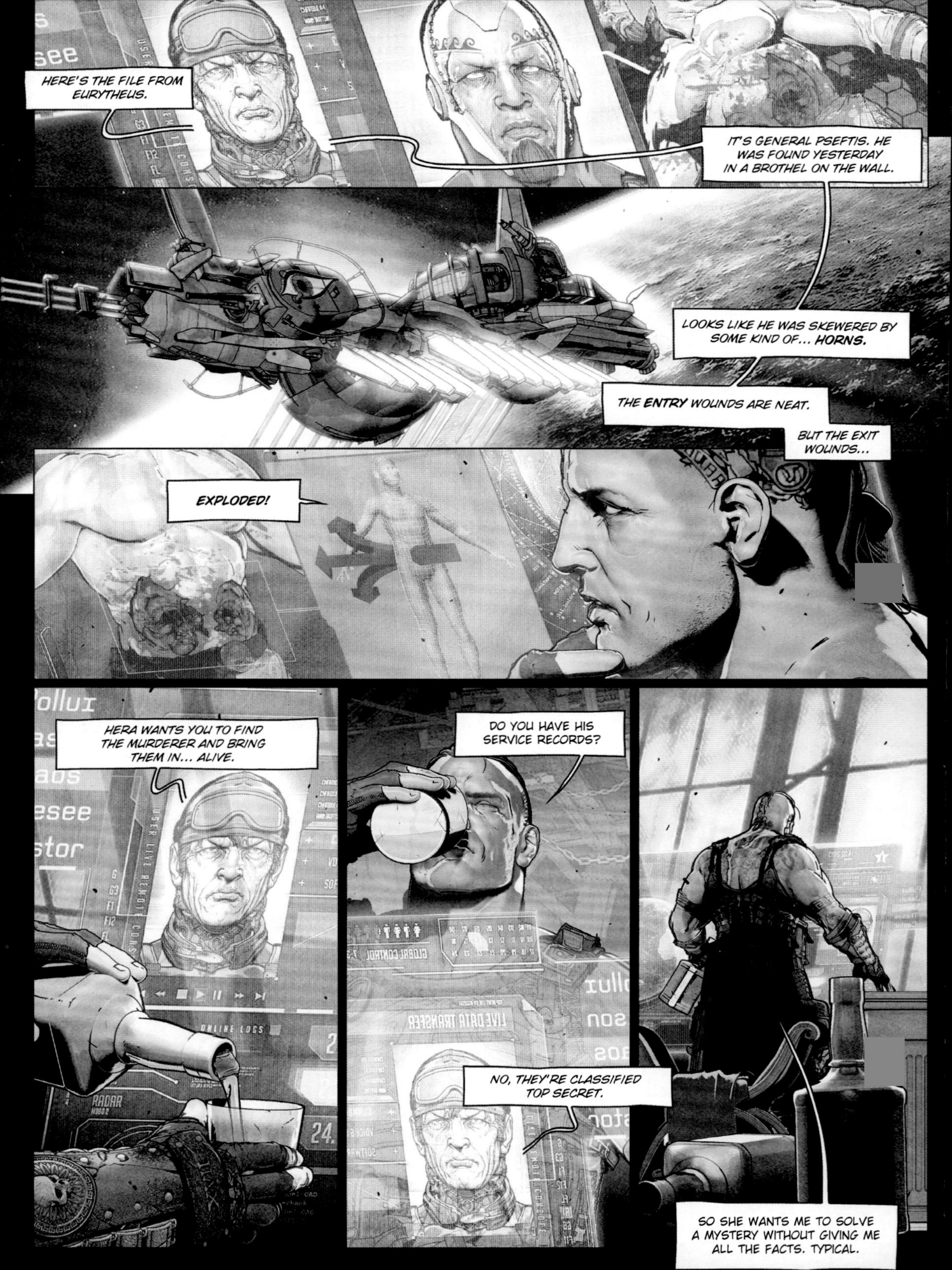
HERE'S THE FILE FROM EURYTHEUS.
IT'S GENERAL PSEFTIS. HE WAS FOUND YESTERDAY IN A BROTHEL ON THE WALL.
LOOKS LIKE HE WAS SKEWERED BY SOME KIND OF... HORNS.
THE ENTRY WOUNDS ARE NEAT.
BUT THE EXIT WOUNDS...
EXPLODED!
HERA WANTS YOU TO FIND THE MURDERER AND BRING THEM IN... ALIVE.
DO YOU HAVE HIS SERVICE RECORDS?
NO, THEY'RE CLASSIFIED TOP SECRET.
SO SHE WANTS ME TO SOLVE A MYSTERY WITHOUT GIVING ME ALL THE FACTS. TYPICAL.

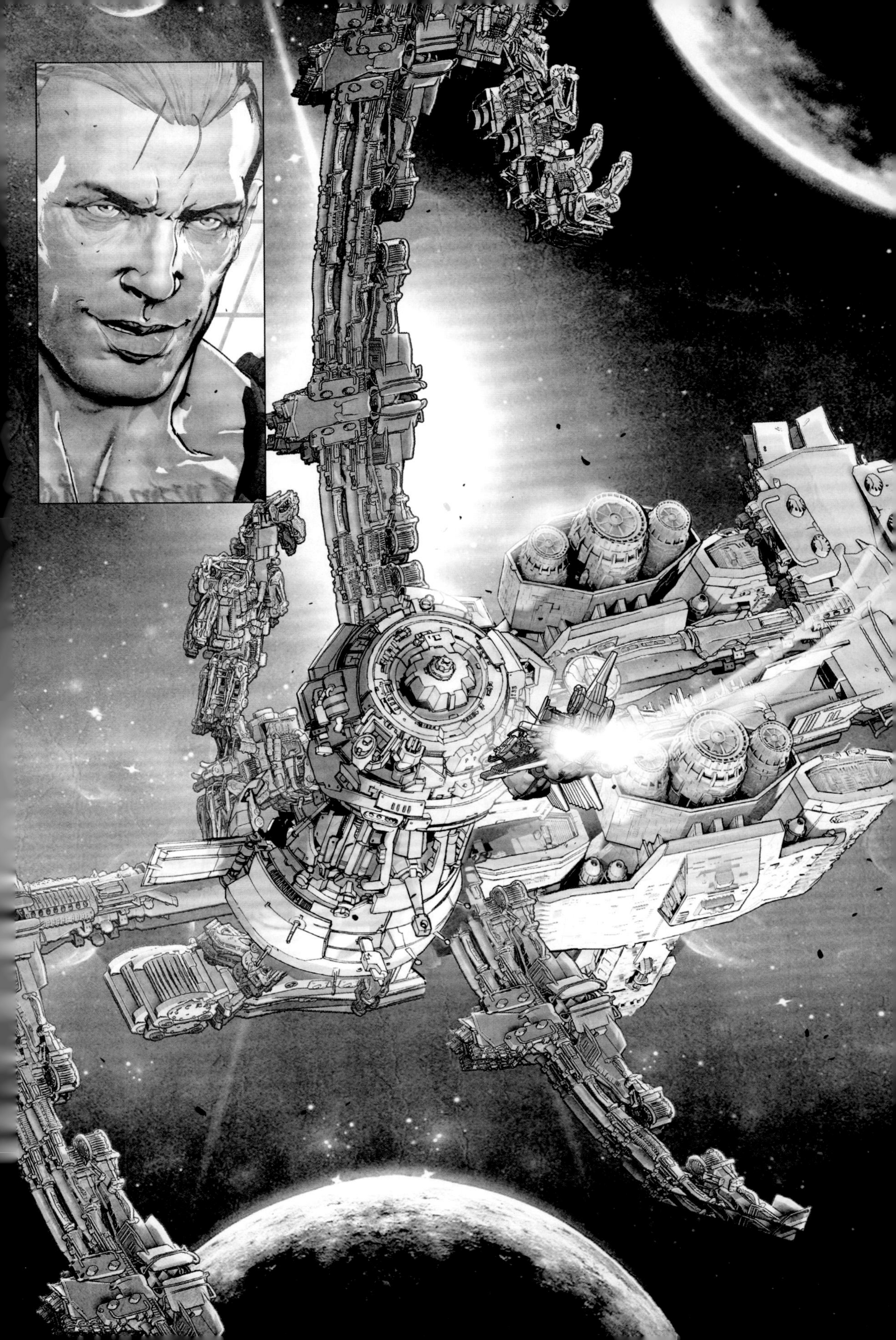

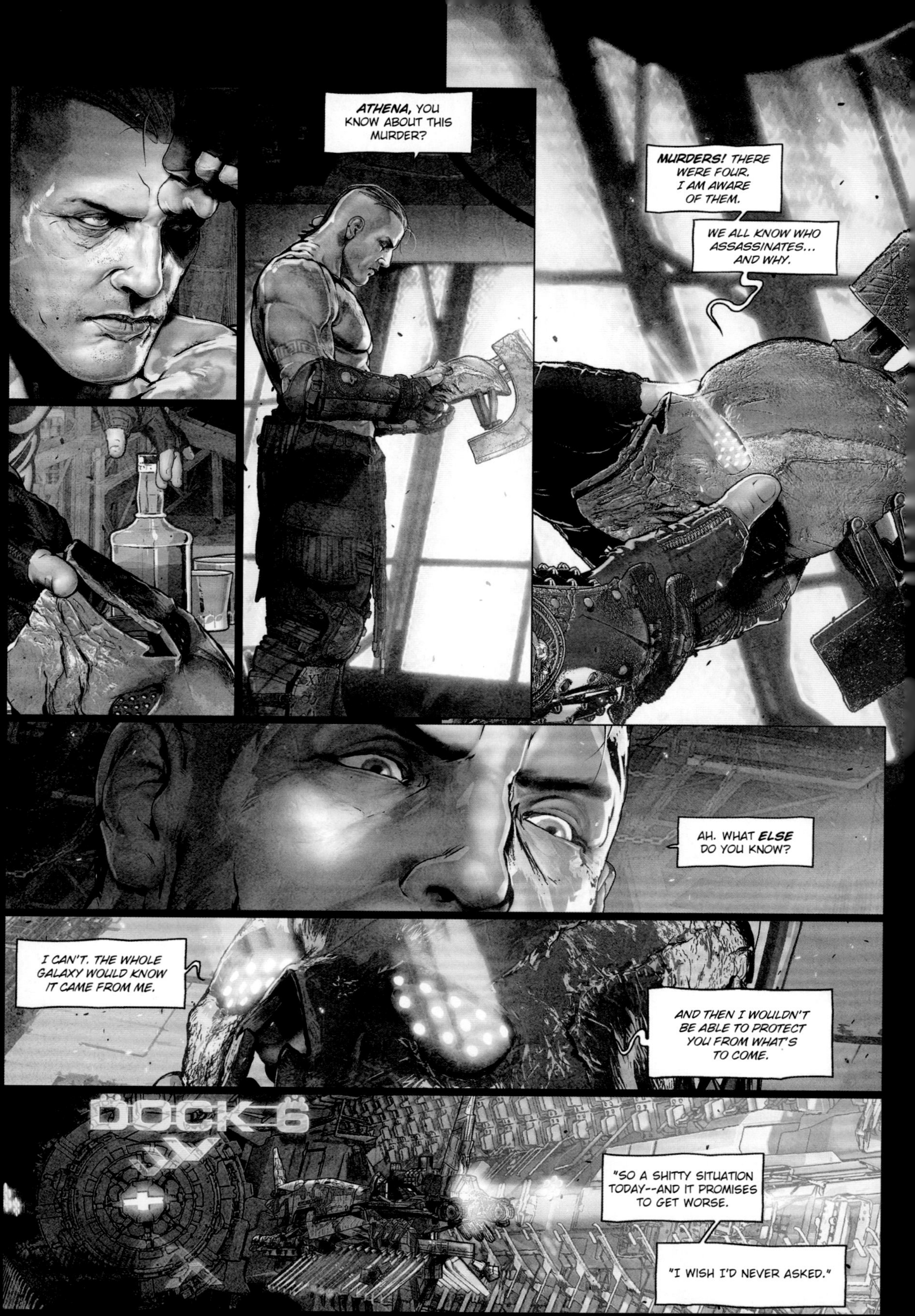
ATHENA, YOU KNOW ABOUT THIS MURDER?
MURDERS! THERE WERE FOUR. I AM AWARE OF THEM.
WE ALL KNOW WHO ASSASSINATES... AND WHY.
AH. WHAT ELSE DO YOU KNOW?
I CAN'T. THE WHOLE GALAXY WOULD KNOW IT CAME FROM ME.
AND THEN I WOULDN'T BE ABLE TO PROTECT YOU FROM WHAT'S TO COME.
DOCK 6
"SO A SHITTY SITUATION TODAY--AND IT PROMISES TO GET WORSE.
"I WISH I'D NEVER ASKED."

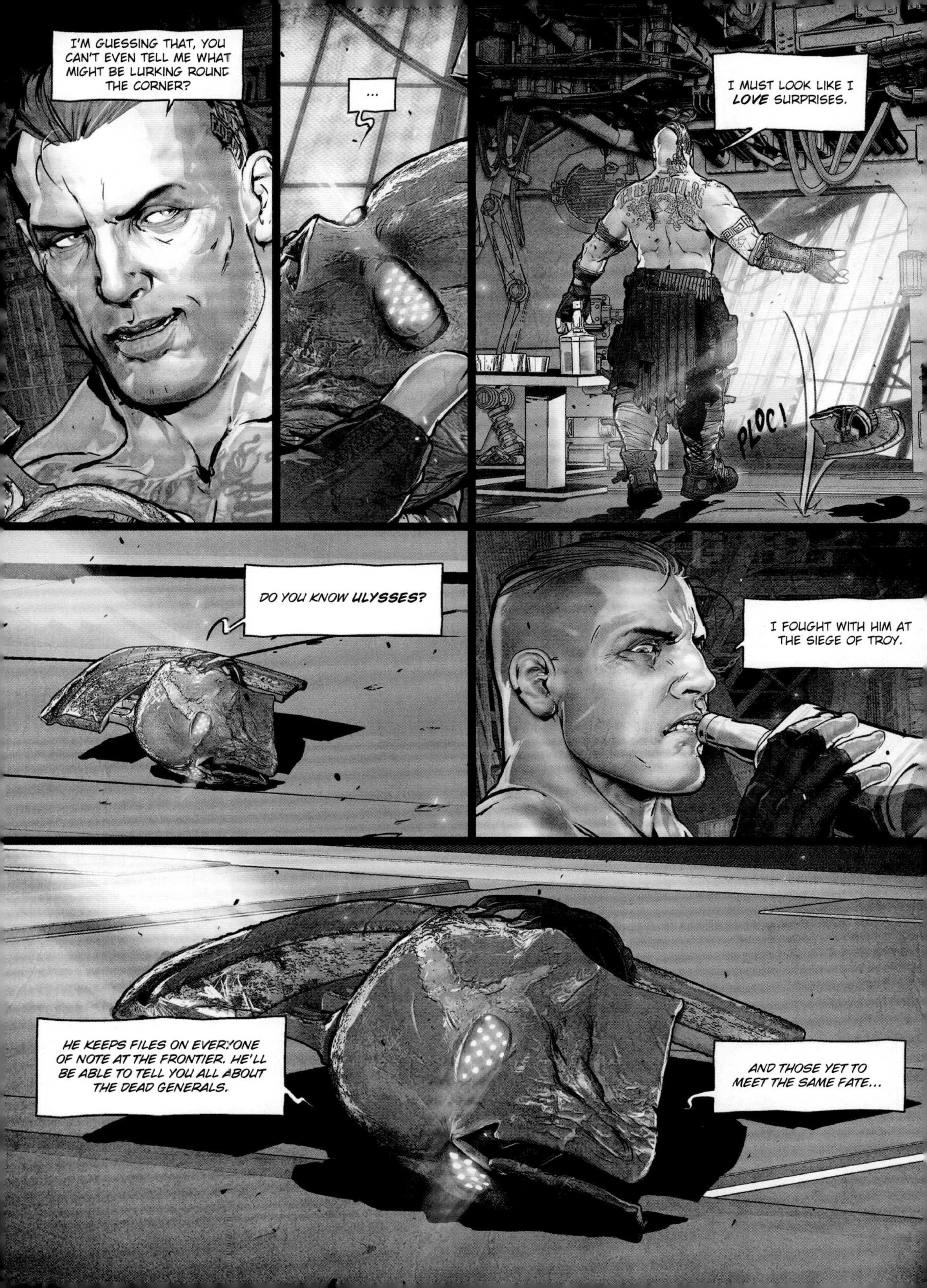

I'M GUESSING THAT, YOU CAN'T EVEN TELL ME WHAT MIGHT BE LURKING ROUND THE CORNER?
...
I MUST LOOK LIKE I **LOVE** SURPRISES.
PLOC!
DO YOU KNOW ***ULYSSES?***
I FOUGHT WITH HIM AT THE SIEGE OF TROY.
HE KEEPS FILES ON EVERYONE OF NOTE AT THE FRONTIER. HE'LL BE ABLE TO TELL YOU ALL ABOUT THE DEAD GENERALS.
AND THOSE YET TO MEET THE SAME FATE...

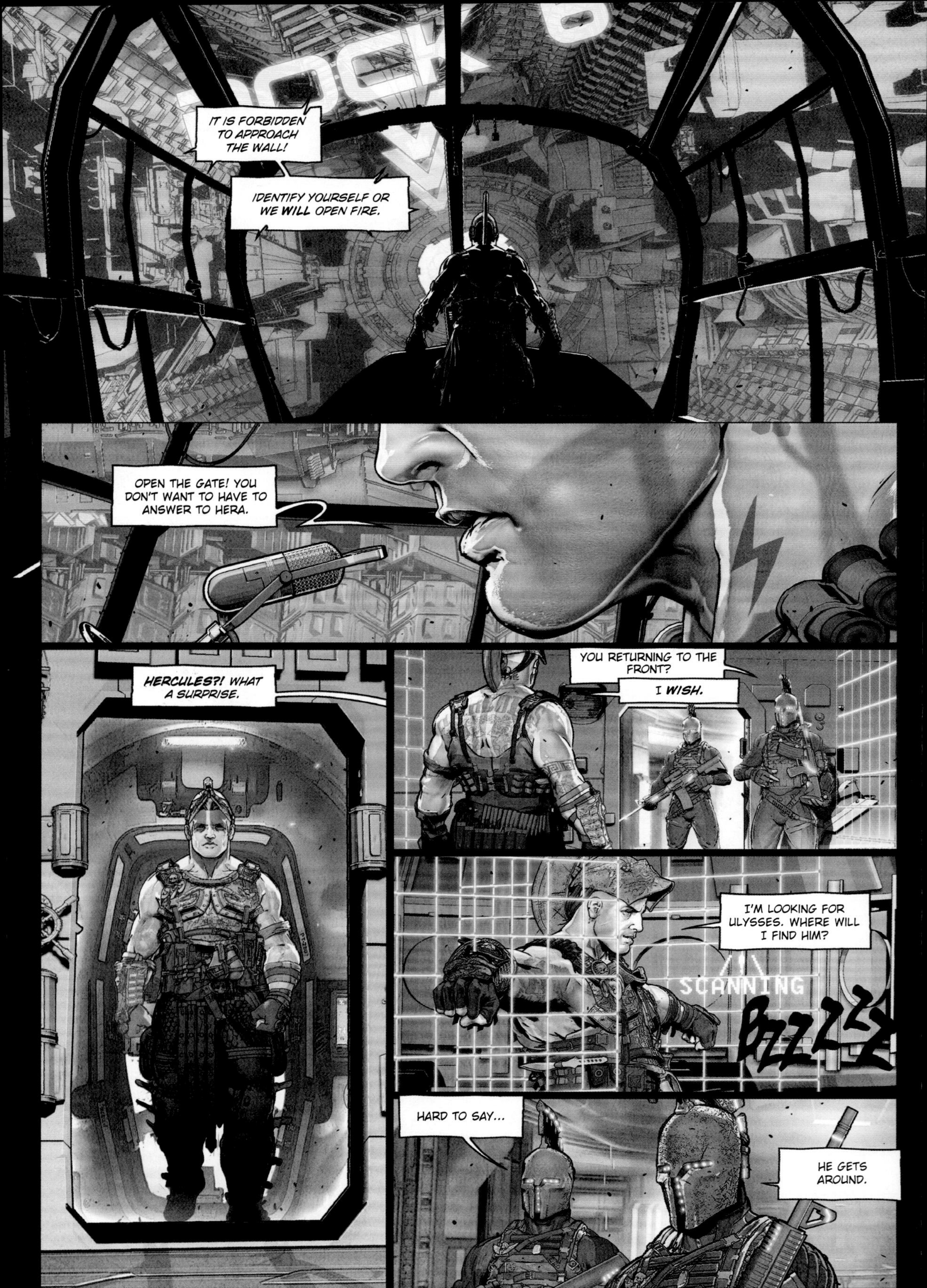
DOCK 6
IT IS FORBIDDEN TO APPROACH THE WALL!
IDENTIFY YOURSELF OR WE WILL OPEN FIRE.
OPEN THE GATE! YOU DON'T WANT TO HAVE TO ANSWER TO HERA.
HERCULES?! WHAT A SURPRISE.
YOU RETURNING TO THE FRONT?
I WISH.
I'M LOOKING FOR ULYSSES. WHERE WILL I FIND HIM?
SCANNING
BZZZZZ
HARD TO SAY...
HE GETS AROUND.

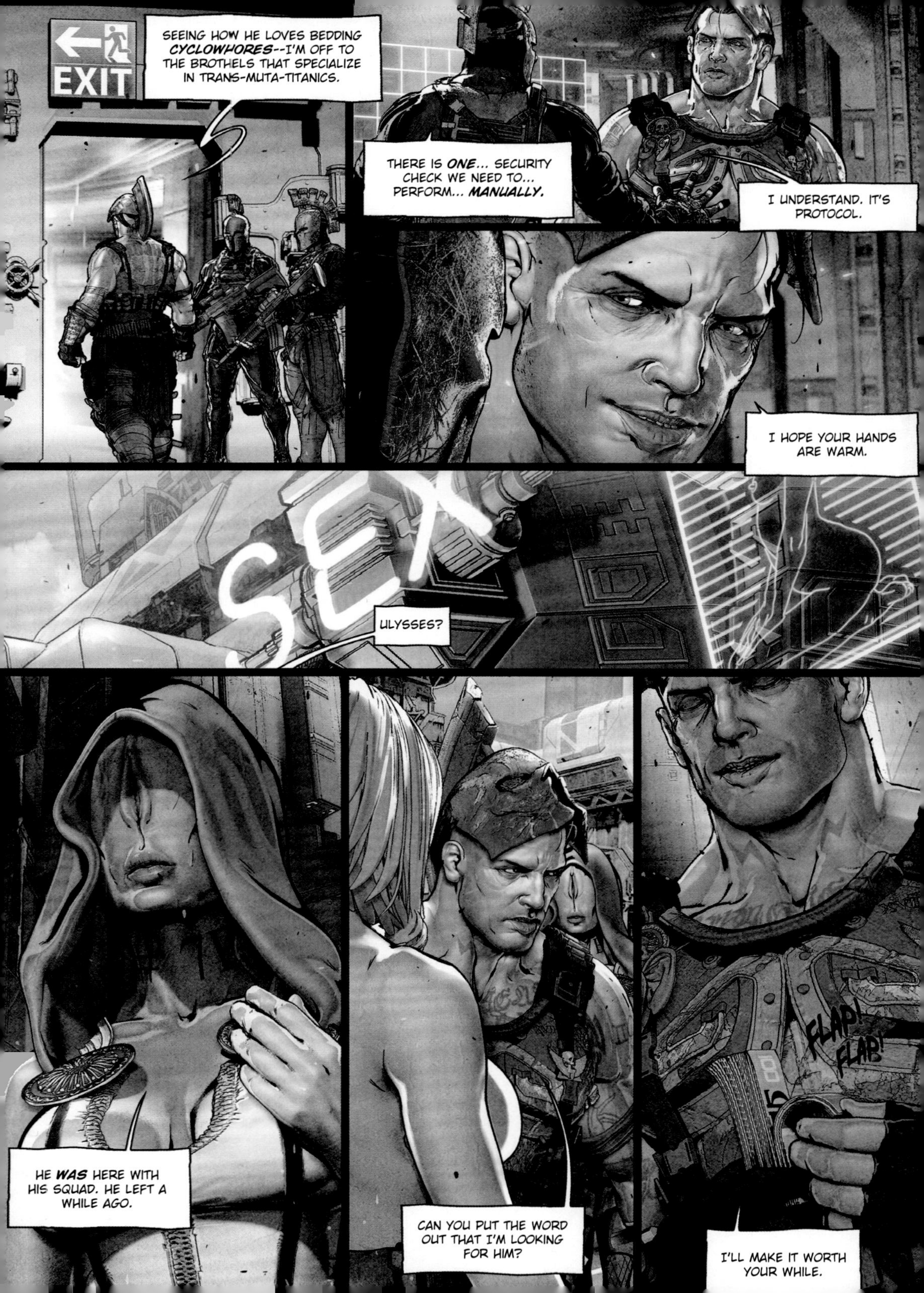
EXIT
SEEING HOW HE LOVES BEDDING CYCLOWHORES--I'M OFF TO THE BROTHELS THAT SPECIALIZE IN TRANS-MUTA-TITANICS.
THERE IS ONE... SECURITY CHECK WE NEED TO... PERFORM... MANUALLY.
I UNDERSTAND. IT'S PROTOCOL.
I HOPE YOUR HANDS ARE WARM.
SEX
ULYSSES?
HE WAS HERE WITH HIS SQUAD. HE LEFT A WHILE AGO.
CAN YOU PUT THE WORD OUT THAT I'M LOOKING FOR HIM?
FLAP! FLAP!
I'LL MAKE IT WORTH YOUR WHILE.

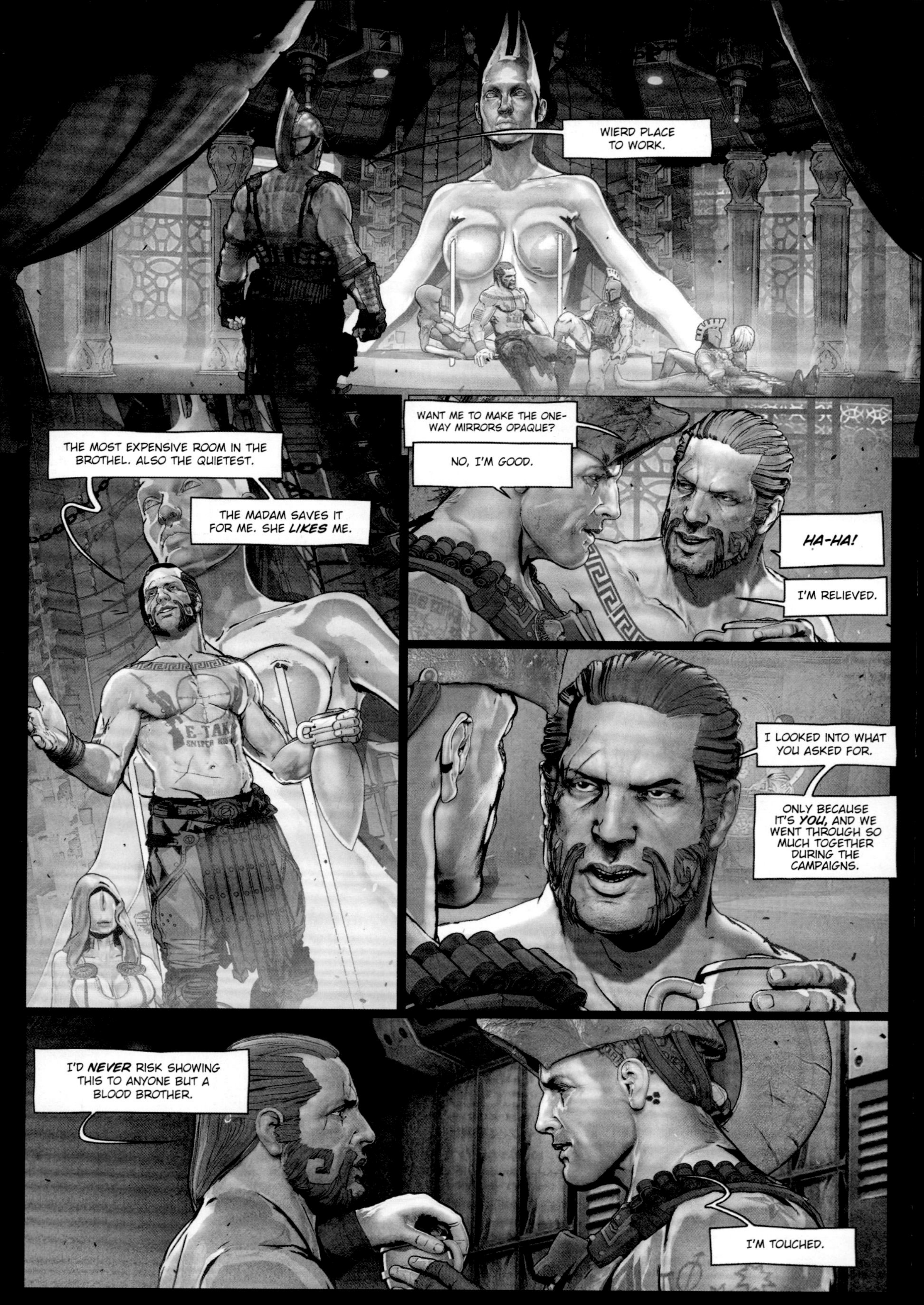
WIERD PLACE TO WORK.
THE MOST EXPENSIVE ROOM IN THE BROTHEL. ALSO THE QUIETEST.
THE MADAM SAVES IT FOR ME. SHE LIKES ME.
WANT ME TO MAKE THE ONE-WAY MIRRORS OPAQUE?
NO, I'M GOOD.
HA-HA!
I'M RELIEVED.
I LOOKED INTO WHAT YOU ASKED FOR.
ONLY BECAUSE IT'S YOU, AND WE WENT THROUGH SO MUCH TOGETHER DURING THE CAMPAIGNS.
I'D NEVER RISK SHOWING THIS TO ANYONE BUT A BLOOD BROTHER.
I'M TOUCHED.

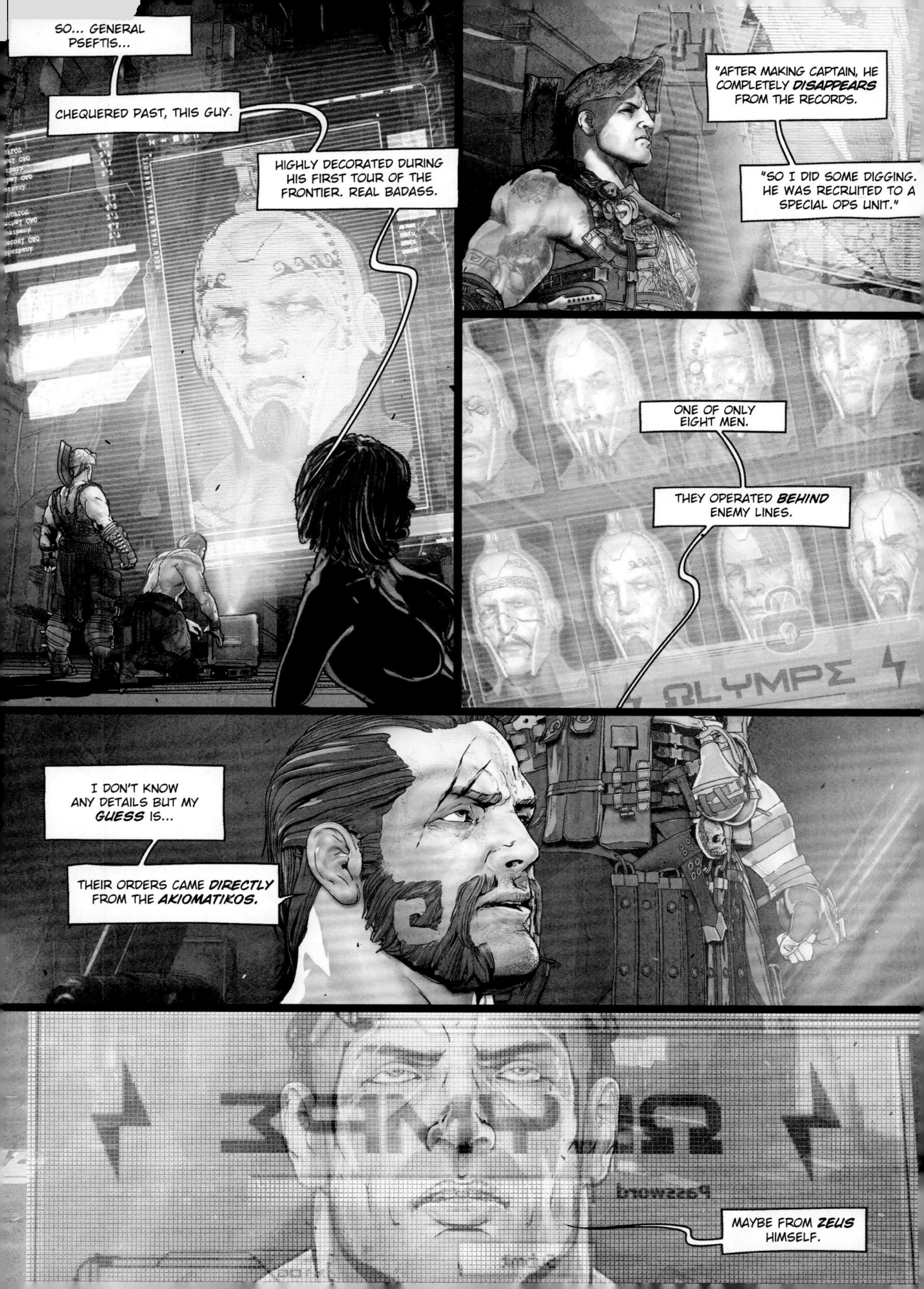
SO... GENERAL PSEFTIS...
CHEQUERED PAST, THIS GUY.
HIGHLY DECORATED DURING HIS FIRST TOUR OF THE FRONTIER. REAL BADASS.
"AFTER MAKING CAPTAIN, HE COMPLETELY DISAPPEARS FROM THE RECORDS.
"SO I DID SOME DIGGING. HE WAS RECRUITED TO A SPECIAL OPS UNIT."
ONE OF ONLY EIGHT MEN.
THEY OPERATED BEHIND ENEMY LINES.
ΩLYMPΣ
I DON'T KNOW ANY DETAILS BUT MY GUESS IS...
THEIR ORDERS CAME DIRECTLY FROM THE AKIOMATIKOS.
MAYBE FROM ZEUS HIMSELF.

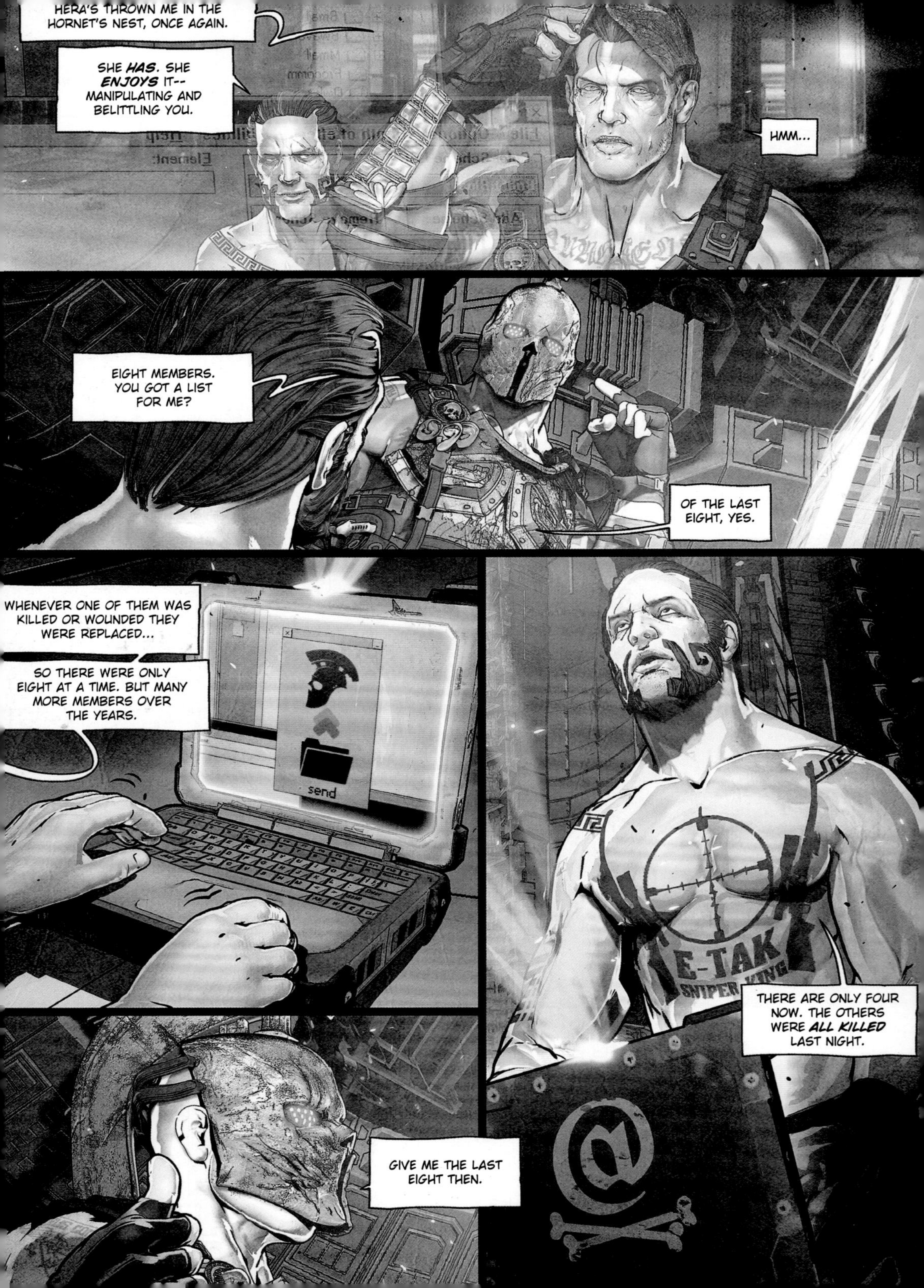
HERA'S THROWN ME IN THE HORNET'S NEST, ONCE AGAIN.
SHE HAS. SHE ENJOYS IT-- MANIPULATING AND BELITTLING YOU.
HMM...
EIGHT MEMBERS. YOU GOT A LIST FOR ME?
OF THE LAST EIGHT, YES.
WHENEVER ONE OF THEM WAS KILLED OR WOUNDED THEY WERE REPLACED...
SO THERE WERE ONLY EIGHT AT A TIME. BUT MANY MORE MEMBERS OVER THE YEARS.
send
E-TAK
SNIPER KING
THERE ARE ONLY FOUR NOW. THE OTHERS WERE ALL KILLED LAST NIGHT.
GIVE ME THE LAST EIGHT THEN.

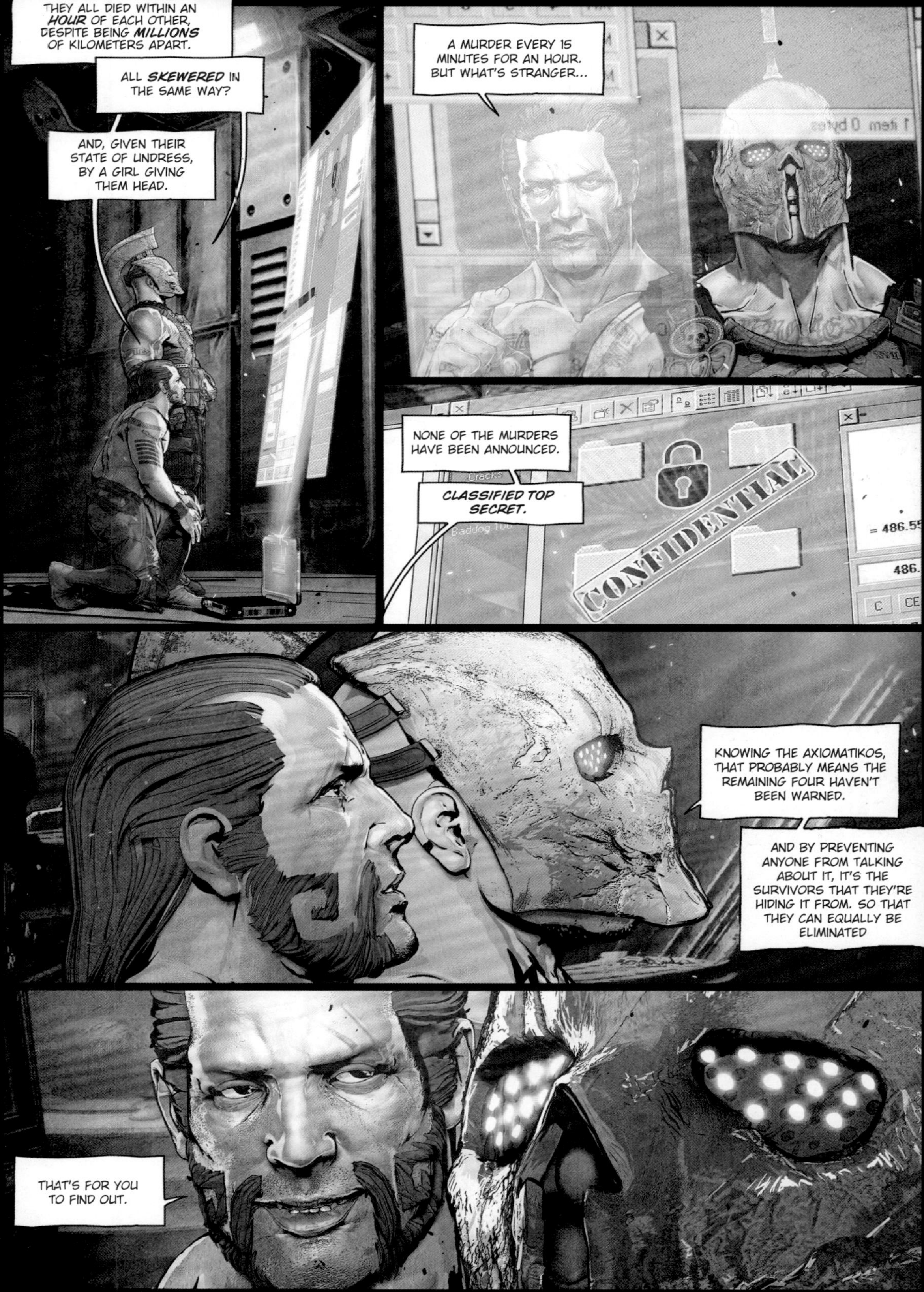
THEY ALL DIED WITHIN AN *HOUR* OF EACH OTHER, DESPITE BEING *MILLIONS* OF KILOMETERS APART.
ALL *SKEWERED* IN THE SAME WAY?
AND, GIVEN THEIR STATE OF UNDRESS, BY A GIRL GIVING THEM HEAD.
A MURDER EVERY 15 MINUTES FOR AN HOUR. BUT WHAT'S STRANGER...
1 item 0 bytes
NONE OF THE MURDERS HAVE BEEN ANNOUNCED.
CLASSIFIED TOP SECRET.
CONFIDENTIAL
KNOWING THE AXIOMATIKOS, THAT PROBABLY MEANS THE REMAINING FOUR HAVEN'T BEEN WARNED.
AND BY PREVENTING ANYONE FROM TALKING ABOUT IT, IT'S THE SURVIVORS THAT THEY'RE HIDING IT FROM. SO THAT THEY CAN EQUALLY BE ELIMINATED
THAT'S FOR YOU TO FIND OUT.

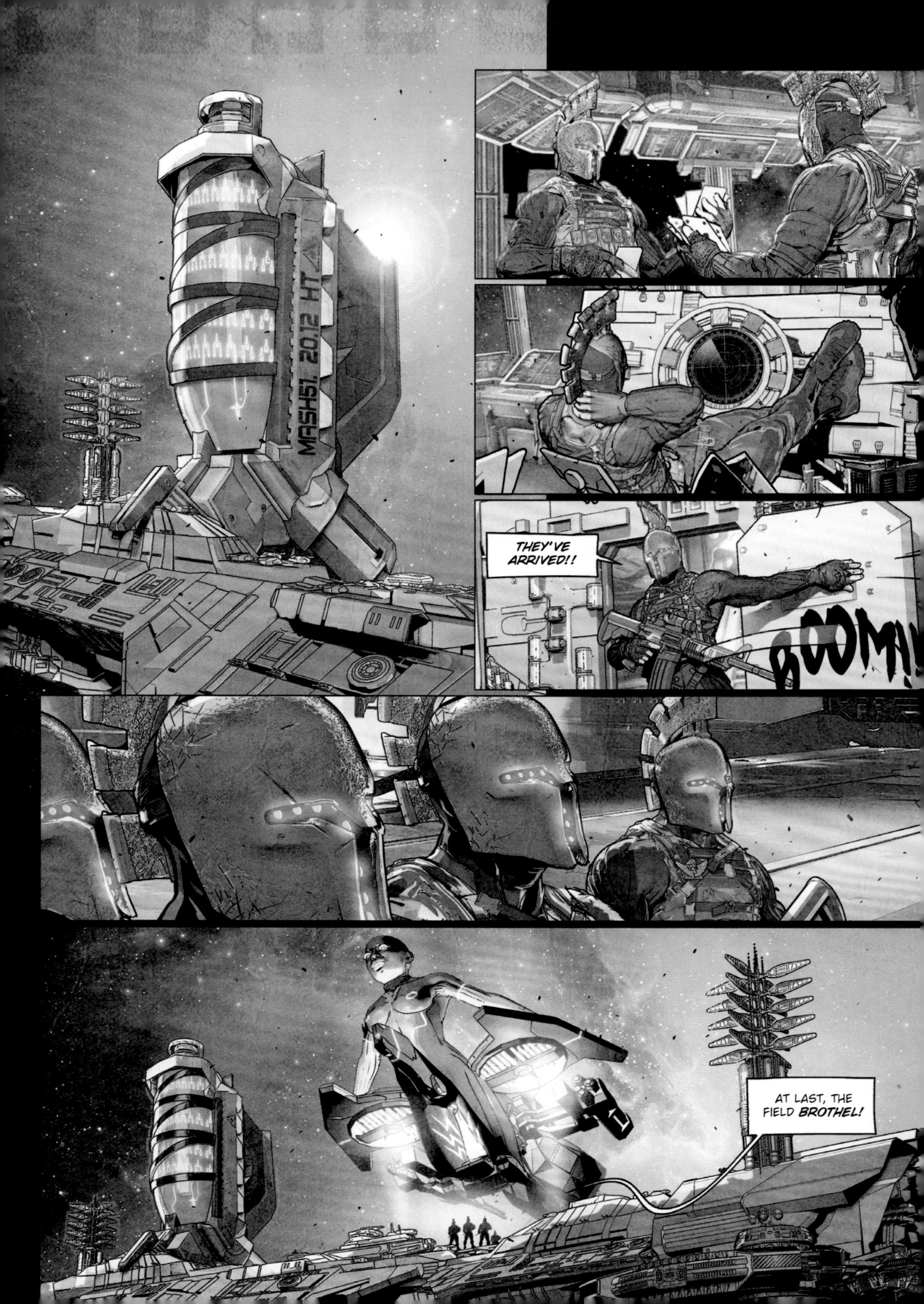
MASH51. 20.12 HT
THEY'VE ARRIVED!!
BOOM!!
AT LAST, THE FIELD *BROTHEL!*

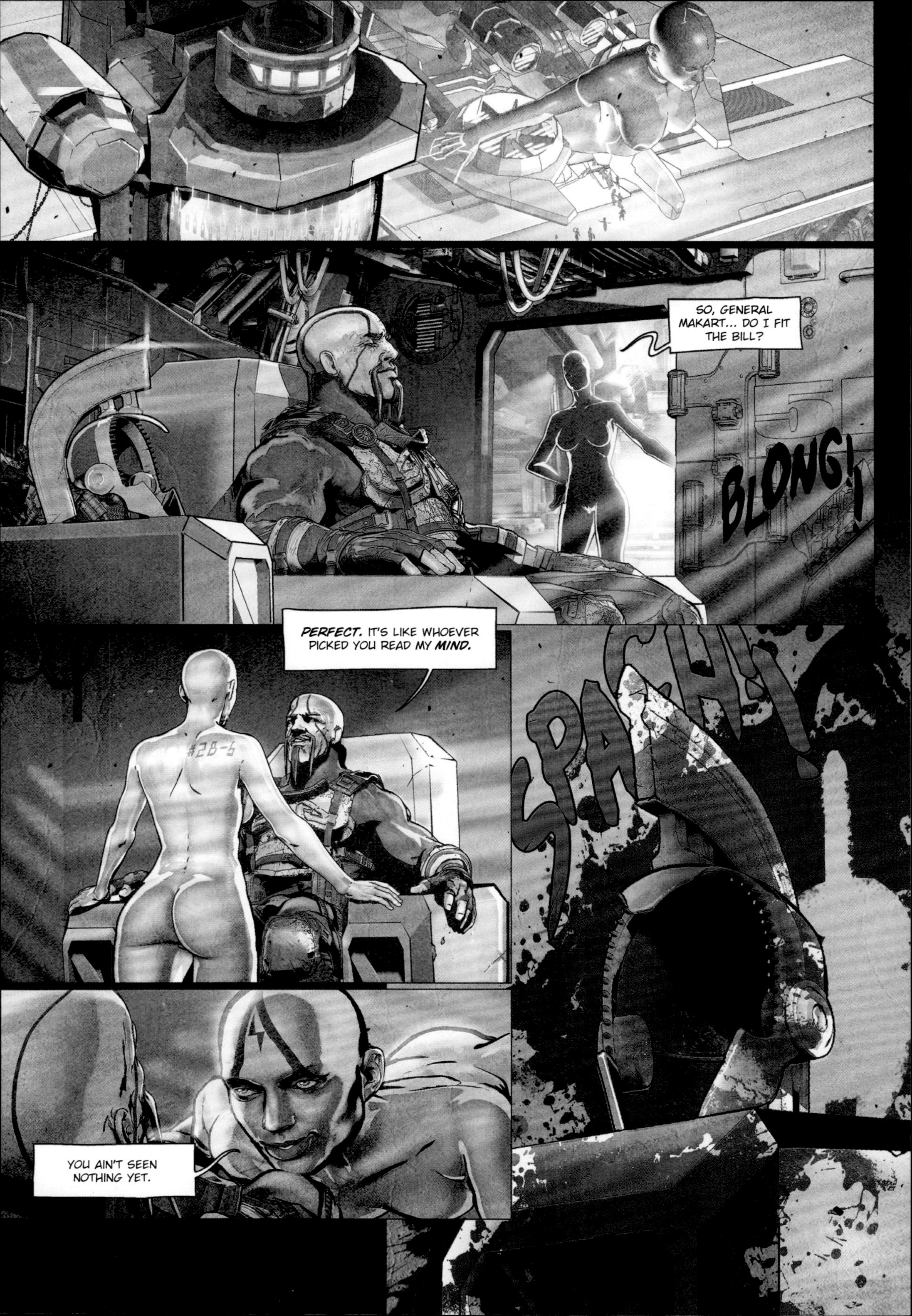
SO, GENERAL MAKART... DO I FIT THE BILL?
BLONG!
PERFECT. IT'S LIKE WHOEVER PICKED YOU READ MY MIND.
#28-6
YOU AIN'T SEEN NOTHING YET.
SPACH!

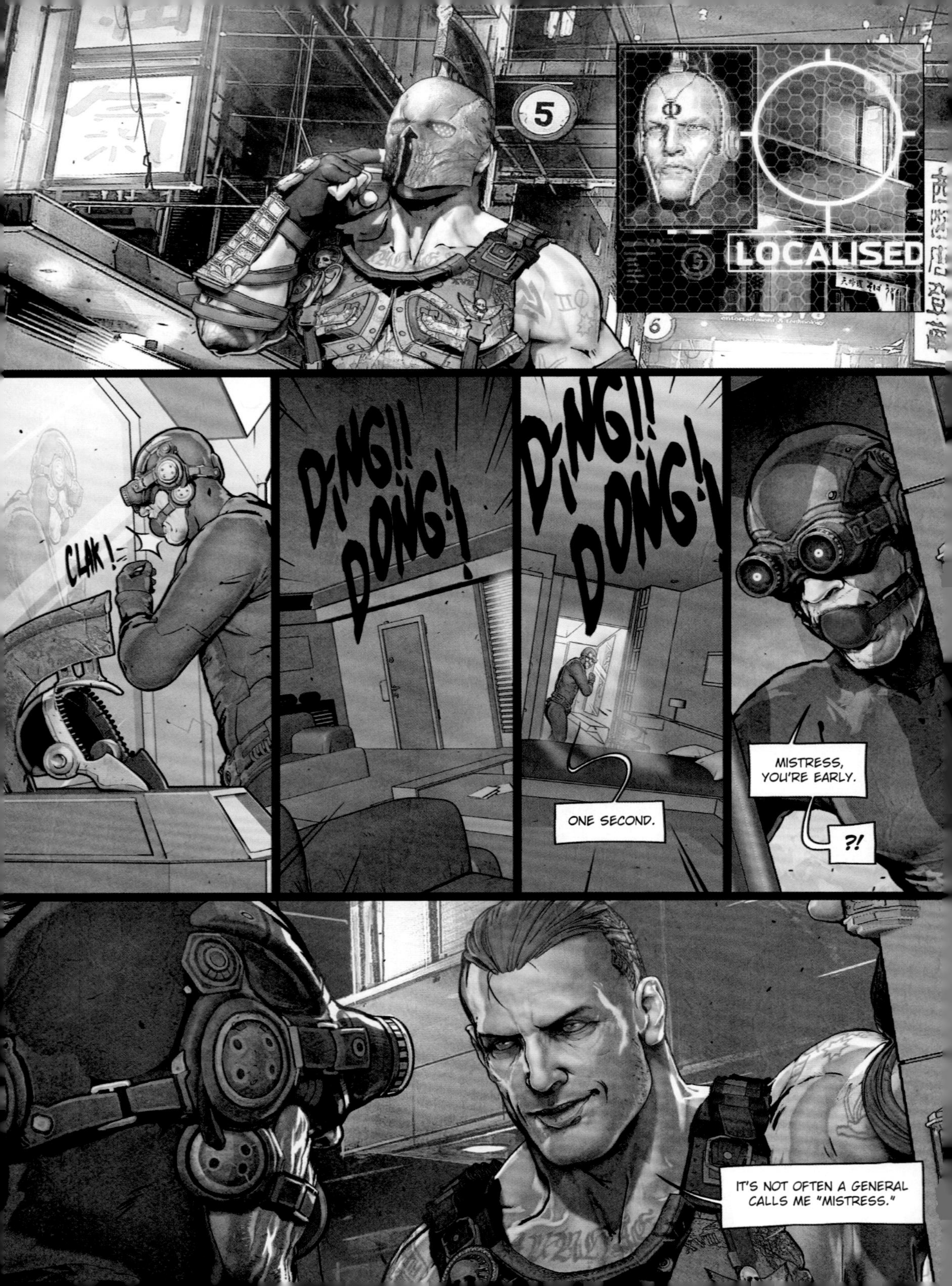
5
LOCALISED
6
CLAK!
DING!! DONG!!
DING!! DONG!!
ONE SECOND.
MISTRESS, YOU'RE EARLY.
?!
IT'S NOT OFTEN A GENERAL CALLS ME "MISTRESS."

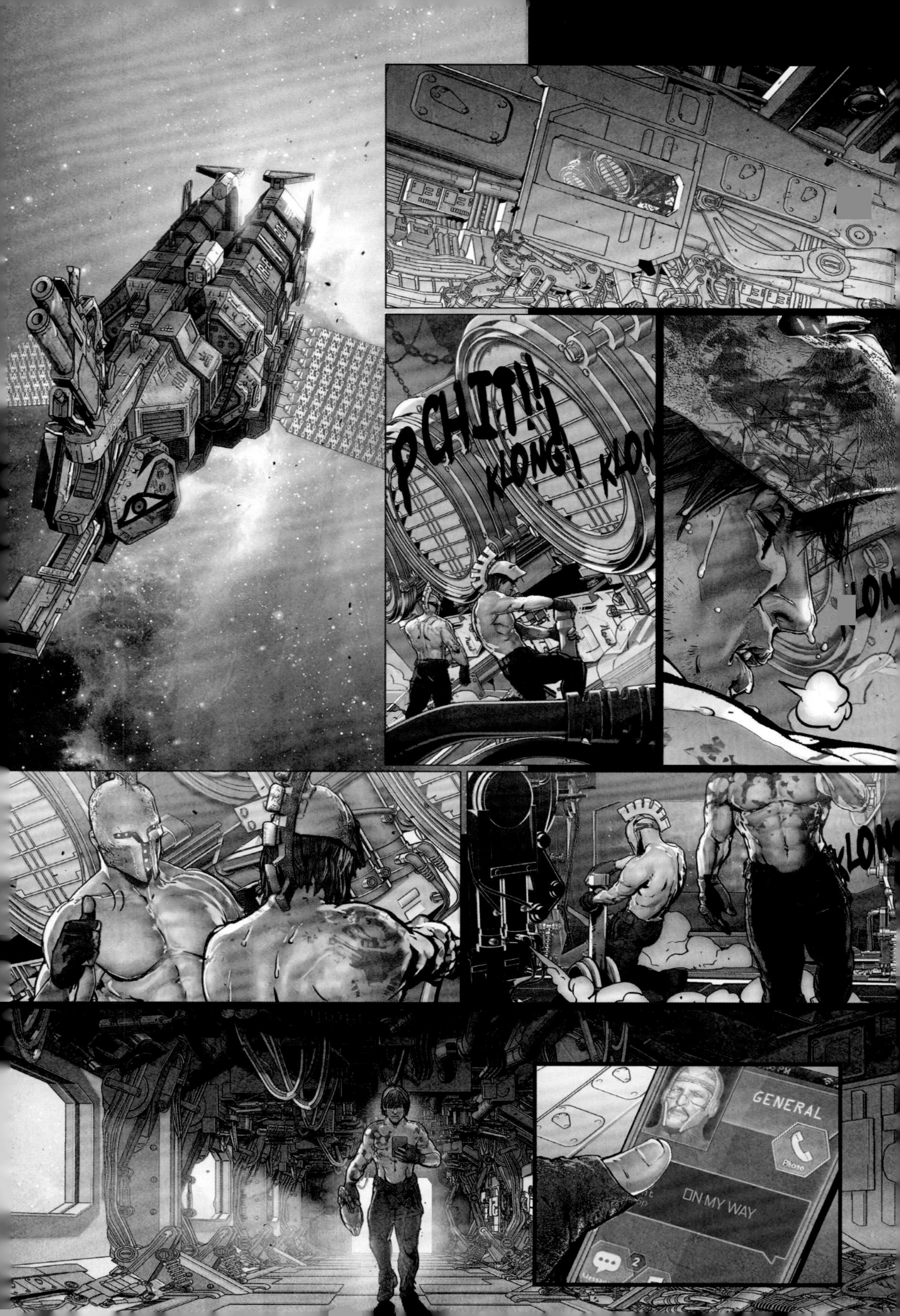
PCHIT!!
KLONG!
KLON
KLON
KLONG
GENERAL
Phone
ON MY WAY

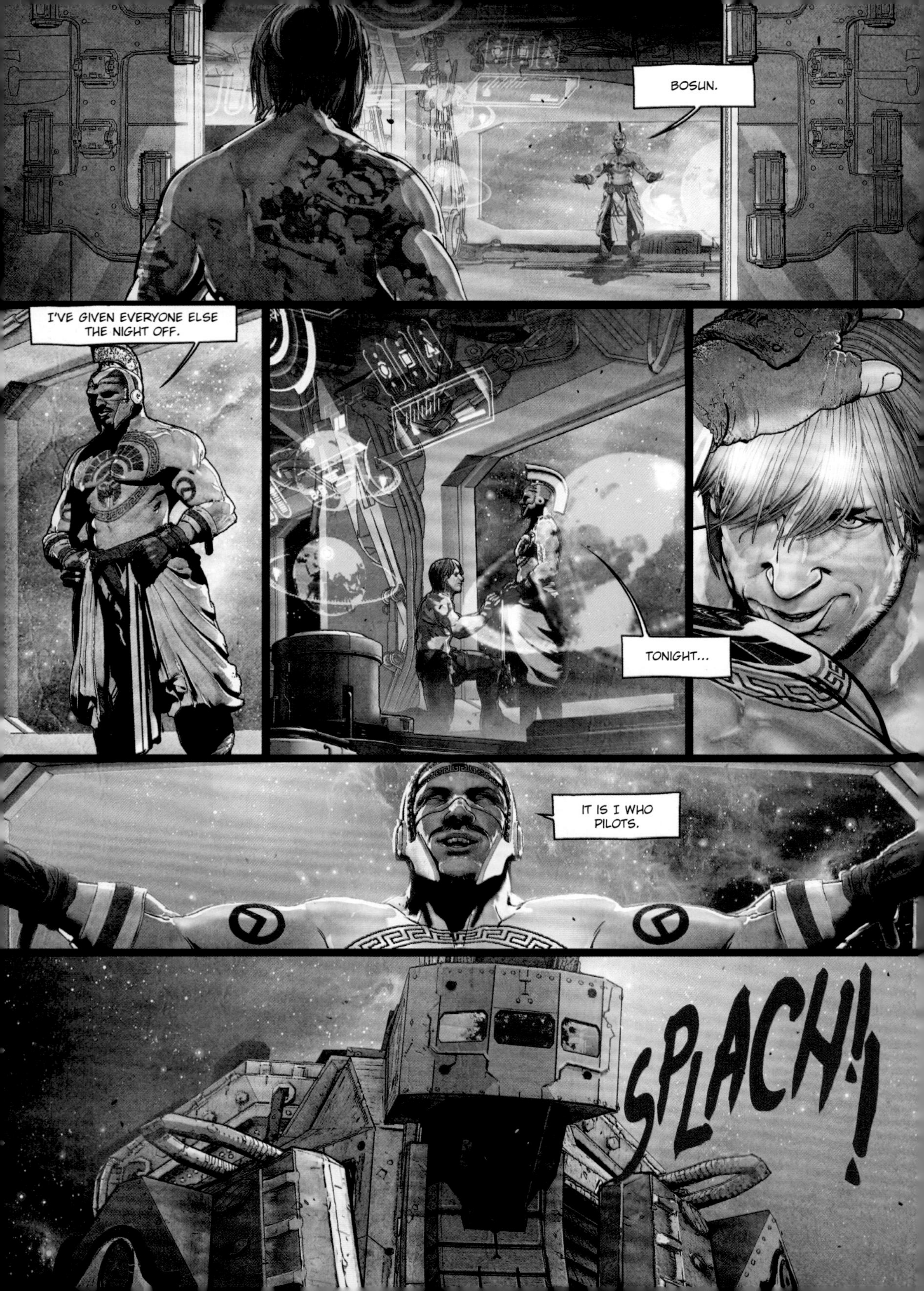
BOSUN.
I'VE GIVEN EVERYONE ELSE THE NIGHT OFF.
TONIGHT...
IT IS I WHO PILOTS.
SPLACH!!

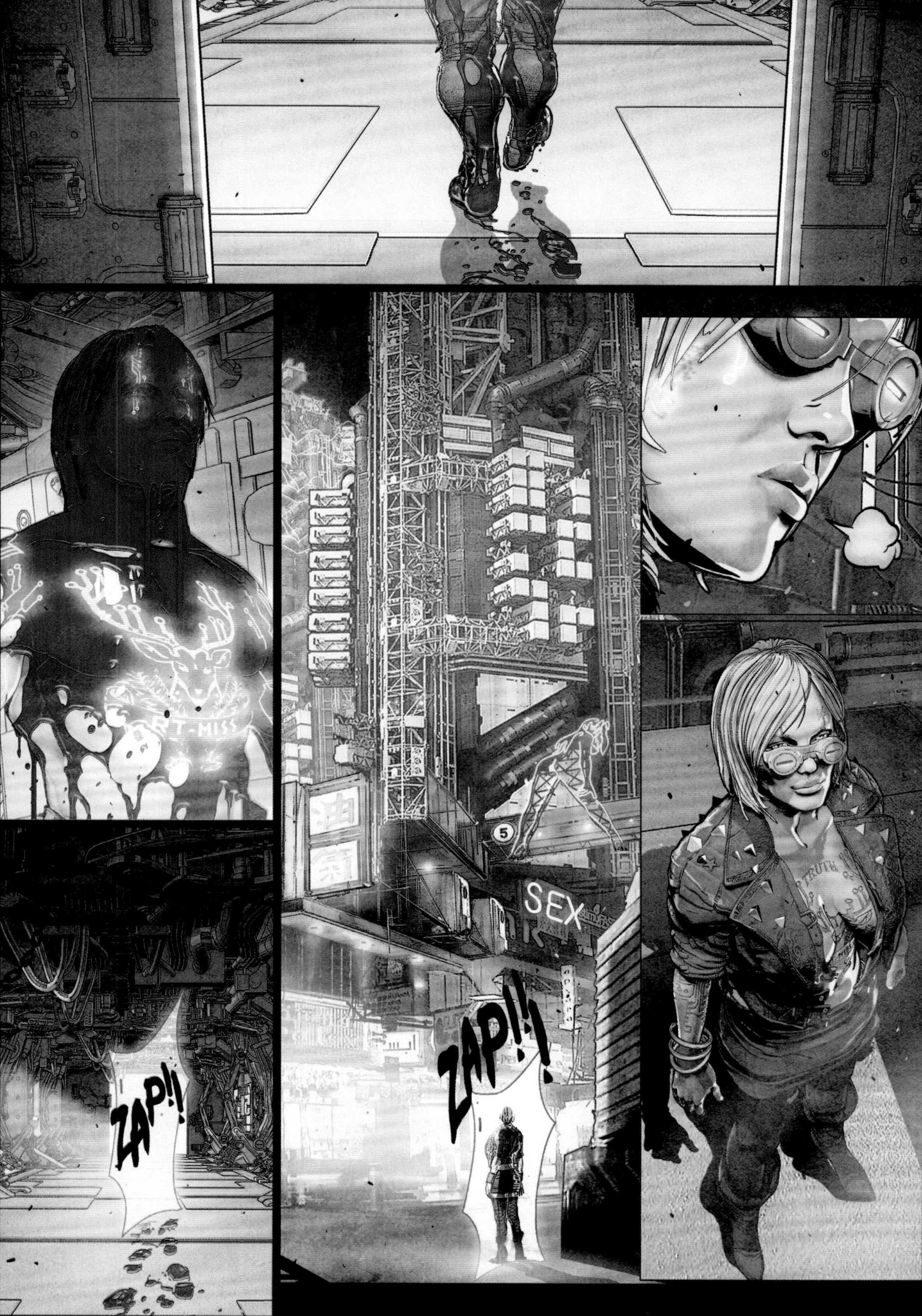
SEX
ZAP!!
ZAP!!

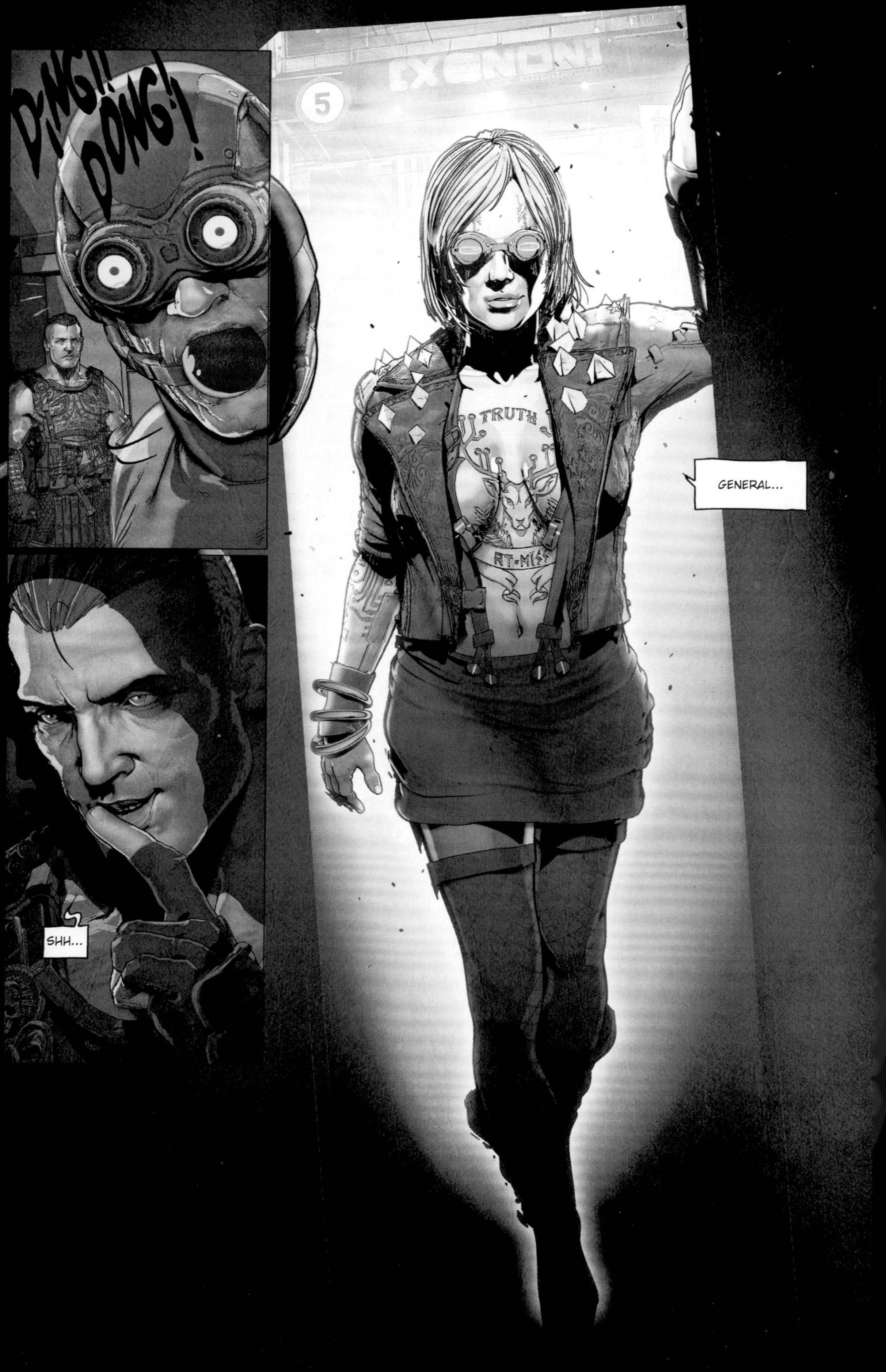
DING!! DONG!!
5
GENERAL...
SHH...

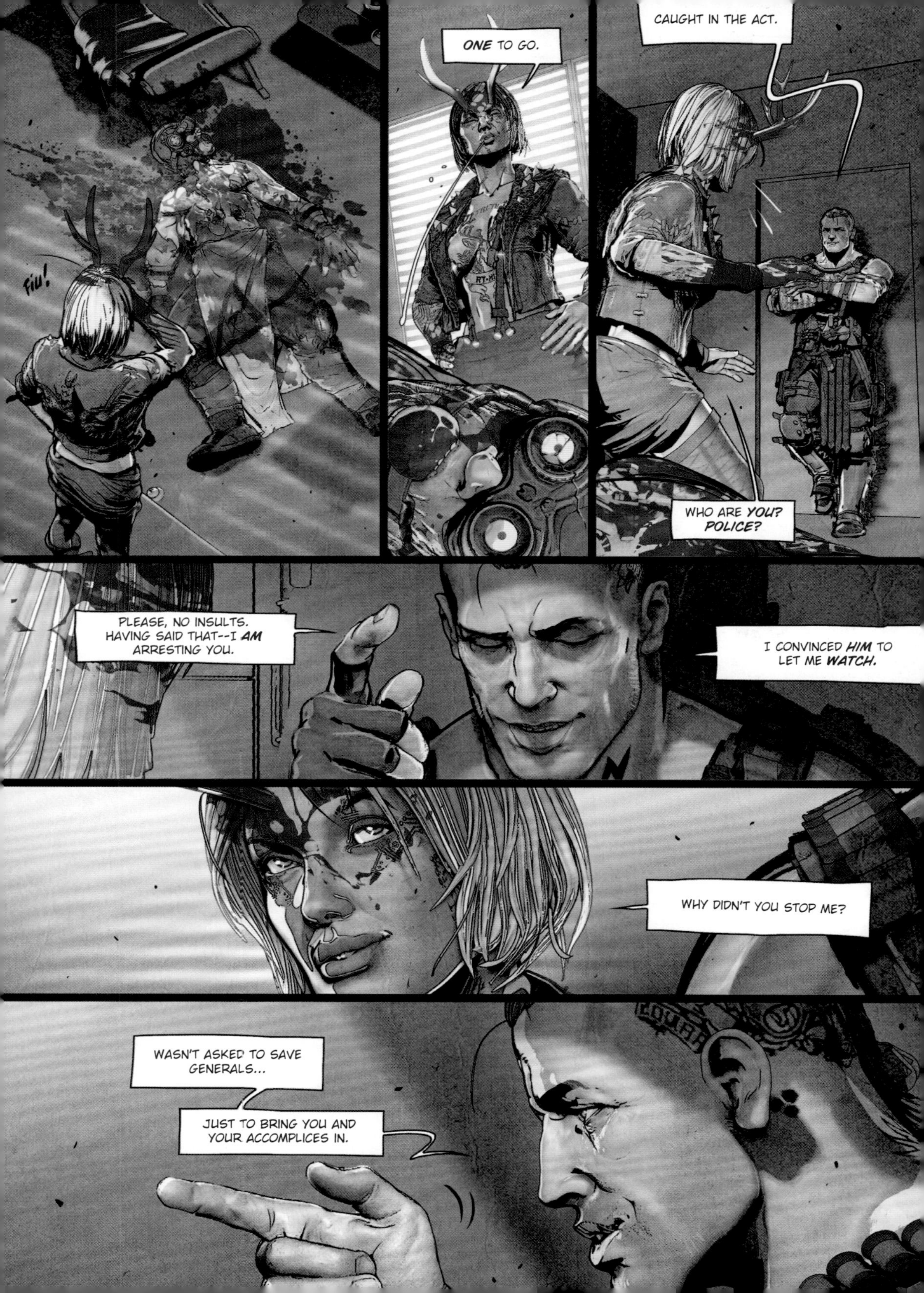
FIU!
ONE TO GO.
CAUGHT IN THE ACT.
WHO ARE YOU? POLICE?
PLEASE, NO INSULTS. HAVING SAID THAT--I AM ARRESTING YOU.
I CONVINCED HIM TO LET ME WATCH.
WHY DIDN'T YOU STOP ME?
WASN'T ASKED TO SAVE GENERALS...
JUST TO BRING YOU AND YOUR ACCOMPLICES IN.

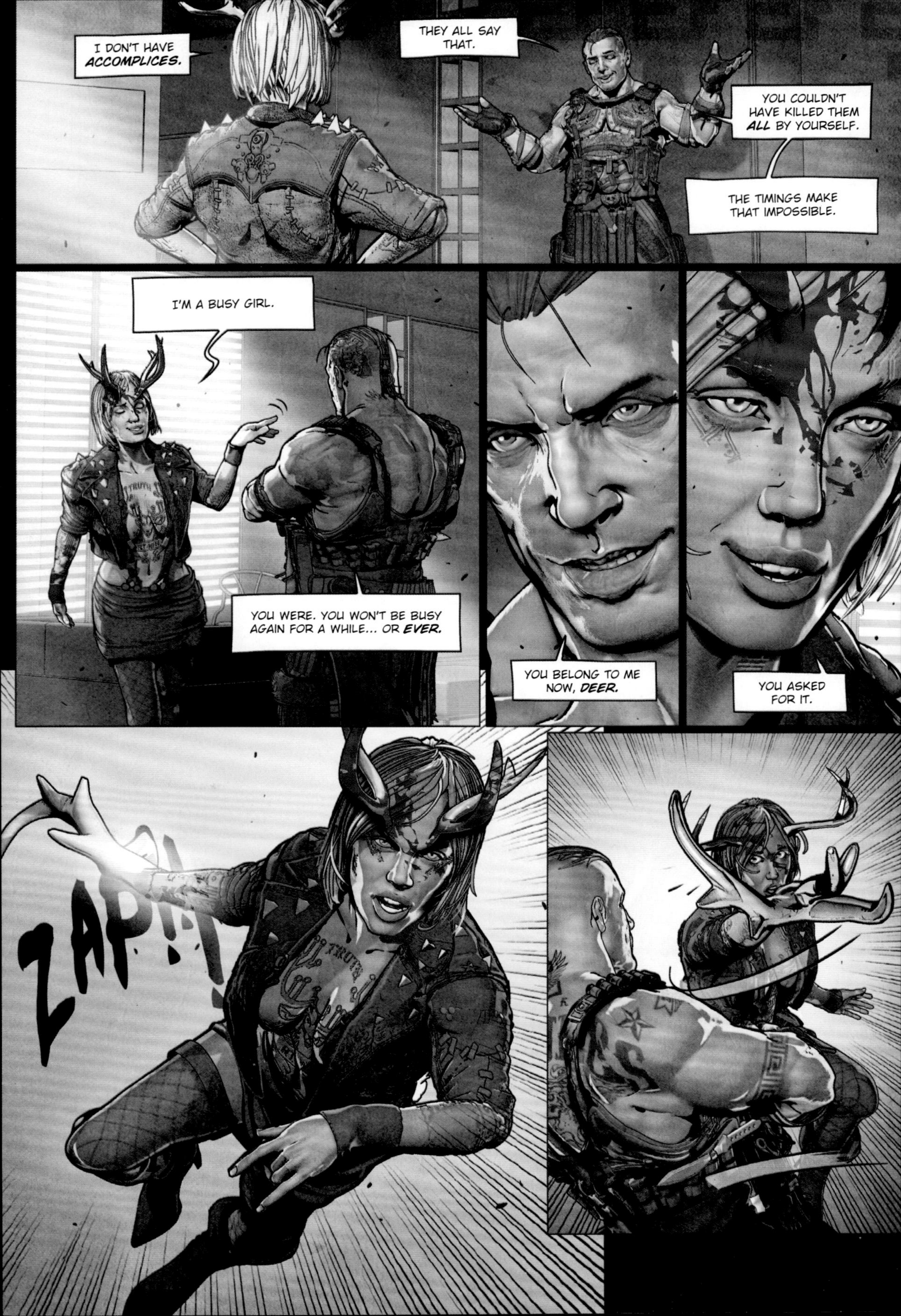
I DON'T HAVE ACCOMPLICES.
THEY ALL SAY THAT.
YOU COULDN'T HAVE KILLED THEM ALL BY YOURSELF.
THE TIMINGS MAKE THAT IMPOSSIBLE.
I'M A BUSY GIRL.
YOU WERE. YOU WON'T BE BUSY AGAIN FOR A WHILE... OR EVER.
YOU BELONG TO ME NOW, DEER.
YOU ASKED FOR IT.
ZAP!!

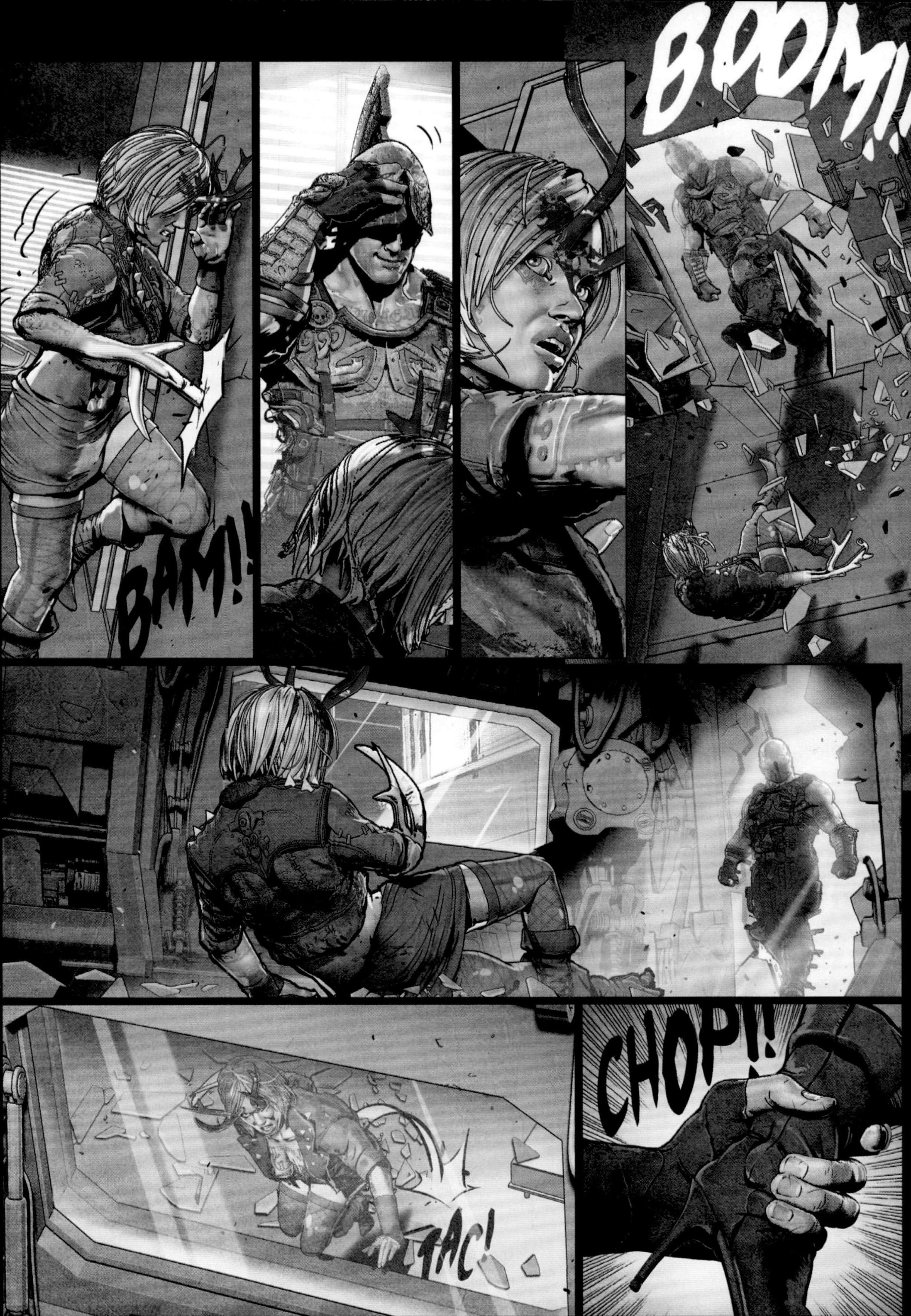
BAM!!
BOOM!!
CHOP!!
TAC!

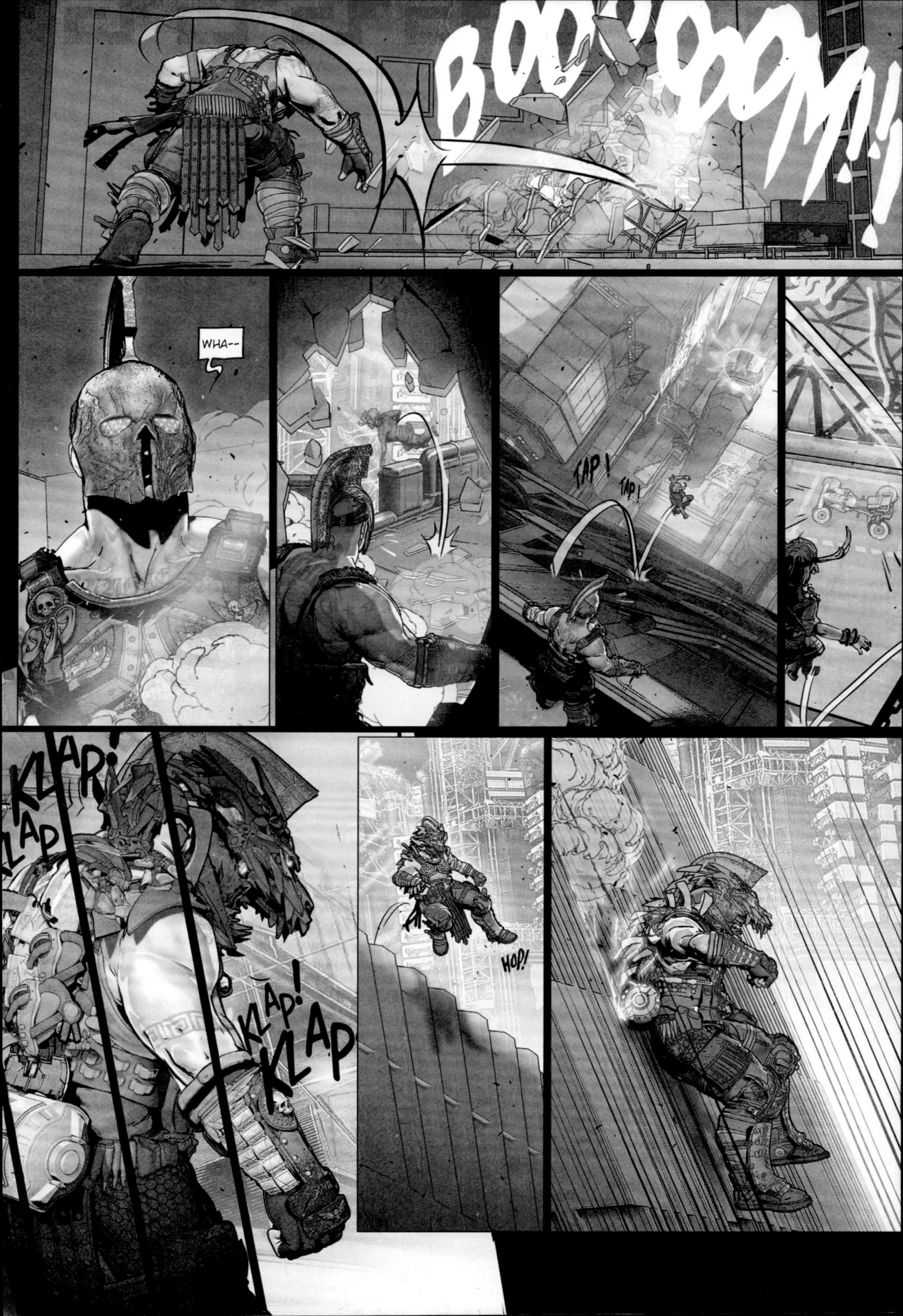
BOOOOOM!!
WHA--
TAP!
TAP!
KLAP!
KLAP
HOP!
KLAP!
KLAP

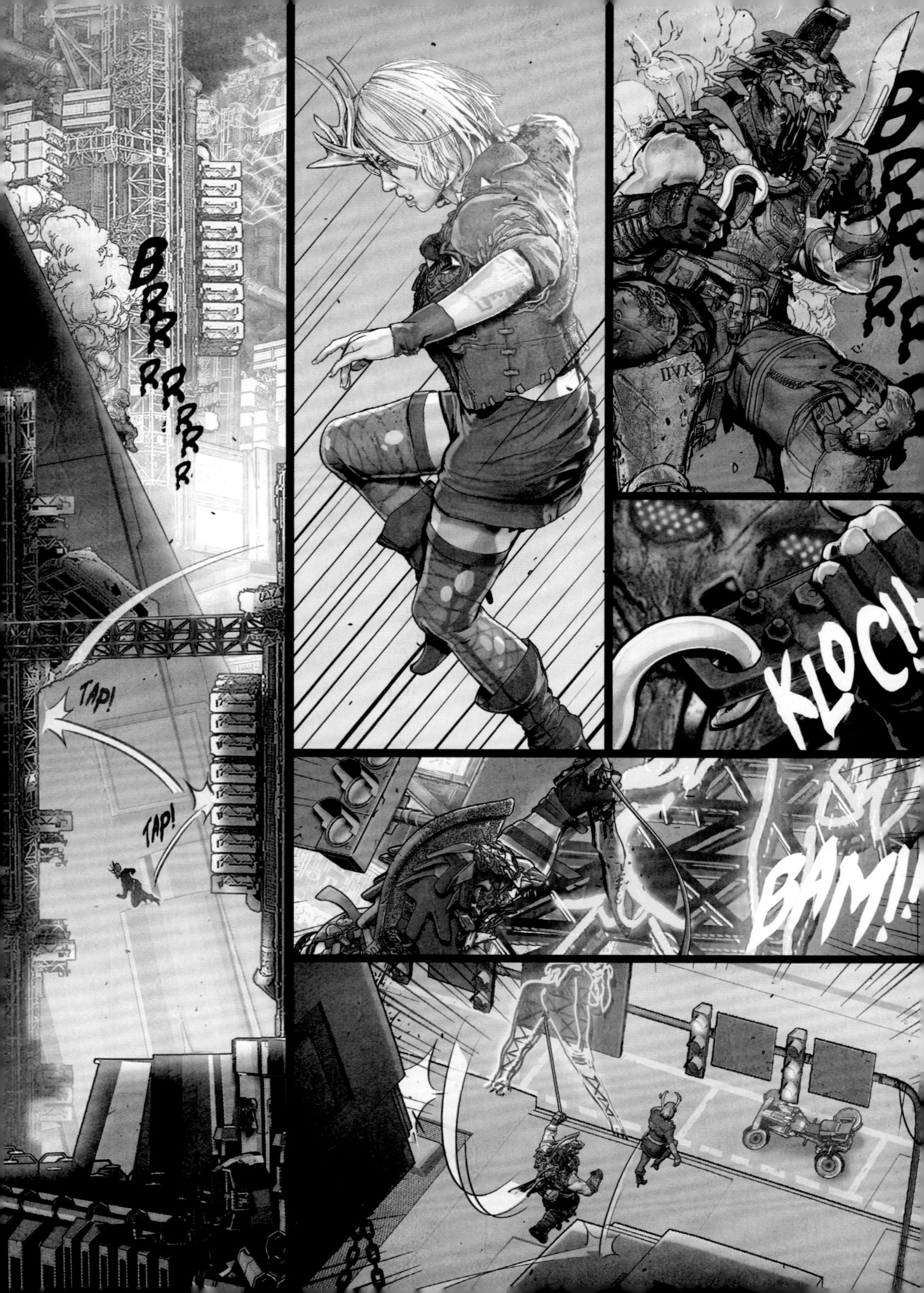
BRRRRRRRRR
TAP!
TAP!
BRRRRR
KLOC!!
BAM!!

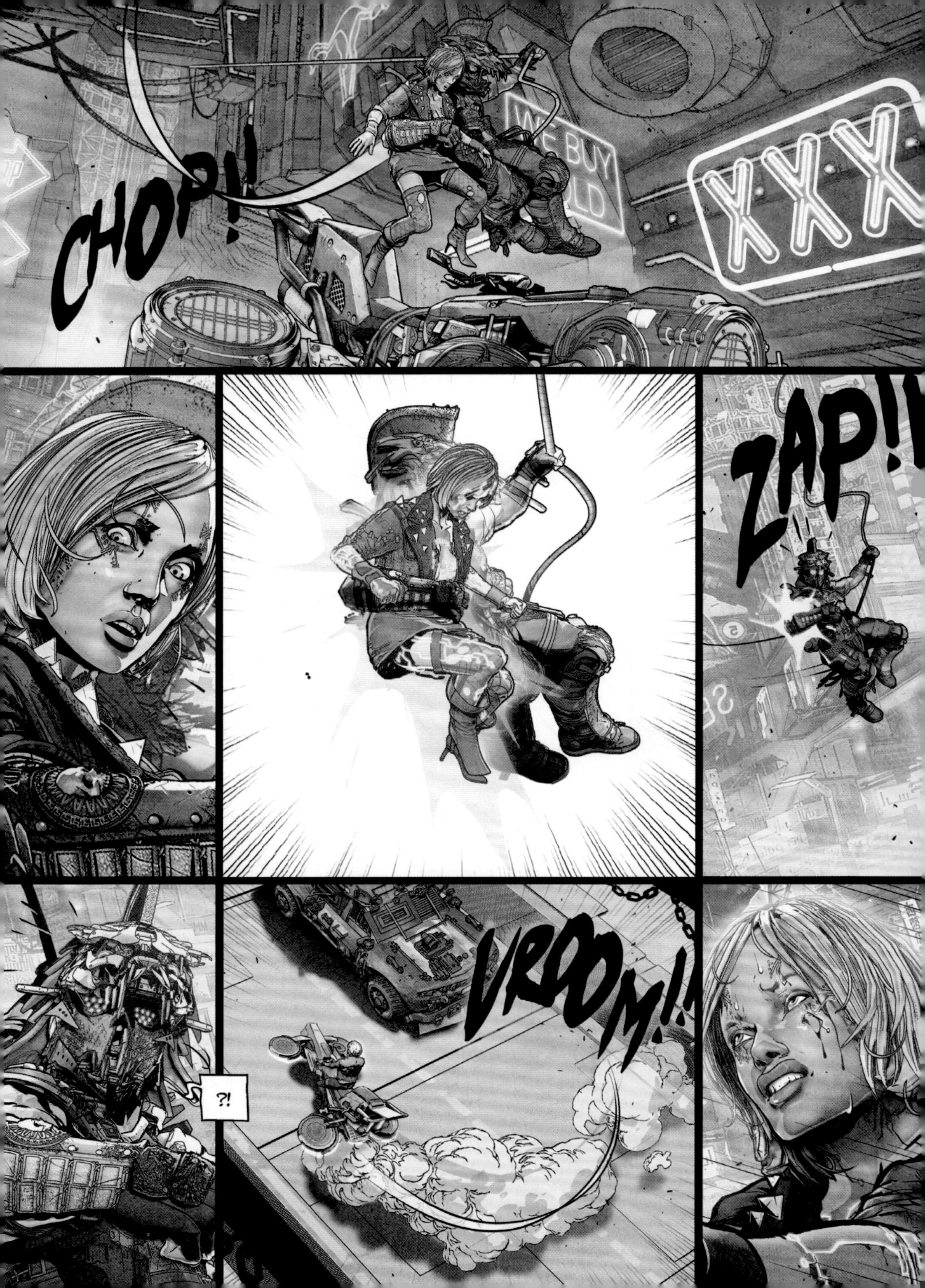

WE BUY
GOLD
XXX
CHOP!!
ZAP!!
VROOM!!
?!

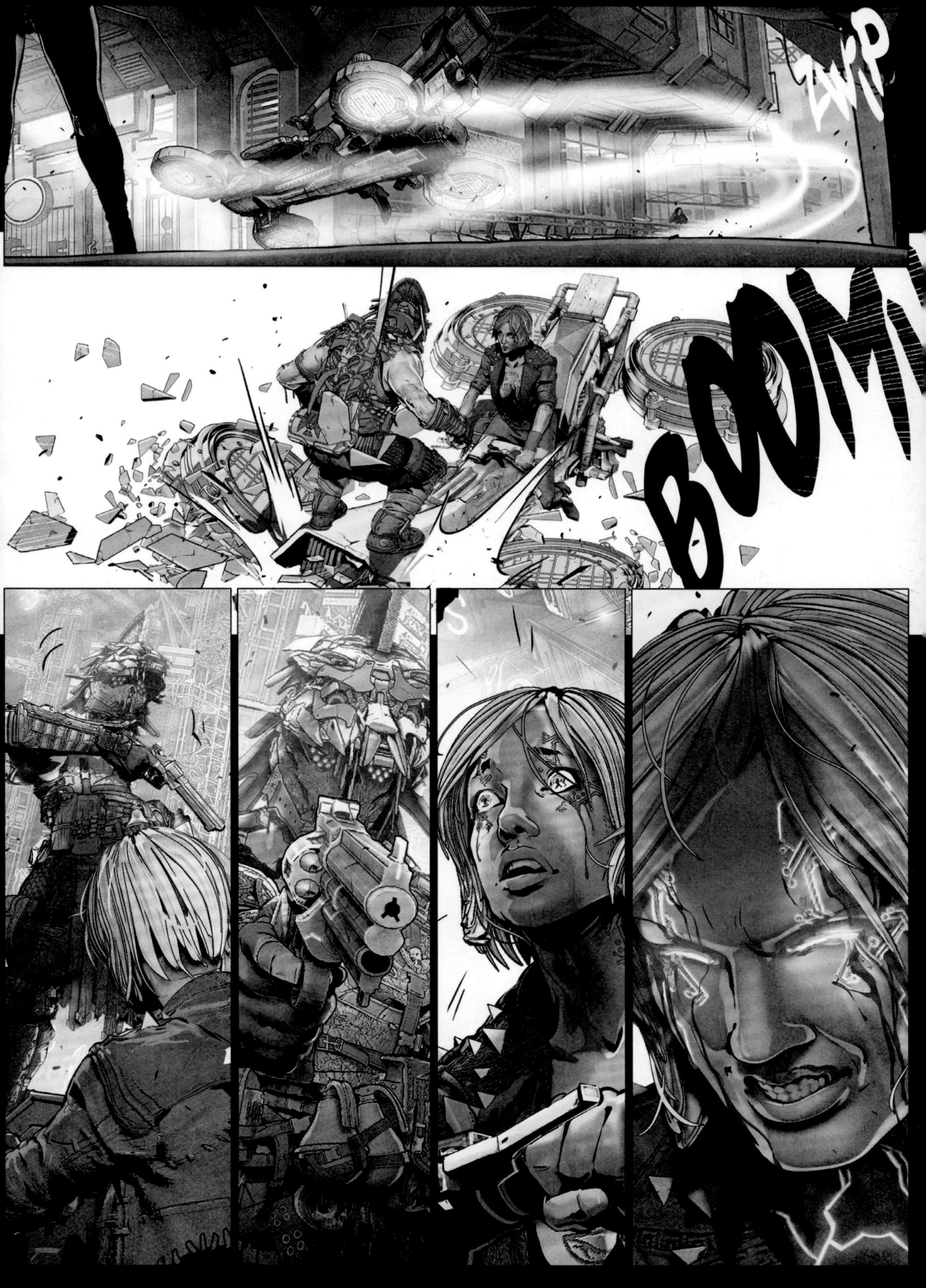
ZWIP
BOOM

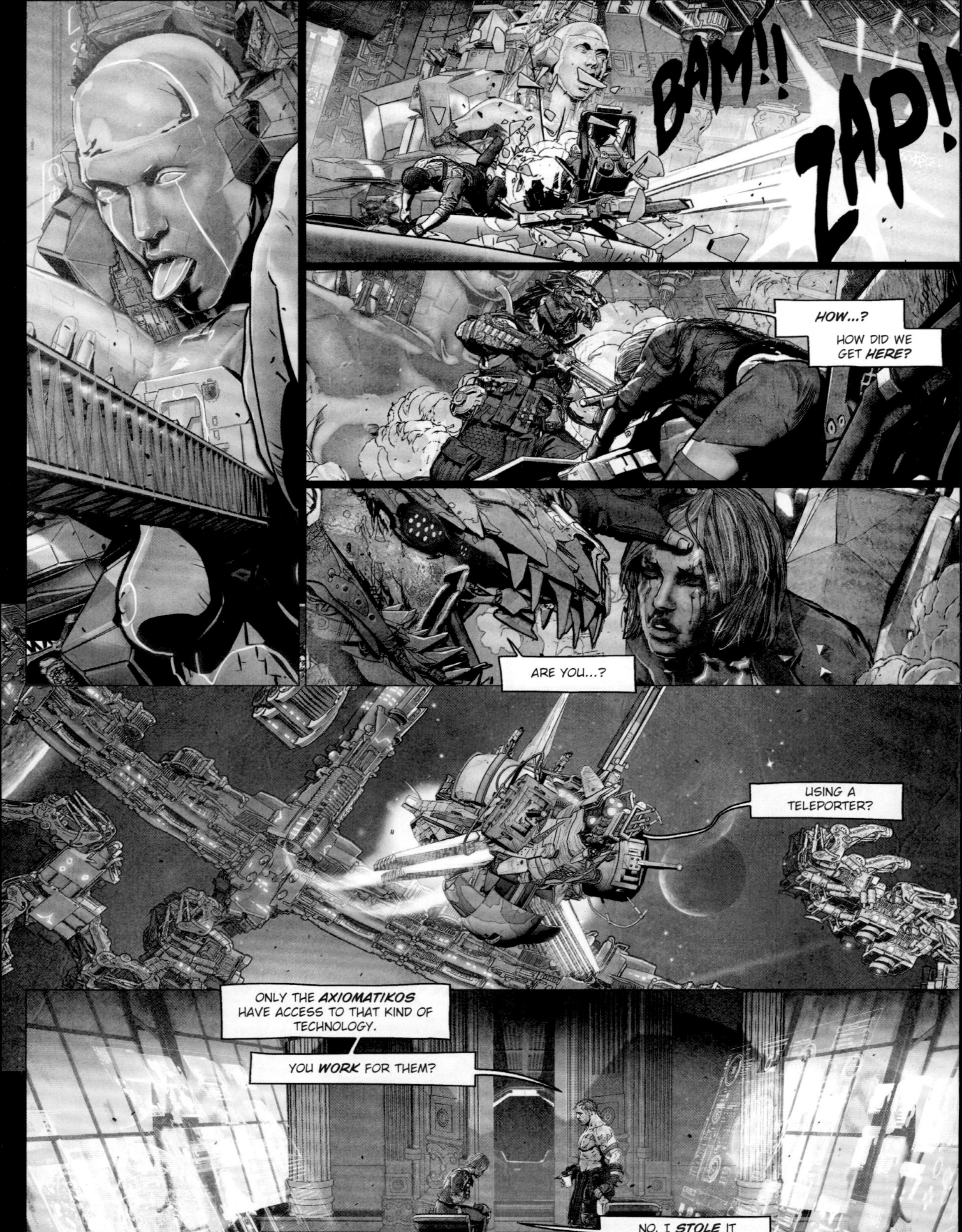
BAM!!
ZAP!!
HOW...?
HOW DID WE GET HERE?
ARE YOU...?
USING A TELEPORTER?
ONLY THE AXIOMATIKOS HAVE ACCESS TO THAT KIND OF TECHNOLOGY.
YOU WORK FOR THEM?
NO, I STOLE IT FROM THEM.

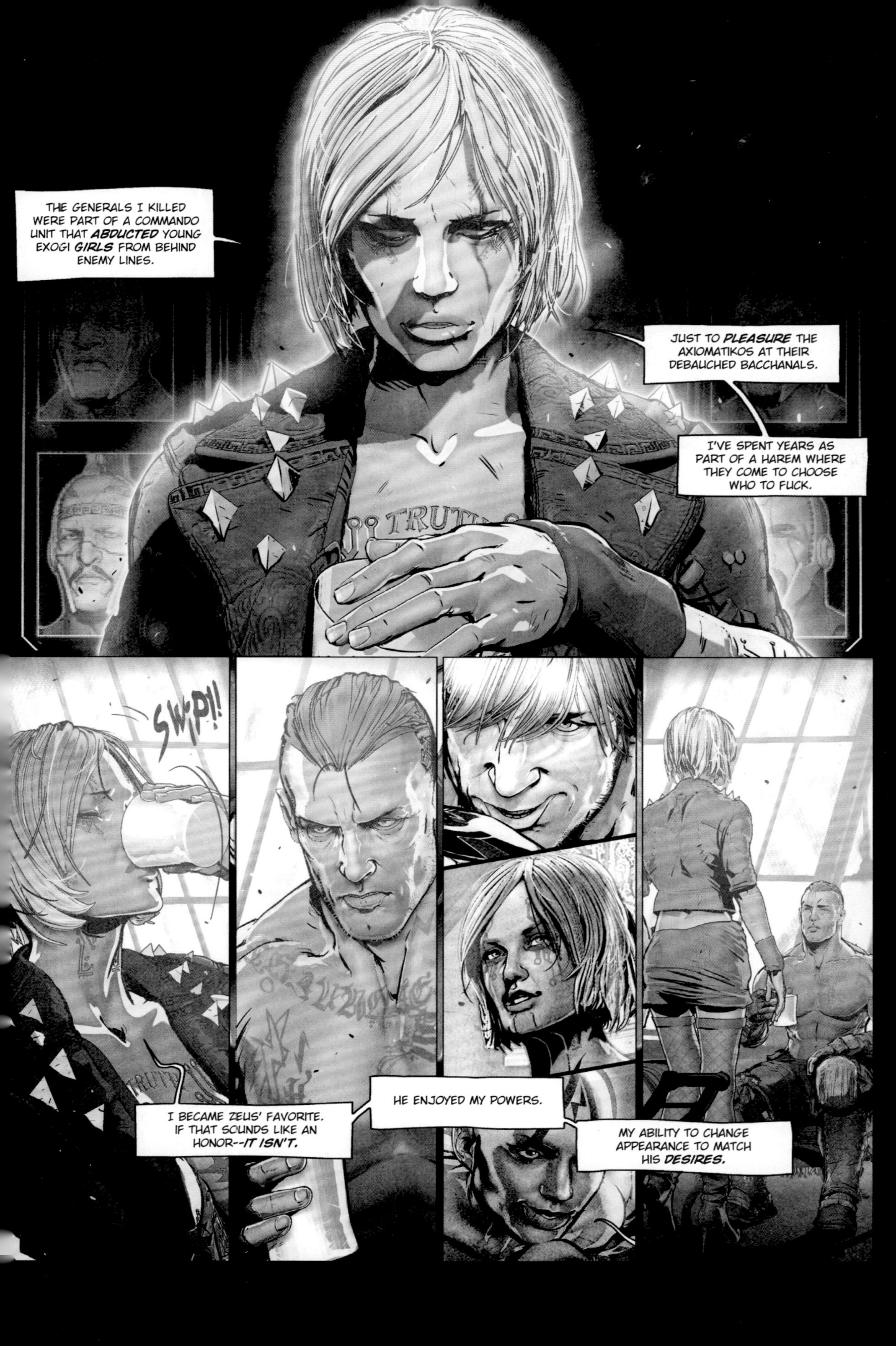
THE GENERALS I KILLED WERE PART OF A COMMANDO UNIT THAT ABDUCTED YOUNG EXOGI GIRLS FROM BEHIND ENEMY LINES.
JUST TO PLEASURE THE AXIOMATIKOS AT THEIR DEBAUCHED BACCHANALS.
I'VE SPENT YEARS AS PART OF A HAREM WHERE THEY COME TO CHOOSE WHO TO FUCK.
SWIP!!
I BECAME ZEUS' FAVORITE. IF THAT SOUNDS LIKE AN HONOR--IT ISN'T.
HE ENJOYED MY POWERS.
MY ABILITY TO CHANGE APPEARANCE TO MATCH HIS DESIRES.

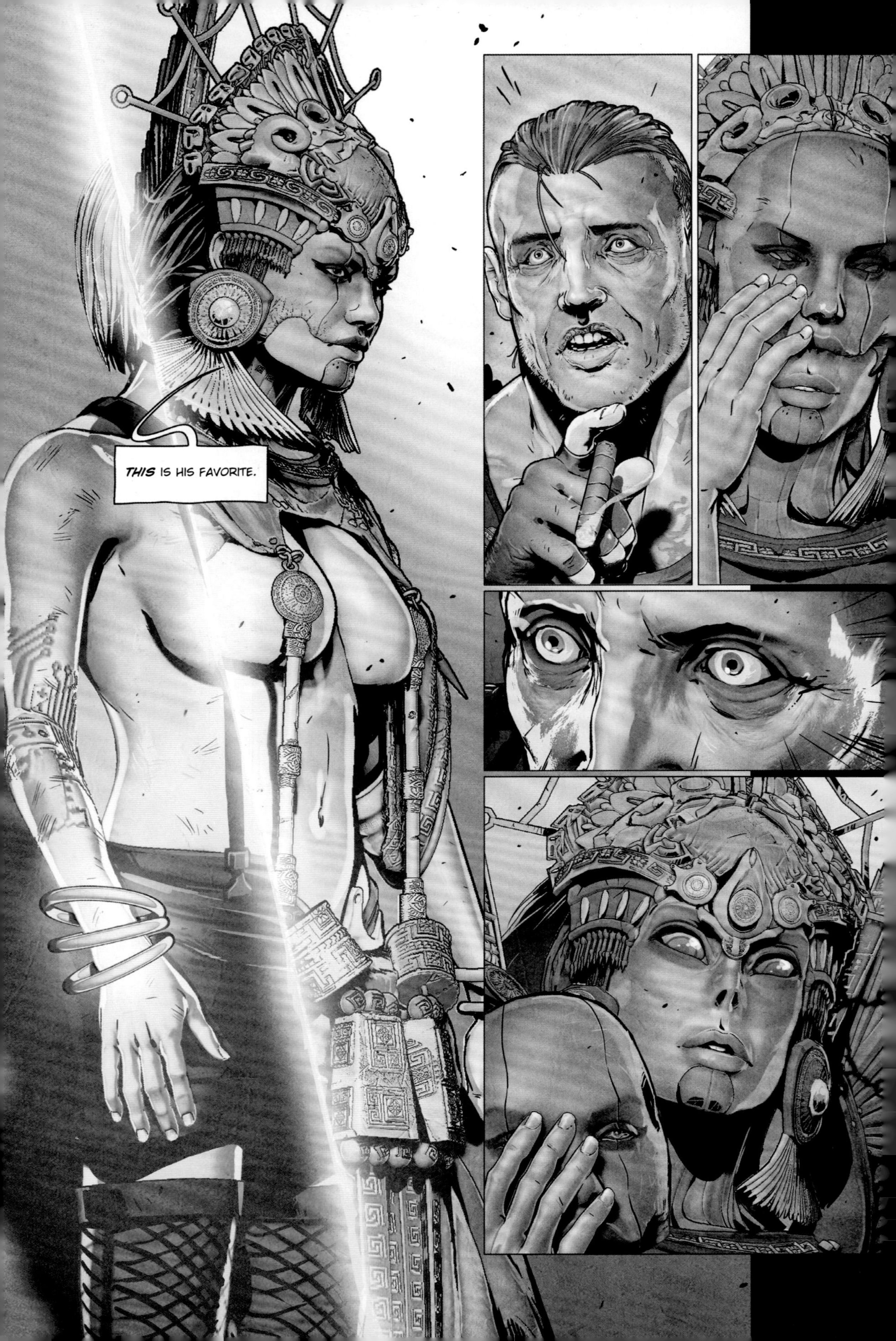

THIS IS HIS FAVORITE.

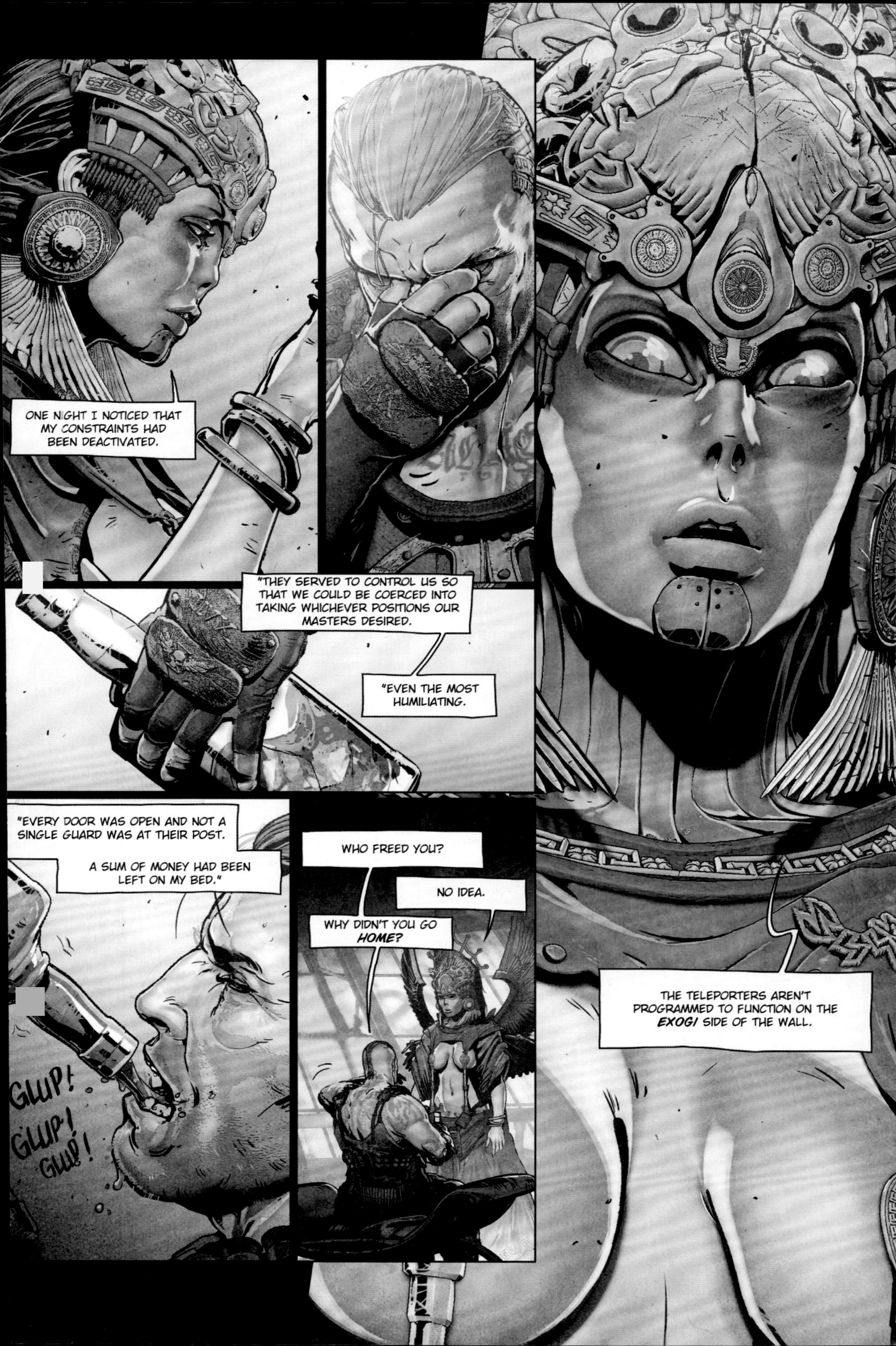
ONE NIGHT I NOTICED THAT MY CONSTRAINTS HAD BEEN DEACTIVATED.
"THEY SERVED TO CONTROL US SO THAT WE COULD BE COERCED INTO TAKING WHICHEVER POSITIONS OUR MASTERS DESIRED.
"EVEN THE MOST HUMILIATING.
"EVERY DOOR WAS OPEN AND NOT A SINGLE GUARD WAS AT THEIR POST.
A SUM OF MONEY HAD BEEN LEFT ON MY BED."
GLUP! GLUP! GLUP!
WHO FREED YOU?
NO IDEA.
WHY DIDN'T YOU GO *HOME?*
THE TELEPORTERS AREN'T PROGRAMMED TO FUNCTION ON THE *EXOGI* SIDE OF THE WALL.

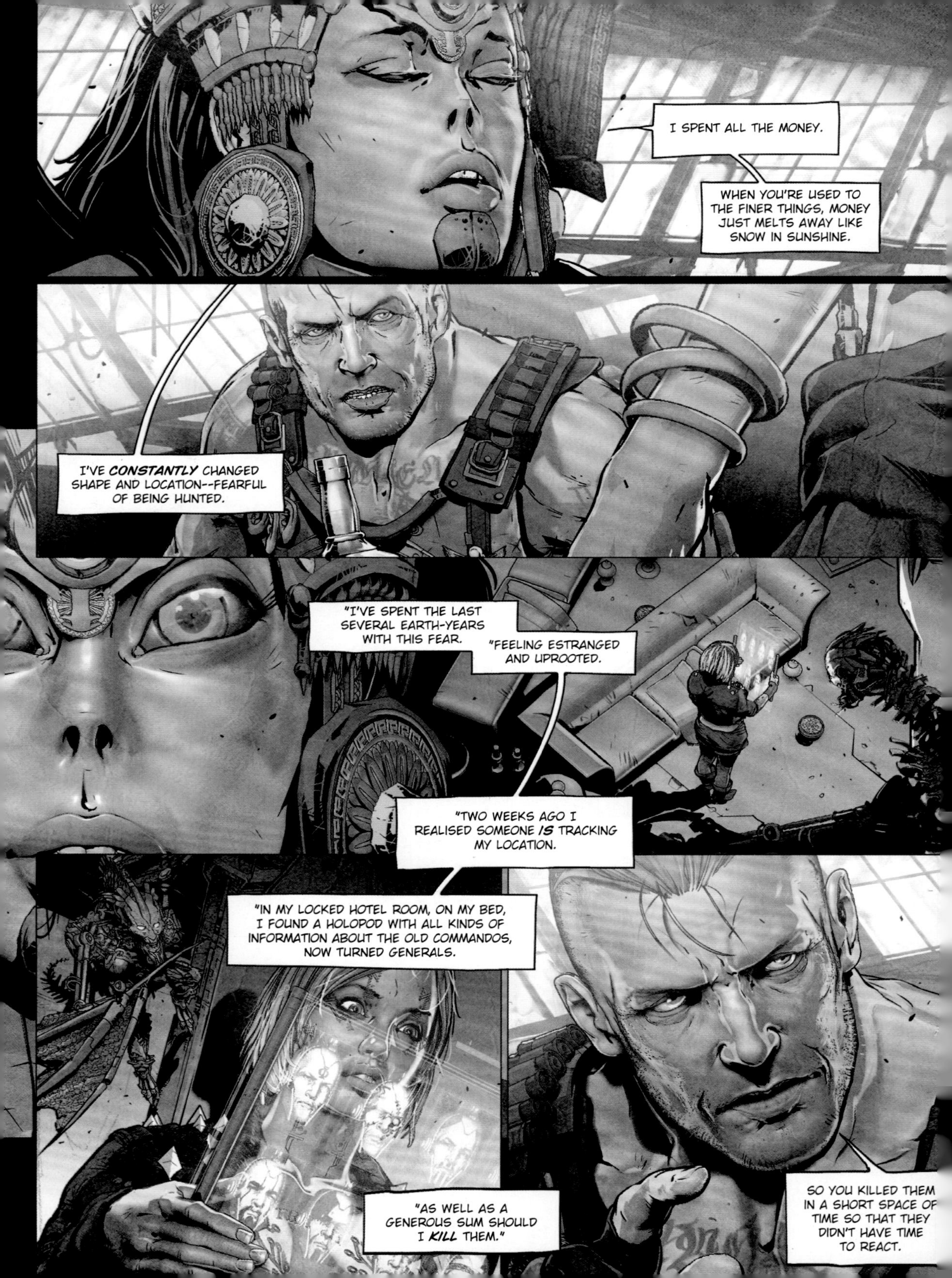
I SPENT ALL THE MONEY.
WHEN YOU'RE USED TO THE FINER THINGS, MONEY JUST MELTS AWAY LIKE SNOW IN SUNSHINE.
I'VE CONSTANTLY CHANGED SHAPE AND LOCATION--FEARFUL OF BEING HUNTED.
"I'VE SPENT THE LAST SEVERAL EARTH-YEARS WITH THIS FEAR.
"FEELING ESTRANGED AND UPROOTED.
"TWO WEEKS AGO I REALISED SOMEONE IS TRACKING MY LOCATION.
"IN MY LOCKED HOTEL ROOM, ON MY BED, I FOUND A HOLOPOD WITH ALL KINDS OF INFORMATION ABOUT THE OLD COMMANDOS, NOW TURNED GENERALS.
"AS WELL AS A GENEROUS SUM SHOULD I KILL THEM."
SO YOU KILLED THEM IN A SHORT SPACE OF TIME SO THAT THEY DIDN'T HAVE TIME TO REACT.

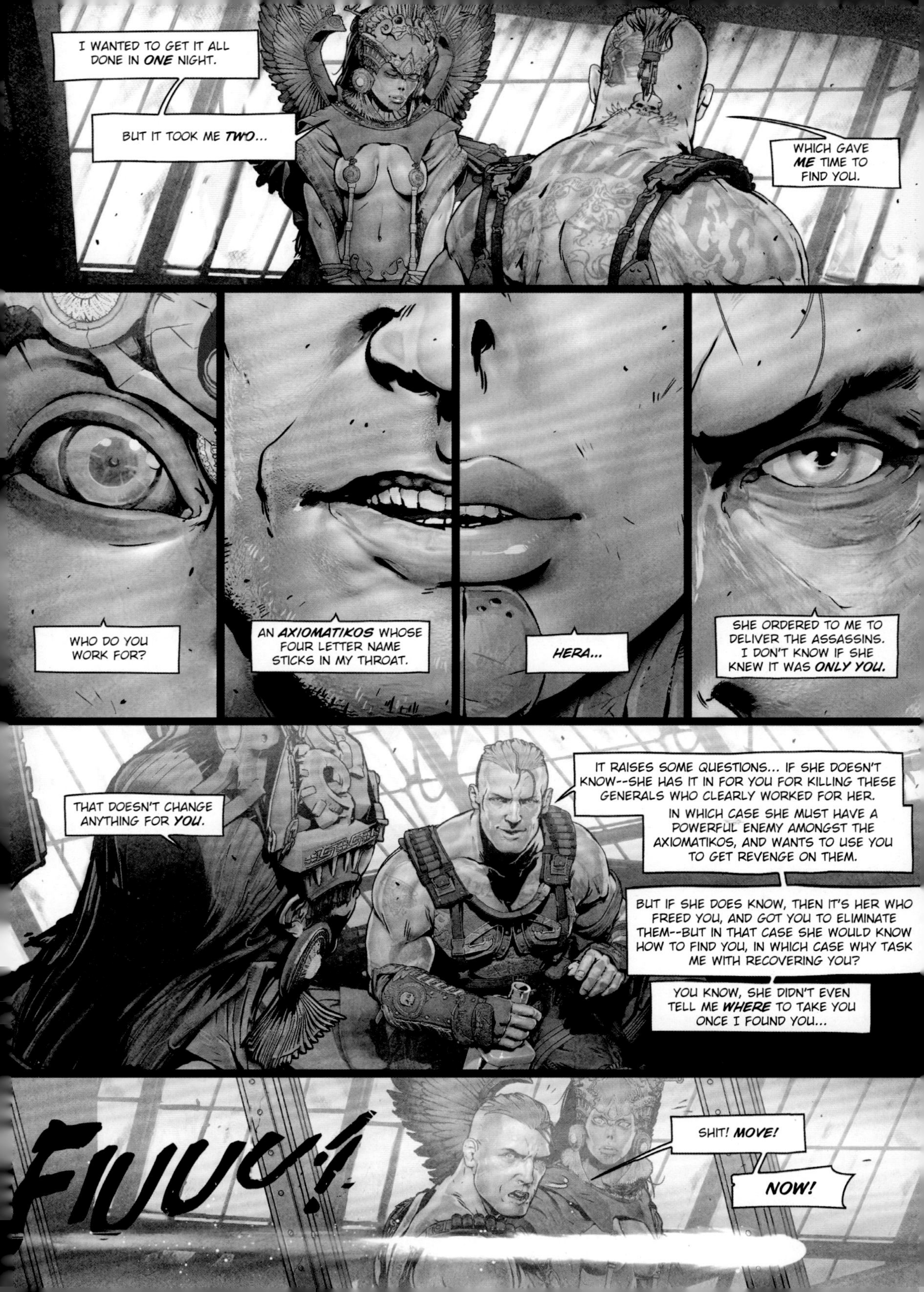
I WANTED TO GET IT ALL DONE IN ONE NIGHT.
BUT IT TOOK ME TWO...
WHICH GAVE ME TIME TO FIND YOU.
WHO DO YOU WORK FOR?
AN AXIOMATIKOS WHOSE FOUR LETTER NAME STICKS IN MY THROAT.
HERA...
SHE ORDERED TO ME TO DELIVER THE ASSASSINS. I DON'T KNOW IF SHE KNEW IT WAS ONLY YOU.
THAT DOESN'T CHANGE ANYTHING FOR YOU.
IT RAISES SOME QUESTIONS... IF SHE DOESN'T KNOW--SHE HAS IT IN FOR YOU FOR KILLING THESE GENERALS WHO CLEARLY WORKED FOR HER.
IN WHICH CASE SHE MUST HAVE A POWERFUL ENEMY AMONGST THE AXIOMATIKOS, AND WANTS TO USE YOU TO GET REVENGE ON THEM.
BUT IF SHE DOES KNOW, THEN IT'S HER WHO FREED YOU, AND GOT YOU TO ELIMINATE THEM--BUT IN THAT CASE SHE WOULD KNOW HOW TO FIND YOU, IN WHICH CASE WHY TASK ME WITH RECOVERING YOU?
YOU KNOW, SHE DIDN'T EVEN TELL ME WHERE TO TAKE YOU ONCE I FOUND YOU...
FIUUU!
SHIT! MOVE!
NOW!

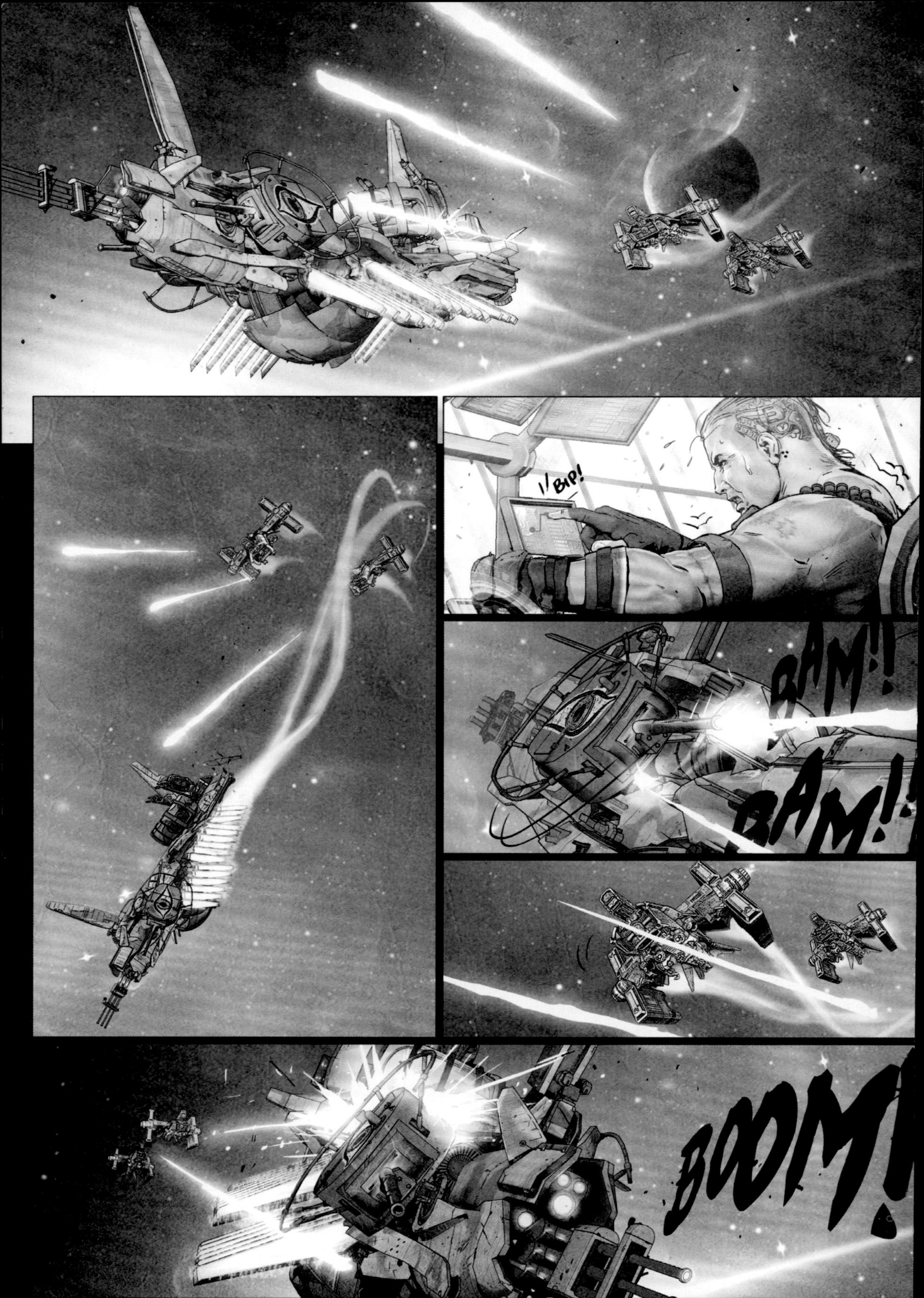

BIP!
BAM!!
BAM!!
BOOM!!

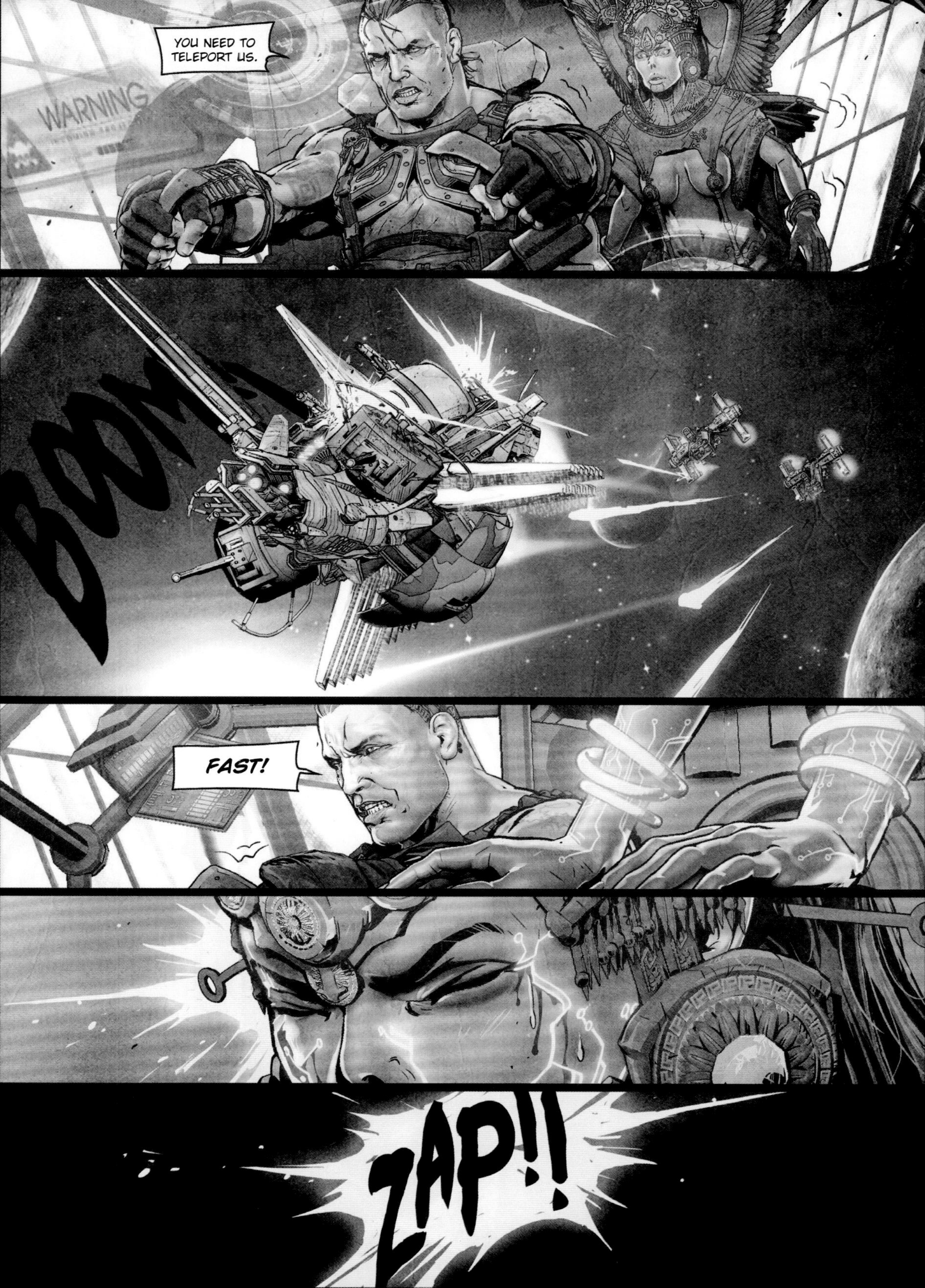
YOU NEED TO TELEPORT US.
WARNING
BOOM!!
FAST!
ZAP!!

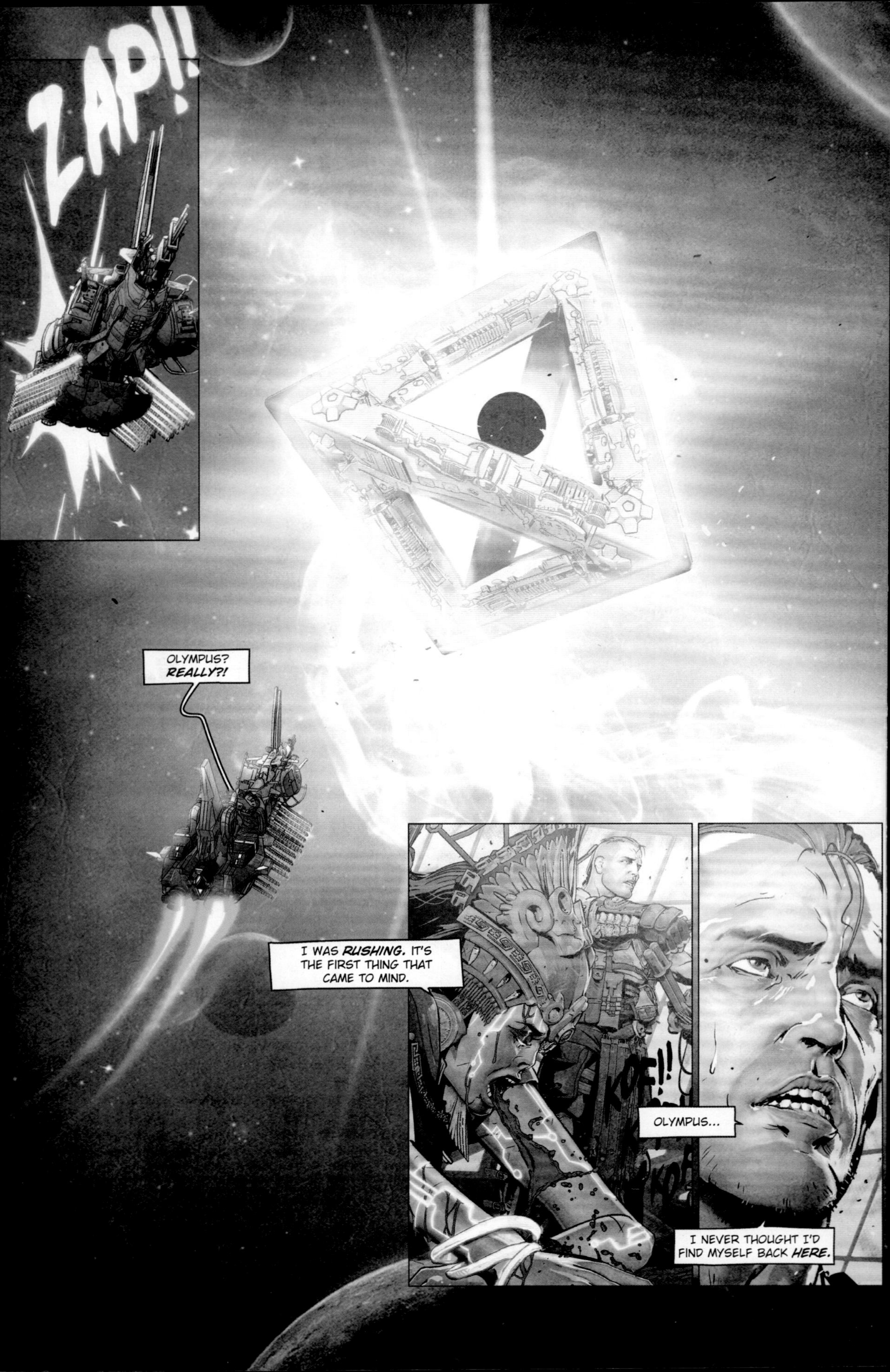
ZAP!!
OLYMPUS? *REALLY?!*
I WAS *RUSHING.* IT'S THE FIRST THING THAT CAME TO MIND.
KOF!!
OLYMPUS...
I NEVER THOUGHT I'D FIND MYSELF BACK *HERE.*

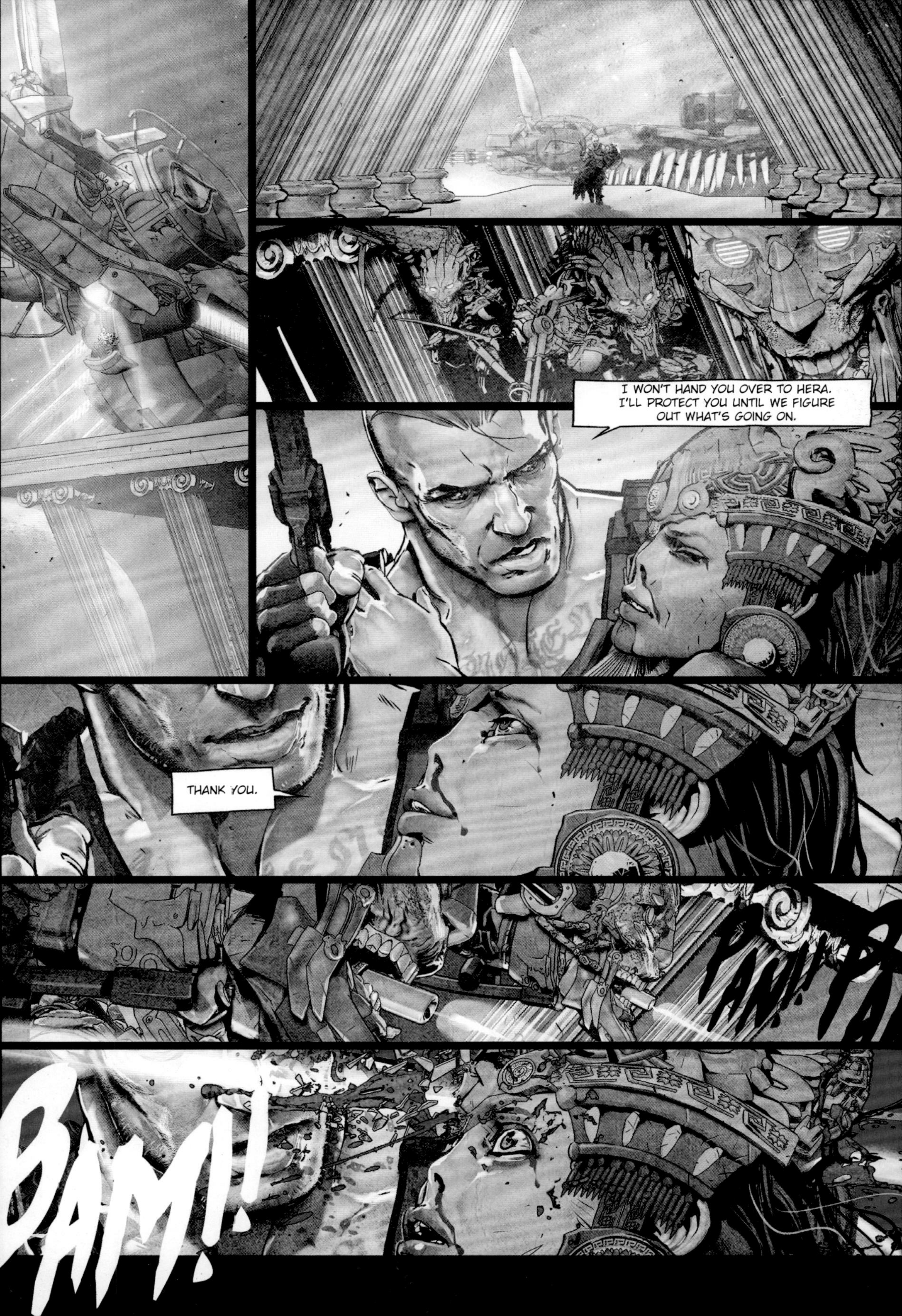
I WON'T HAND YOU OVER TO HERA. I'LL PROTECT YOU UNTIL WE FIGURE OUT WHAT'S GOING ON.
THANK YOU.
BAM!

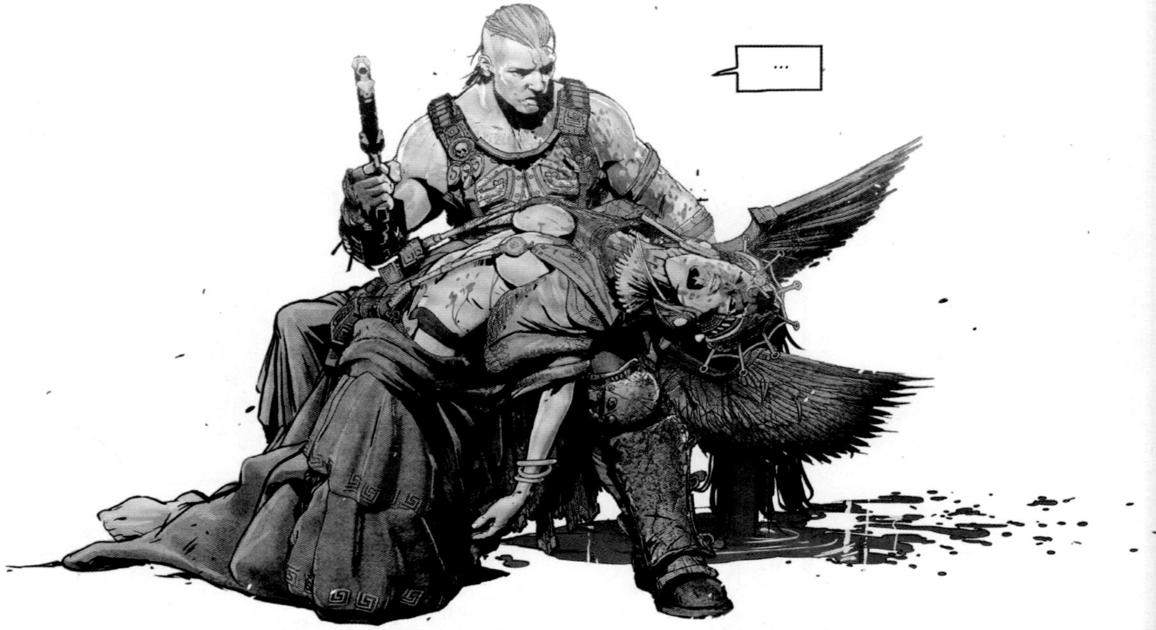
...

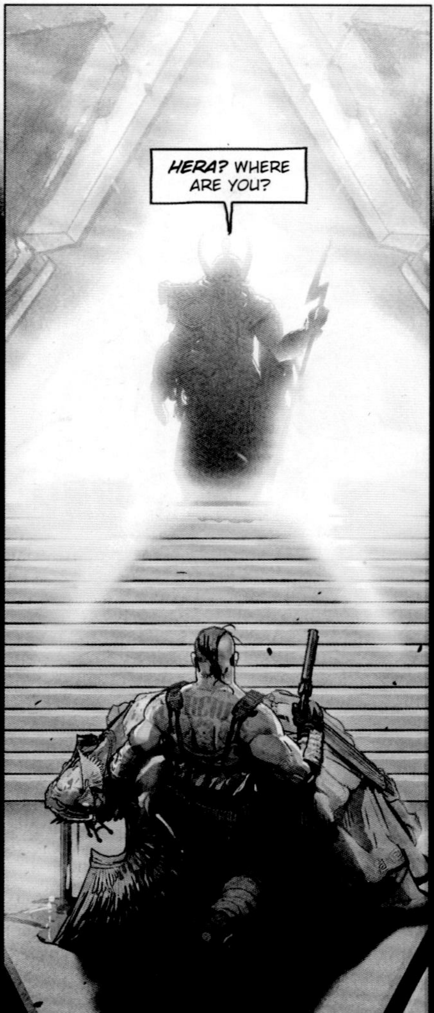
HERA? WHERE ARE YOU?

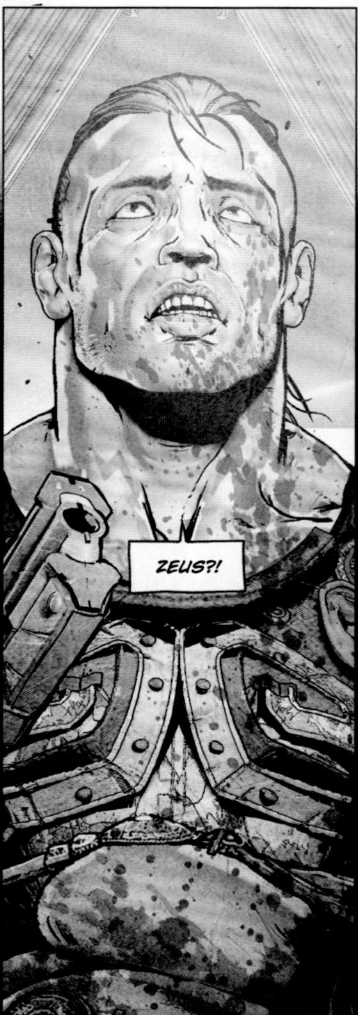
ZEUS?!

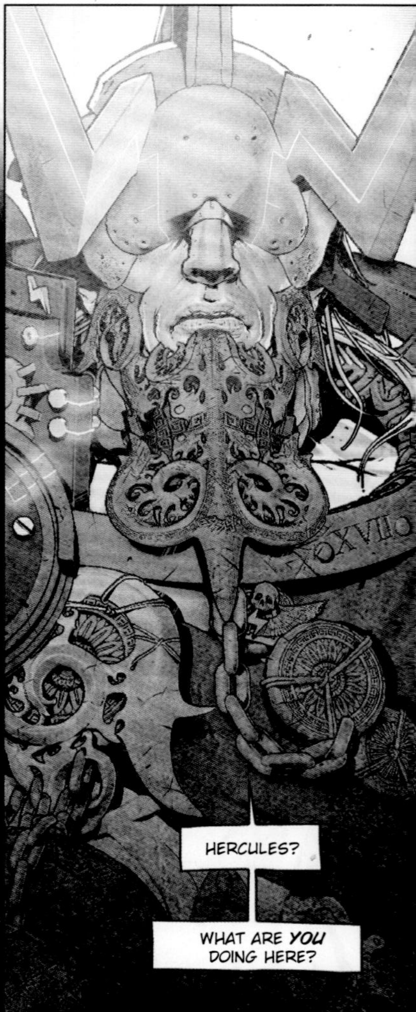
HERCULES?
WHAT ARE YOU DOING HERE?

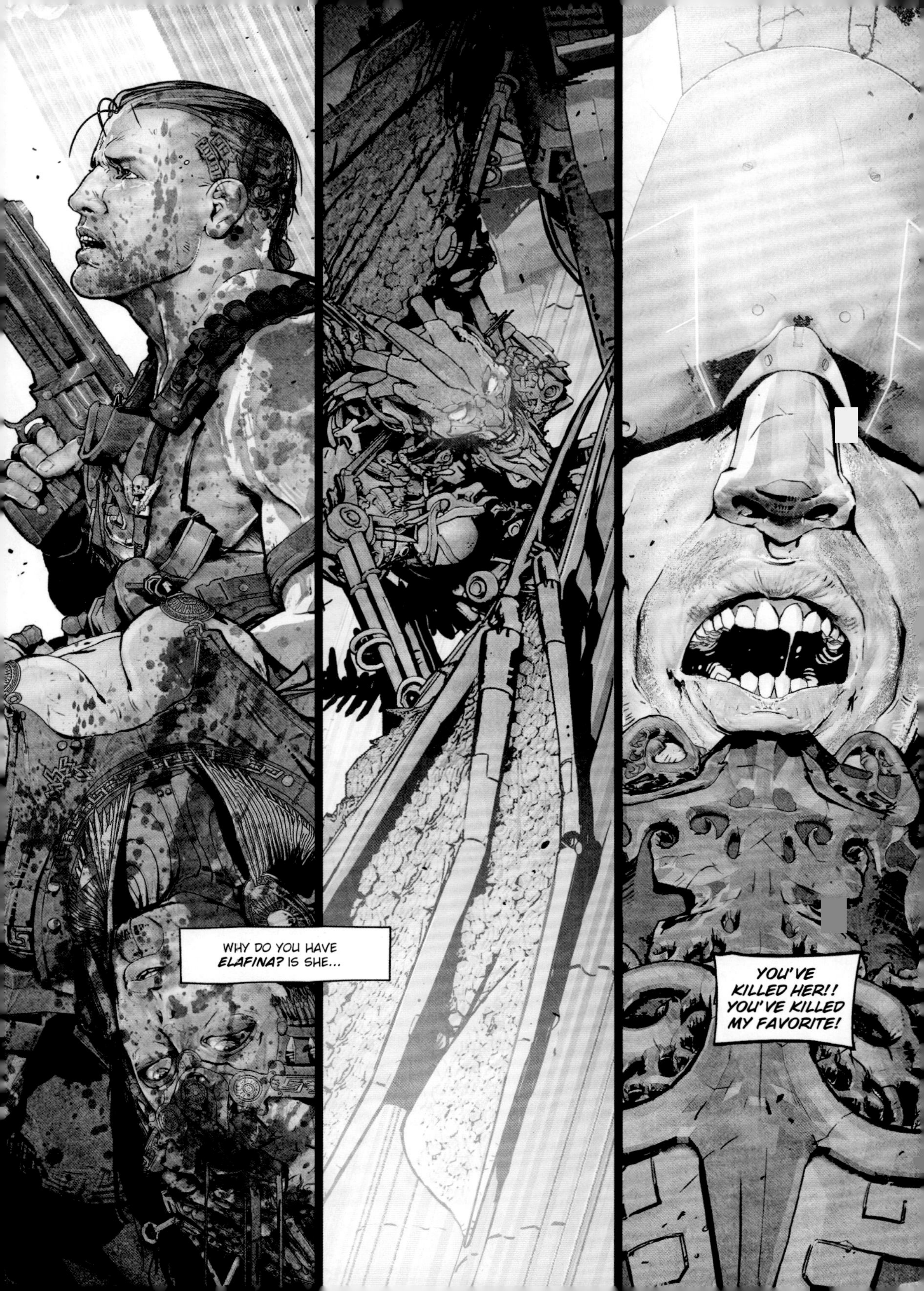
WHY DO YOU HAVE *ELAFINA?* IS SHE...
YOU'VE KILLED HER!! YOU'VE KILLED MY FAVORITE!

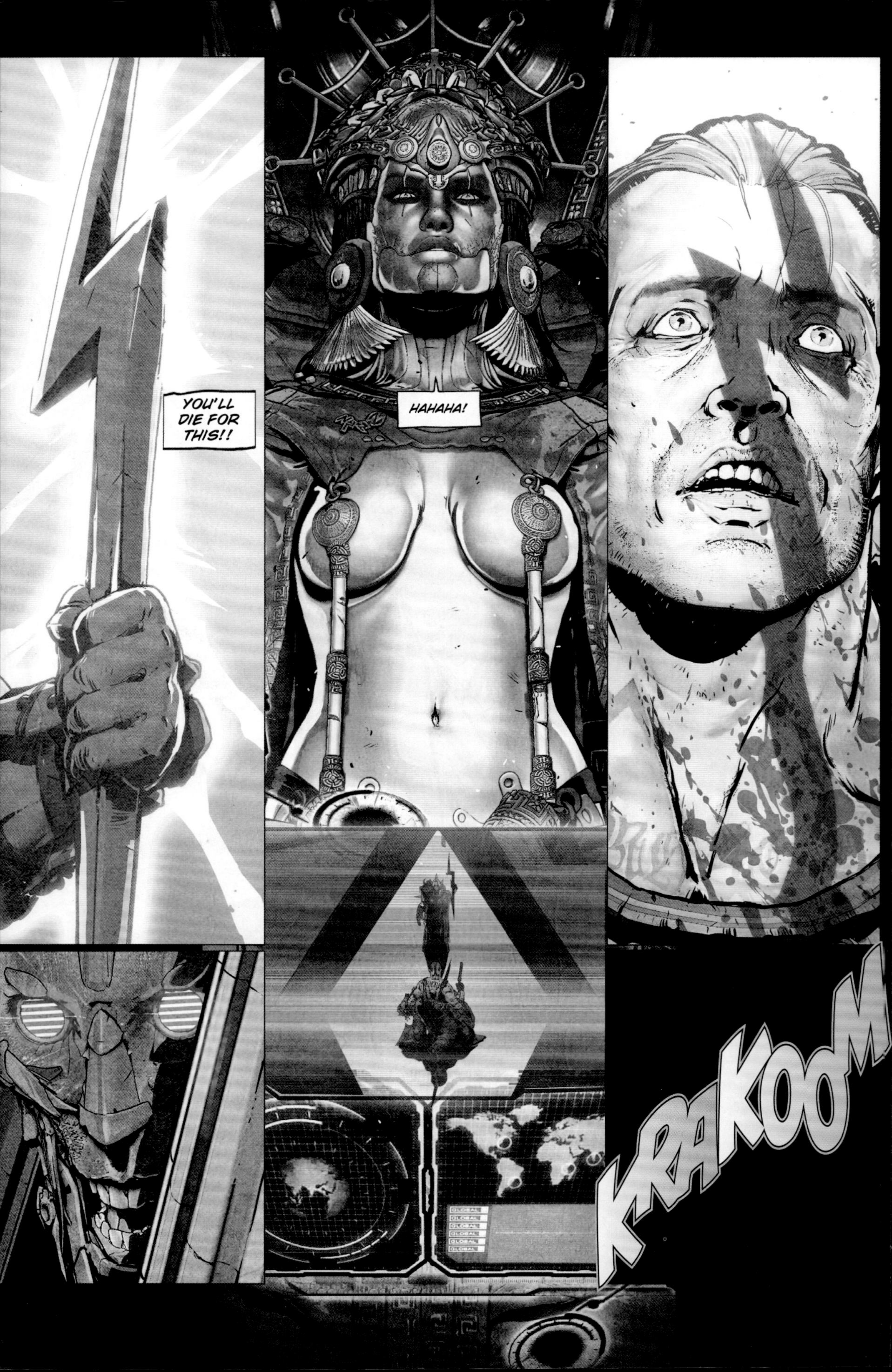
YOU'LL DIE FOR THIS!!
HAHAHA!
KRAKOOM
GLOBAL
GLOBAL
GLOBAL
GLOBAL
GLOBAL
GLOBAL

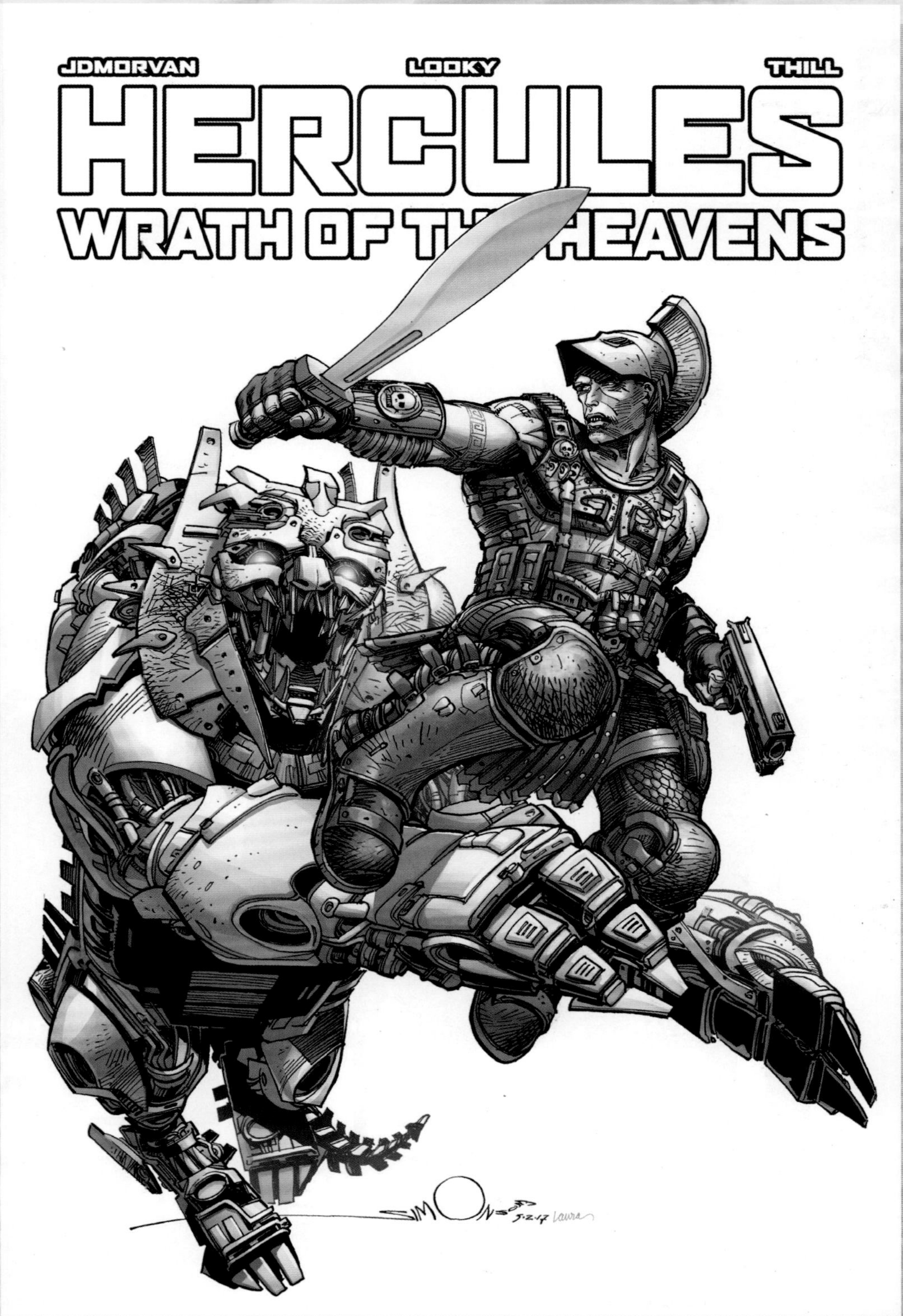
JDMORVAN
LOOKY
THILL
HERCULES
WRATH OF TH HEAVENS

#1 COVER A

WALTER SIMONSON & LAURA MARTIN

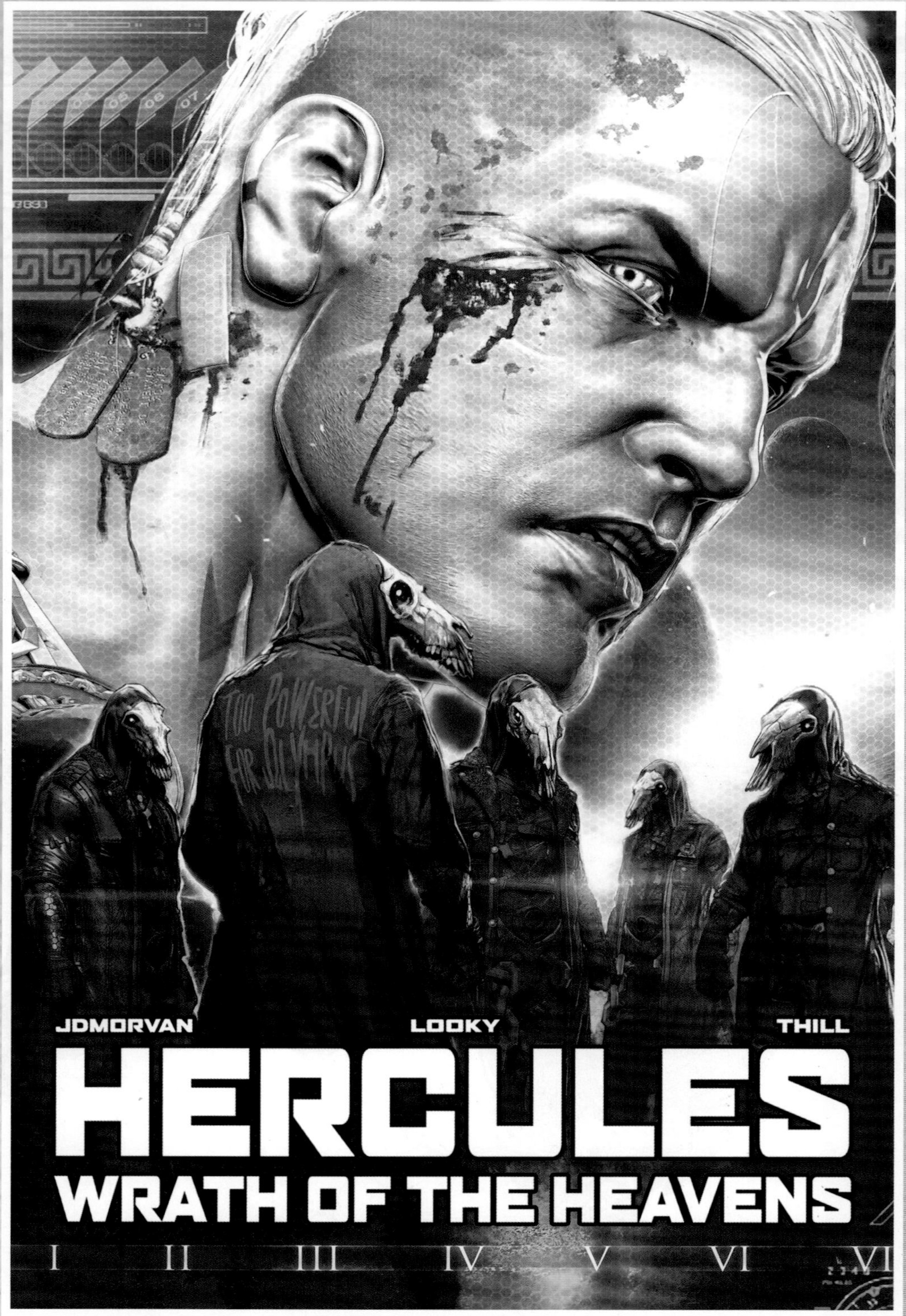
JDMORVAN
LOOKY
THILL
HERCULES
WRATH OF THE HEAVENS
I II III IV V VI

#2 COVER A
LOOKY & OLIVIER THILL

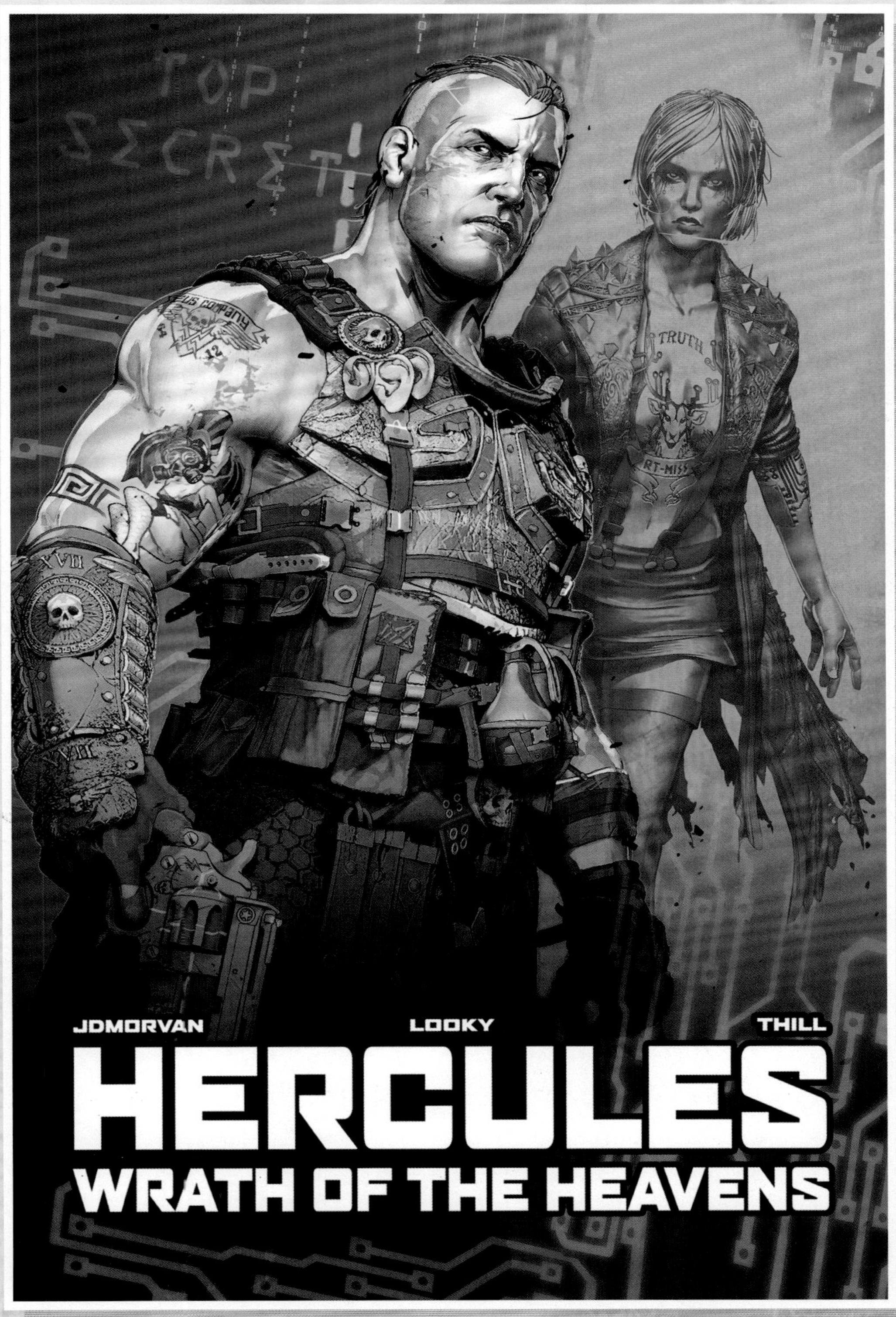
TOP SECRET
TRUTH
JDMORVAN
LOOKY
THILL
HERCULES
WRATH OF THE HEAVENS

#4 COVER A
LOOKY & OLIVIER THILL

CREATORS

WRITER:

JDMORVAN

Jean-David Morvan studied arts at the Institut Saint-Luc in Brussels, before moving on to the Academy of Fine Arts. After first trying his hand at being a comics artist, he soon realised that his true strength is storytelling. JD has since gone on to win multiple awards and nominations for his works. His previous credits include *Wolverine: Saudade*, *Naja*, *Spy Games* and *Wake*. He resides in Reims, France.

ARTIST:

LOOKY

Looky is a self-taught French comic book artist. He made his professional debut when he took over art duties on the fantasy series *Nocturnes Rouges* in 2008. He stuck with fantasy and contributed to *La Geste des Chevaliers Dragons* and modern renditions of *Snow White (Blanche Neige)* and *Beauty and the Beast (La Belle et la Bête)*.

ARTIST:

OLIVIER THILL

Olivier Thill is a graphic designer and character modeller from France. *Hercules: Wrath of The Heavens* is his first comic.